SPECIAL DRAWING RIGHTS (SDR) AND THE FEDERAL RESERVE

VOLUME 1.

SIR PATRICK BIJOU

Copyright © 2021 by Sir Patrick Bijou All rights reserved.

**Cover design: Copyright © 2021 by Sir Patrick Bijou
All rights reserved**

This document is geared towards providing exact and reliable information about the topic and issue covered. The publication is sold with the idea that the publisher is not required to render accounting, officially permitted, or otherwise, qualified services. If advice is necessary, legal, or professional, a practiced individual in the profession should be ordered.

From a Declaration of Principles which was accepted and approved equally by a Committee of the American Bar Association and a Committee of Publishers and Associations.

In no way is it legal to reproduce, duplicate, or transmit any part of this document in either electronic means or printed format. Recording of this publication is strictly prohibited and any storage of this document is not allowed unless with written permission from the publisher. All rights reserved.

The information provided herein is stated to be truthful and consistent, in that any liability, in terms of inattention or otherwise, by any usage or abuse of any policies, processes, or directions contained within is the solitary and utter responsibility of the recipient reader. Under no circumstances will any legal responsibility or blame be held against the publisher for any reparation, damages, or monetary loss due to the information herein, either directly or indirectly.

Respective authors own all copyrights not held by the publisher.

The information herein is offered for informational purposes solely and is universal as so. The presentation of the information is without a contract or any type of guarantee assurance.

The trademarks that are used are without any consent, and the publication of the trademark is without permission or backing by the trademark owner. All trademarks and brands within this book are for clarifying purposes only and are owned by the owners themselves, not affiliated with this document.

Published by BIJOUBOOKS

Table of Contents

ABOUT THE AUTHOR 1
CHAPTER 1 7
INTRODUCTION 7
The SDR's Origins and Characteristics 8
SDR VALUATION 11
Basket of SDR 12
Valuation Method for SDRs Currently In Use 13
Currency Weights in the SDR Basket 16
Interest Rate Of SDR 16
Cancellations and Allocations of SDRs 19
The SDR Department's Operations 22
SDR Holdings at the International Monetary Fund 26
Arrangements for Voluntary SDR Trading 27
Statements Of Financial Position of the SDR Department 31
The establishment of the SDR 32
The Fundamental Principles That Guide SDR Valuation Decisions 34
Criteria for the SDR Basket's Composition 35
Actual Daily Weights and Currency Values 37
SDR Valuation 38
CHAPTER 2 43
Invention Of The Special Drawing Right In The CBDC Era 43

Mr. Xiaochuan Zhou's Recommendations of SDR Reform in 2009 45
SDR Innovation based on CBDC 49
Payment, Clearing and Settlement Infrastructure 49
Intrinsic Value 50
The Issuance and Redemption Mechanism 51
SDR on the Corridor Network 52
The Trading System 53
SDR-denominated Assets 54
Origins And Guiding Principles For SDR Valuation 55
A LEGAL FRAMEWORK FOR THE VALUATION OF SDR 57
A. Export ("gateway") criterion 59
B. Freely usable criterion 59
Currency Selection Criteria 65
The Export Criterion 66
The Freely Usable Criterion 67
Indicators: General Considerations 67
Operational Issues 78
Exchange rates for SDR valuation and Fund operations 80
SDR interest rate 82
Hedging 84
SDR BASKET SIZE 86
OTHER ISSUES FOR THE REVIEW 87
The Discussion Points 91
Annex I. History of SDR Valuation Framework 93

Annex II. Electronic Trading Platforms and Principal Exchange Markets.. 96

Annex III. The Role of Hong Kong SAR as a Global Financial Center: Implications for Freely Usable Assessment.. 98

Annex IV. Renminbi internationalization 101

Underlying Policy measures to Promote RMB Internationalization 104

Gradual opening of the capital account 104

Domestic Financial Reforms 108

Cross-Border Payments Infrastructure and Offshore Liquidity... 109

Annex V. Data Issues Pertaining to the Freely Usable Currency Assessment 111

Board-endorsed Indicators (2011) 111

New proposed indicators 116

CHAPTER 3 .... **120**

SDR: Reserve Currencies and the International Monetary System's Future 120

II.   Analytical Issues... 122

III. International Currencies: The SDR and its Rivals 131

IV. Implications for the Future.............................. 140

V.   Implications of the Evolution of the International Monetary System 146

What is the Future of the SDR as an International Reserve Asset? The Financial System. 158

The Evolution Of Special Drawing Rights (SDRs) 175

Trends in SDR allocation and the global reserve system 178
The IMF, developing countries and SDR creation 180
Proposals for an SDR geared toward development . 184
Analysis of proposals for development SDR 187
CHAPTER 4 189
The Argument For A Development SDR 189
The Argument 'Against' Development SDRS 191
Proposed mechanisms for creating a development SDR 194
Conditions for creating a development SDR and links to debt relief.. 195
Timing the creation of SDR to support developing countries... 197
Proposed Institutional Re-Organization For Creating A Development SDR 199
An assessment of the proposals for a development SDR 201
Development SDRs versus other forms of assistance 201
A global fund versus individual countries' access to more liquid assets... 203
Structuring The Issuance And Management Of New SDR 205
Special drawing rights, the dollar, and the institutionalist approach to reserve currency status . 206
CHAPTER 5 207
Four Approaches To Reserve Currency Status 207

(a) The institutionalist approach to reserve currency status.. 207

(b) How the Federal Reserve, as an institution, enhanced the dollar's reserve status 209

Why SDRs Are Not Currently A Viable Alternative To The Dollar: An Institutionalist Criticism..................... 214

A Criticism Of Eichengreen's Definition Of SDRs..... 217

Why Zhou and Stiglitz want to expand the role of SDRs 220

An Institutionalist Criticism Of SDRs 225

What Is The Federal Reserve Bank And What Do You Need To Know About It?.. 229

Understanding the 1913 Federal Reserve Act.......... 234

The Fed System 235

Current Federal Reserve Board................................ 235

CHAPTER 6 237

How The Federal Reserve Was Formed................... 237

America Before the Federal Reserve........................ 237

J.P. Morgan and the Panic of 1907 238

Learning from Europe... 238

The Great Depression 239

The Post-War Recovery 240

Inflation or Unemployment? 240

The Greenspan Years... 240

5 Need-To-Know Facts About the Federal Reserve 241

How Central Banks Create Money Out From The Thin Air 243

The Central Banks.. 244

SPECIAL DRAWING RIGHTS (SDR) AND THE FEDERAL RESERVE

The Fed 245
How Quantitative Easing Affects You 246
The New Laws of Money 247
How The Federal Reserve Literally Makes Money.... 248
Printing green 248
Magicking green 249
Costs Of Magical Money 249
The other cost is a consequence of reallocating credit.
.... 250
Uncharted waters 250
How The Fed Injects Money Into The Economy 252
QUESTION: IS THE ADMINISTRATION TRYING TO BYPASS CONGRESS IN APPROVING AN SDR ALLOCATION?.. 258
QUESTION: DOES AN SDR ALLOCATION IMPOSE A LARGE FINANCIAL BURDEN ON THE UNITED STATES? 259
QUESTION: WILL THE UNITED STATES BE REQUIRED TO EXCHANGE DOLLARS FOR SDRS WITH ANY IMF MEMBER ON DEMAND?... 260
QUESTION: IS THERE A NEED FOR AN SDR ALLOCATION TO SUPPORT GLOBAL RESERVES? 260
QUESTION: IS THERE A NEED FOR AN SDR ALLOCATION GIVEN THE GLOBAL ECONOMY IS RECOVERING?... 261
QUESTION: IS AN SDR ALLOCATION A CASH GIVEAWAY? 262

QUESTION: DOES AN SDR ALLOCATION ONLY BENEFIT RICH COUNTRIES, AS OPPOSED TO THE COUNTRIES THAT NEED IT? 262

QUESTION: IS THERE TRANSPARENCY AND ACCOUNTABILITY IN HOW SDRS ARE USED? 263

QUESTION: IS AN SDR ALLOCATION A LIFELINE FOR DICTATORS? 263

QUESTION: WILL AN SDR ALLOCATION PUT AT RISK THE DOLLAR'S RESERVE CURRENCY STATUS? .. 264

CONCLUSION **264**

ABOUT THE AUTHOR

Sir Patrick Bijou is Senior Judge for the ICJ-ICC, Ambassador for the United Nations, a British investment banker, philanthropist, and a published author. Sir Patrick specializes in the debt capital markets, private placements, equities, derivatives and futures trading. He has worked with multiple leading banks such as Wells Fargo, Deutsche Bank, Credit Agricole CIB, Merrill Lynch and others, apart from trading on Wall Street.

He has over four decade's experience in the financial field and has worked with numerous prolific clients, including governments, banking institutions, and corporations. He is also a renowned author and has published over 21 books across several genres.

Sir Patrick was born in Georgetown, Guyana, South America. At the age of five, he came to Britain when his father obtained a scholarship to study and has remained in the U.K. ever since. Having been brought up in London, he spent part of his education in England and completed his education in the USA, where he obtained his degrees in Business Studies and later an MBA in Economic and International banking.

As a notable investment banker, he has also worked on Wall Street, and is a skillful and highly experienced Tier 1 trader in the derivative and bond markets, and he also established MTN desks within various significant banks. He became responsible for the setup of the MTN & Private Placement Desk and dealer functions within Lloyds Bank PLC, and was the first trader for Lloyd's treasury to increase the portion of self-led deals significantly from 4% to 32% in 2002.

Sir Patrick has tailored funding and investments for many different clients, including governments, banks and financial institutions, and has implemented over $16.B funding for socio-economic and humanitarian projects.

He has excelled as an investment banker and was awarded many accolades such as the Multiple Recipient, of the Wells Fargo "Valley of the Stars" award throughout his illustrious career. He was also distinguished by receiving the Wells Fargo "Circle of Stars" award, and was a Member of Wells Fargo's "Millionaire Club" and "Champion Circle". This further propelled him to then become the notable banker he is today. He was finally awarded his most distinguished accolade of all, a knighthood, for his services to banking and philanthropy.

His expertise is so profound that he was headhunted for a position within the International Court of Justice Redemption Department for his finance and international law proficiency to become a member of the Panel of Arbitrators of the International Centre for the Settlement of Investment Disputes. He currently sits as a Senior Judge of the ICJ-ICC. Sir Patrick manages to fit all these activities into his current role as Fund Manager for LWPCapital, and is also distinguished as being a U.N. Ambassador.

He is also a Global Ambassador for the International Rights and Welfare Association (IRAWA), and Ambassador of the Royal

Diplomatic Club. In May 2021, he was appointed Ambassador by The Academy of Universal Global Peace USA as a member of the governing board/trustees and awarded The Human Excellency Award and Presidency of the Commonwealth Entrepreneurs Club.

One of his most significant career achievements was creating a line of credit for international supply chains and SMEs for the public sector and government funding through PPP. He also helped create the Contract for Difference (CFD) economic phenomena and credit leverage ratio concepts, regarded as hugely pioneering, which all banks and trading institutions have adopted today.

His journey into content writing has allowed him to become an exceptionally motivated and enthusiastic author and professional communicator, experienced in proactive campaign-driven and responsive communications.

His platforms are at Credit Suisse Geneva and DBS Singapore, where he manages high yield investments with attractive returns for selective high net worth clients.

"Coming together is a beginning, keeping together is progress, and working together is a success."

Sir Patrick Bijou

BOOK DESCRIPTION

This book would help you understand how ***Special Drawing Right And The Federal Reserve Works***. It also discusses the various process and the SDR's origin and characteristics and shows you how you can put that knowledge to good use. SDRs were devised in response to concerns about the limitations of gold and dollars as the sole means of settling international accounts. The SDRs contribute to growth in global liquidity by enhancing the standard reserve currencies. Once you have a clear understanding of what Special Drawing Rights mean then you will understand its impact on the economy.

SDRs were established with the goal of subjecting international liquidity control for the first time to international dialogue and determination. The Special Drawing Right (SDR) is not a currency, nor is it a claim on the IMF. I argue that institutions can enhance a currency's reserve status by creating liquid markets and by intervening quickly in financial crises. This book describes extensively how best Special Drawing Right Works and *as you read you'll discover:*

1. The SDR's Origins And Characteristics
2. The SDR Department's Operations
3. Origins And Guiding Principles For SDR Valuation
4. The Evolution Of Special Drawing Rights (SDRs)
5. The Argument For A Development SDR
6. Four Approaches To Reserve Currency Status
7. Understanding The 1913 Federal Reserve Act
8. How The Federal Reserve Was Formed
9. How The Fed Injects Money Into The Economy

And More.

CHAPTER 1

INTRODUCTION

International reserve assets, such as special drawing rights (SDRs), were established in 1969 to supplement the growth of other reserve assets, which were deemed insufficient to finance the expansion of international trade and finance under the Bretton Woods system in the postwar period, as well as to support the Bretton Woods fixed exchange rate system. The SDR was established with the goal of subjecting international liquidity control for the first time to international dialogue and determination. The Special Drawing Right (SDR) is not a currency, nor is it a claim on the IMF. Instead, it is a prospective claim on the freely useable currencies of IMF members. It is possible for the IMF to allocate SDRs to members (participants) on an unconditional basis, allowing them to use them to obtain freely useable currencies in order to achieve a balance of payments need without imposing economic policy measures or incurring repayment obligations.

Following a brief introduction to the SDR's history and characteristics, this chapter describes the procedures that are used to value the SDR and compute its yield value (SDR interest rate). Following that, it examines the rules for the allocation and cancellation of SDRs. It also describes the operations of the SDR Department, as well as the nature and history of voluntary SDR trading arrangements, with a particular emphasis on the IMF's crucial role. Finally, Others draws attention to the distinction between the General and SDR Departments of the International Monetary Fund, as depicted in the SDR Department's balance sheet.

The SDR's Origins and Characteristics

It was during the 1960s that the Bretton Woods fixed exchange rate system came under increasing pressure due to the lack of a mechanism for limiting the accumulation of reserves required to finance the expansion of world trade and financial development. As a result of the continued growth in worldwide U.S. dollar reserves necessitating a constant deficit in the United States balance of payments, the dollar's value was under threat. Gold production was an inadequate and unreliable source of reserve supplies. The world community has decided to establish a new international reserve asset under the aegis of the International Monetary Fund (IMF).

Following the introduction of the SDR, the International Monetary Fund (IMF) formed the SDR Department to oversee all SDR transactions. In order to supplement existing reserve assets, the International Monetary Fund (IMF) created the SDR, which can only be held and used by participants in the SDR Department, the IMF through the General Resources Account (GRA), and certain designated official entities referred to as "prescribed holders."

The Articles of Agreement of the International Monetary Fund (IMF) mandate that the General Department and the SDR Department be maintained completely separate. It is not permissible to use any assets or property held by one department to satisfy the liabilities, obligations, or losses of the IMF incurred by another department in the course of its operations and transactions, except in the case of reimbursement of the General Department for expenses incurred by the SDR Department in the course of its business. Although all current IMF members are also members of the SDR Department, it is not required that an IMF member be a member of the SDR Department. Participants' holdings of SDRs are included in their international reserves, along with their gold, foreign exchange, and reserve position in the International Monetary Fund. Almost exclusively, the SDR is used in transactions with the International Monetary Fund, and it is also used as the unit of account for the IMF and a number of other international organizations.

The value of the SDR as a reserve asset is derived from the pledges of members to exchange SDRs for freely useable currencies and to fulfill certain duties associated with the proper operation of the SDR Department. SDRs is not a liability of the International Monetary Fund. As a middleman between holders of SDRs in a voluntary but controlled market, the IMF helps to ensure the SDR's claim on freely useable currencies. Members may also utilize SDRs outside of this market to acquire foreign exchange in a transaction if they reach an agreement with another participant or group of participants. Participants are under no obligation to maintain any specific level of SDR holdings as a result of current Executive Board decisions. Since September 1987, the SDR market has been predominantly supported by voluntary SDR trading contracts between parties (VTAs). A number of members and one prescribed holder have volunteered to buy and sell SDRs in accordance with the terms of their separate arrangements. As a last resort, the IMF can activate the designation mechanism if there is inadequate capacity under the voluntary trade arrangements: IMF members with a solid balance of payments and reserves position may be designated by the IMF to acquire SDRs from members with weak external positions. This designation procedure acts as a safety net to ensure the SDR's liquidity and reserve asset status. In this way, the SDR Department's work, like that of the General Department, is founded on the principles of reciprocity and intergovernmental collaboration.

The value of the SDR, as well as its yield, are determined by the exchange rate system in use at the time. Initially, this was the Bretton Woods fixed exchange rate system, but it has since changed to a basket of currencies. SDR basket, as revised on October 1, 2016, consists of five freely usable currencies: the

United States dollar, the European Union's single currency, the Chinese yuan, the Japanese yen, and the British pound. The value of the SDR is determined daily as the total of precise amounts of the five basket currencies valued in U.S. dollars, using exchange rates quoted in the London market at noon each day. The SDR's worth in US dollars is updated on a daily basis on the IMF Finances website.

After years of being fixed and below market, the SDR interest rate is now market-based and computed on a weekly basis. Unless the weighted average falls below the 0.050 percent floor for the SDR interest rate, it is calculated using a weighted average of representative interest rates on short-term government debt in the money markets of the SDR basket of currencies, in which case the weighted average is calculated using the SDR interest rate (5 basis points). Although both the valuation and the yield of the SDR are related to the prevailing markets for their component exchange rates and interest rates, there is no market for the SDR itself in which excess supply or demand pressure can be alleviated by modifications in the price, or value, of the SDR. Instead, the International Monetary Fund (IMF) regulates the flow of SDRs to guarantee that there is sufficient liquidity in the system. Members participating in the SDR Department may be allocated SDRs in proportion to their IMF quotas by the IMF under specified conditions (Article XV (1) and Article XVIII), subject to the approval of 85 percent of the IMF's voting power. On April 30, 2016, there were only three regular allocations of SDRs and one exceptional allocation, bringing the total number of general allocations to four. Following the entry into force of the Fourth Amendment, the IMF made two allocations in 2009: one general allocation to meet a long-term global need for reserves while also aiding in the mitigation of the effects of the global financial crisis, and a special allocation following the passage of the Fourth Amendment to allow all members of the SDR Department to participate in the

SDR system on an equal footing. The International Monetary Fund's (IMF) allocation of SDRs provides each recipient country with an asset that is completely free of charge. A member earns interest on its holdings and pays interest on its cumulative allocations, but the interest rates on the two accounts are equivalent, and the payments are therefore equal as long as the member's cumulative allocations match the amount of SDRs that the member has in possession of. A country's SDRs can be converted into freely useable currencies at a rate defined by the SDR basket's value, allowing it to use these assets.

Countries that use their SDRs and, as a result, hold less SDRs than their cumulative allocations pay interest at the SDR interest rate on the difference between their cumulative allocations and their current holdings. Countries that possess more SDRs than their cumulative allocations and are therefore net creditors in the SDR system get interest on the excess SDR holdings in the same proportion as their cumulative allocations. The SDR Department is in charge of keeping track of all SDR transactions, holdings, and allocations, among other things.

SDR VALUATION

The system by which the SDR is valued has exhibited a high degree of consistency, and it has only been updated in response to significant shifts in the relative importance of other currencies in the world economy. Following the introduction of the euro in 1999, the present standards for the value of SDRs were established. Until the 1980s, when the SDR valuation basket was reduced from 16 to 5 currencies, and before that, when the SDR was linked to the value of gold, the criteria that guided the 2000 decision were in existence. Following the most current assessment, which finished in November 2015, the Executive Board opted to add the Chinese yuan in the SDR basket, which became effective on October 1, 2016. As a result, the current SDR basket is comprised of five currencies: The United States dollar, the euro, the Chinese yuan, the Japanese yen, and the pound sterling, among others.

Basket of SDR

It's the 16 members of the International Monetary Fund (IMF) who represented at least one percent of global commerce when the Special Drawing Rights (SDR) were redefined as a currency basket in 1974. A new policy was instituted at the same time, and the interest rate on the SDR was raised to 5 percent. The rate was set semiannually at approximately half the level of a combined market interest rate, which was defined as a weighted average of interest rates on short-term market instruments in France, Germany, Japan, the United Kingdom, and the United States, among other countries.

Because it was difficult and expensive to replicate, as well as because it comprised certain currencies that were not regularly traded, the 16-currency SDR basket proved difficult to administer as a unit of account. As a result of having a lower yield than comparable reserve assets, it also performed poorly as a store of value. For these reasons, the SDR's valuation was simplified in 1981: it would be valued using the same five-currency basket that determined the SDR interest rate, and the interest rate itself would be equivalent to market rates, rather than the complex formula used previously. Over the preceding five years, the valuation basket was defined as a collection of currencies representing the five member countries with the highest levels of exports of goods and services. In response to these modifications, both the SDR valuation and the SDR interest rate baskets were composed of the five freely usable currencies recognized by the IMF at the time: The United States dollar, the Japanese yen, the Deutsche mark, the French franc, and the pound sterling (at the time). The five- currency basket was basic enough to be easily replicated by financial markets while still ensuring that the SDR's value remained relatively steady in the face of large swings in exchange rates, as was the case in 2008. Because of the introduction of the euro in 1999, the Deutsche mark and the French franc were replaced in the SDR basket with an equivalent amount of euros, resulting in a four-currency basket. However, the relative weight of the continental European currencies remained intact. A review of the SDR value conducted in 2015 culminated in a decision to include the Chinese renminbi in the SDR basket on October 1, 2016, which became effective on that day. The Executive Board also agreed to amend the composition of the SDR interest rate basket to include a short-term financial instrument denominated in the Chinese yuan, which was previously absent. The IMF, its members, and other SDR users were given a reasonable amount of time to acclimate to the new SDR basket, which was implemented in phases over a period of time.

Valuation Method for SDRs Currently In Use

After every five years, the Executive Board of the International Monetary Fund examines the value of the Special Drawing Rights (SDR). In five-yearly reviews, the currencies to be included in the SDR valuation basket (along with the criteria for selecting those currencies) are discussed, as well as the relative weights of those currencies, as well as the financial instruments that are used to calculate the SDR interest rate are evaluated. A number of longstanding concepts have driven the revisions, all of which aim to increase the appeal of the SDR as a reserve asset in the future. The Executive Board has broad discretion to decide the method of valuation for the Special Drawing Rights (SDR), according to the Articles of Agreement. Following the introduction of the euro into the SDR basket, the Executive Board revised the criterion for selecting the SDR value basket. By incorporating the euro, the SDR basket includes not only currencies issued by Fund members, but also currencies issued by monetary unions, bringing the total number of currencies in the basket to twenty-five.

SDR currency selection criteria are based on two criteria: the first is based on the proportionate scale of exports; the second requires that a currency be determined by the Fund to be freely usable. The SDR valuation framework was developed in 2000 and includes two criteria for SDR currency selection. In terms of the first criterion, historically, exports have played a significant impact in the selection of SDR baskets. In order to reflect countries' relative importance in global commerce, to provide an appropriate capacity to supply reserve assets, and to limit the number of currencies in the basket, this size-related "gateway" currency selection criterion has been implemented.

It was established by the Executive Board in 2000 that currencies in the SDR basket must be freely useable as a second currency selection criterion. This judgment recognized that a country's proportion of world exports is not always a trustworthy predictor of the amount to which its currency is utilized in international transactions, nor is it an accurate gauge of the depth and breadth of a country's financial markets, as was previously believed. It is possible to take into account several other indicators of a country's financial markets when determining whether a currency is freely usable, such as the level of official reserves held in that currency by other member countries, as well as the breadth and depth of the country's financial markets. This requirement was also consistent with previous Executive Board decisions; for example, one of the goals of the 1980 decision to reduce the number of currencies in the SDR basket from 16 to 5 was to ensure that the basket's currencies had broad and deep foreign exchange markets, which is a key element of the concept of a freely usable currency (also known as a freely convertible currency).

A crucial notion in the IMF's financial operations is the concept of freely available resources, which is defined in its Articles of Agreement (Article XXX(f)). It is expected that members receiving financial assistance from the Fund will be able to meet their balance of payments obligations, either directly because the currency is widely used to make payments for international transactions, or indirectly because it is widely traded in the principal exchange markets.

When the Executive Board met in October 2011, they reviewed ideas for clarifying and maybe modifying the present criteria for expanding the SDR currency basket. The majority of Executive Directors were of the opinion that the criteria for SDR basket selection remained suitable and that the threshold for inclusion in the SDR basket should not be lower. It was highlighted by the Executive Directors, however, that determining free usability would need considerable judgment, which would be framed by the definition of freely usable currency set forth in the Articles of Agreement. Also emphasized was the significance of permitting adjustments in the basket to keep up with changes in the international monetary system, according to a number of Executive Directors. With regard to the 2015 SDR value review, the Executive Board reiterated that the current valuation system, which was first implemented in 2000, was still suitable, and that the two criteria for currency selection continued to be appropriate.

The initial weights of each currency in the SDR basket are also determined via SDR valuation evaluations. For a long time, the weights were determined by a mathematical equation. A new technique for estimating the currency weight of SDR units was approved by the Board of Directors in the 2015 SDR review. Among the longstanding concerns about the previous formula were its relatively high weight on exports and limited coverage of financial flows. The new formula intended to address these concerns while preserving a simple, transparent formula and wide stability in the currency weights. Exports and a composite financial indicator are given equal weights in the new formula. The latter additionally broadens the scope of financial flows' representativeness by covering not only official reserves (as was previously the case), but also foreign exchange market turnover, international banking liabilities, and international debt securities, among other things.

Currency Weights in the SDR Basket

	2000 Review	2005 Review	2010 Review[1]
U.S. Dollar	45	44	41.9
Euro	29	34	37.4
Japanese Yen	15	11	9.4
Pound Sterling	11	11	11.3

It was on October 1, 2016, that the new SDR valuation and SDR interest rate basket took effect.

The initial weights of the currencies in the basket are determined by the Executive Board every five years, although the weights alter over time in response to changes in exchange rates. Amounts in specific currencies that are consistent with the initial weights are established as soon as the decision becomes effective. On the basis of these fixed currency amounts, further daily valuations of the SDR are computed. Exchange rate fluctuations impact the relative weights of the component currencies, with appreciating currencies receiving a larger part of the basket as a result of the fluctuation in the exchange rate.

Interest Rate Of SDR

When calculating the interest charged to members on no concessional IMF loans from the IMF's general resources, the SDR interest rate is used as the basis for calculating the interest paid to members on their remunerated creditor positions in the IMF (reserve tranche positions and claims under borrowing agreements), as well as the interest paid to members on their SDR holdings and the interest charged on the SDR allocation. The SDR interest rate is determined on a weekly basis and is based on a weighted average of representative interest rates on short-term financial debt instruments in the money markets of the SDR basket currencies, except when the weighted average falls below the floor for the SDR interest rate of 0.050 percent, in which case the floor for the SDR interest rate is applied (5 basis points). When the valuation technique for the SDR is reviewed on a five-year cycle, it is also examined to see if any of the financial instruments that are used to determine the SDR interest rate are still in use. On two main criteria, representativeness and risk characteristics, the Executive Board has agreed:

It is important that the financial instruments in the interest rate basket be broadly representative of the range of financial instruments that are actually available to investors in a particular currency, and that the interest rate on the instruments is responsive to changes in underlying credit conditions in the corresponding money market.

- The financial instruments included in the interest rate basket should have characteristics that are similar to the official standing of the SDR itself, that is, they should have a credit risk profile of the highest quality and be fully comparable to that of government paper available on the market, or, in the absence of appropriate official paper, comparable to the credit risk on prime financial instruments.
- The financial instruments included in the interest rate basket should have characteristics that are similar to the official standing of the SDR itself, that is, they should have a credit risk profile of It is also important that instruments represent the actual reserve asset selection made by reserve managers in terms of the shape of the financial instrument, its liquidity, and its maturity, for instance.

SPECIAL DRAWING RIGHTS (SDR) AND THE FEDERAL RESERVE

Interest Rates on the SDR and Its Financial Instrument Components, 2005—15. (Percent a year)

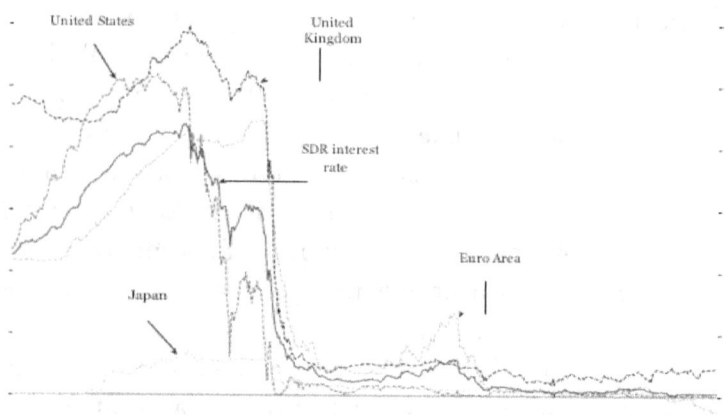

Since the beginning of October 2016, the following are the benchmark rates for the five currencies:

- Dollar: three-month Treasury notes issued by the United States. In the Eurozone, the European Central Bank publishes a three-month rate for euro area central government bonds with credit ratings of AA and higher.
- Chinese renminbi: The China Central Depository and Clearing Co. Ltd. publish a 3-month benchmark rate for China Treasury bonds that is used as a benchmark for the country's debt.
- Japanese yen: Japanese Treasury discount notes maturing in three months
- Pound sterling: three-month Treasury notes issued by the United Kingdom.

As previously stated, the SDR interest rate is determined by taking a weighted average of the yields on these instruments and averaging them out for each week, except that the SDR interest rate is subject to a minimum floor of 5 basis points. A diagram depicting changes in the SDR interest rate since the 2000 review may be seen at Figure 4.2.

Cancellations and Allocations of SDRs

Under the Articles of Agreement (Articles XV (1) and XVIII), the Executive Board of the International Monetary Fund (IMF) has the authority to create unconditional liquidity by allocating SDRs to member countries that participate in the SDR Department in proportion to their IMF quotas in the SDR Department. Each member receives an unconditional international reserve asset as a result of such a division of resources. If a member's SDR holdings exceed the amount of his or her net cumulative allocation, the member will receive interest on the excess. The opposite is true: if it has less SDRs than its net cumulative allocation, it is obligated to pay interest on the difference. The Articles of Agreement also provide for the cancellation of SDRs, however no cancellations have been place to yet. The International Monetary Fund (IMF) is prohibited from allocating SDRs to itself or to designated holders.

In making decisions on general allocations of SDRs, as required by the Articles of Agreement, the International Monetary Fund has sought to meet the long-term global need to supplement existing reserve assets while also promoting the achievement of the IMF's objectives, which include avoiding economic stagnation and deflation and preventing excess demand and inflation in the economy. Generally speaking, decisions on SDR general allocations are made for successive basic periods of up to five years.

The decision on a general allocation of SDRs is made in accordance with a predetermined method. Firstly once it has been determined that a proposal for an SDR allocation has widespread support among SDR members, the Managing Director is required to make such a proposal at least 6 months before the start of a basic period, or within 6 months of receiving a request for a proposal from the Executive Board or Board of

Governors, or at such other times as specified by Article XVIII. Second, if a request for an allocation is made, the proposal must be approved by the Executive Committee. Third, the Board of Governors has the authority to accept or amend the plan if a majority of 85 percent of its total voting power votes in favor of doing so.

SDR allocations are a type of unconditional liquidity that is available at any time. In order to obtain their proportional share of a general allocation, participants in the SDR Department are not required to satisfy any special conditions. In addition, following such an allocation, they will have the ability to use the newly allocated SDRs when they have a balance of payments requirement or when they need to adjust the composition of their reserves in order to obtain currency from other participants in transactions by agreement or, if necessary, through the designation plan, or both. According to to current Executive Board decisions, there is no duty to maintain a specific amount of SDR holdings in any single currency. Therefore, participants of the SDR system have access on demand to freely useable currencies on an unconditional basis with no set maturity, as long as they meet the requirements of the system.

General SDR allocations have only been made three times in the past three years. The first allocation, which totaled SDR 9.3 billion, was distributed in 1970—72; the second, which totaled SDR 12.1 billion, was delivered in 1979—81; and the third, which totaled SDR 12.1 billion, was distributed in 1980—81. Following these two allocations, the overall cumulative SDR allocations reached 21.4 billion SDRs. It was announced on August 28, 2009, that the third general SDR allocation will be made in order to fulfill the long-term global need for reserves while also assisting in mitigating the impacts of the global financial crisis. An amount of SDR 161.2 billion was made available to assist liquidity-constrained countries in dealing with the aftermath of the global financial crisis by limiting their need to adjust through contractionary policies and by allowing them greater flexibility to pursue countercyclical policies in the face of deflationary risks. Using extra SDR reserves rather than borrowed reserves, it was determined that systemic stability would be enhanced in the long run.

Additional to that, on August 10th, 2009, the Fourth Amendment to the Articles of Agreement came into force, which called for a special one-time allocation of SDR 21.5 billion, which was implemented on September 9th, 2009.

The purpose of the special allocation was to enable all members of the IMF SDR Department to participate in the SDR system on an equitable basis, as well as to compensate for the fact that countries that joined the IMF after 1981 constituted more than one-fifth of the current IMF membership at the time, with many of the economies in transition being among those who had not received an SDR allocation at the time of the special allocation. The combined sum of general and exceptional SDR allocations for 2009 brought the overall cumulative SDR allocations to about SDR 204.1 billion.

The SDR allocations for 2009 were disproportionately high, resulting in a more than tenfold rise in SDR holdings globally as a result.

The allocations for 2009 resulted to a considerable rise in reserve coverage for all member nations as a result of the allocations. The industrialized economies received the lion's share of the SDR allocation, accounting for 62 percent of the total due to their greater quota sizes. When evaluated in terms of economic size, on the other hand, low-income nations received the greatest share of the allocation, followed by emerging market economies.

The allocations had a significant influence on the currency composition of nations' reserves as well as on the decisions made by those countries regarding their reserve management. Following the 2009 allocations, over 30% of low- and developing-income countries and emerging market economies chose between September and December 2009 to either sell part of the SDRs against the currencies of other members or utilize them to repay the IMF.

SDR Allocations: General and Special

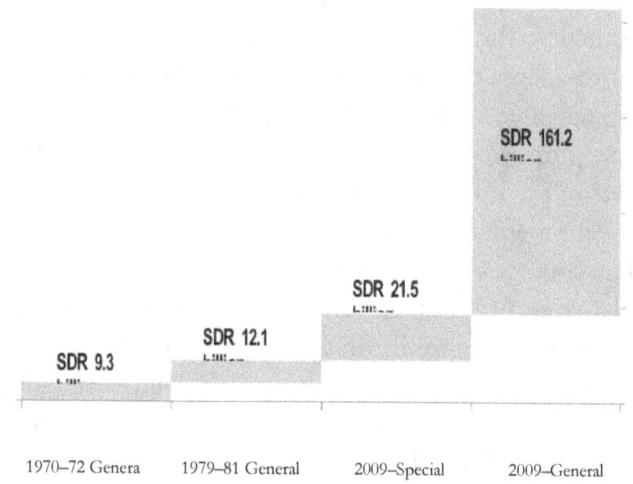

The SDR Department's Operations
Prescription Holders and Participants

SDRs are only provided to IMF members who opt to participate in the SDR Department and agree to abide by the responsibilities of participation. SDRs are not distributed to non-participants. Since the SDR Department was established on April 7, 1980, all members of the IMF have been participants.

In line with the Articles of Agreement and the decisions taken by the IMF Executive Board and Board of Governors, SDRs may be used by IMF members and the IMF itself to finance economic development projects. SDRs are not permitted to be held by private companies or individual investors. Other SDR holders include the International Monetary Fund (IMF), which holds SDRs through the General Resources Account

(GRA) inside the General Department, as well as international organizations and monetary institutions that have been prescribed by the IMF.

Members, nonmembers, member nations that are not participants in the SDR Department, organizations that execute the tasks of a central bank for more than one member and other official bodies are all subject to the IMF's prescribing authority. As of April 30, 2016, a total of 15 organizations had been certified as "prescribed holders" under the law. It is possible for these companies to purchase and utilize SDRs in transactions by agreement as well as in activities with other participants and holders. They are not permitted to obtain SDR allocations or to utilize SDRs in "transactions with designation," on the other hand. In general, there is no mechanism for specified holders to begin transactions in SDRs with the General Resources Account in the General Resources Account.

Flows of SDRs and the IMF's Central Role in the World Economy

According to the Articles of Agreement, participants may trade SDRs for foreign currency among themselves, and the Executive Board has the authority to allow any additional activities. With this authority come to a series of decisions from the IMF, which permit a wide variety of transactions involving SDR Department participants and designated holders, including loans, pledges, gifts and swaps as well as futures and forward operations. The Articles of Agreement permits the exchange of SDRs for other currencies between participating countries. SDRs are a possible claim on the freely usable currencies of IMF members when employed in such activities; however, they are not a claim against the IMF when used in such operations. It is used as the unit of account by the International Monetary Fund and a number of other international organizations.

SPECIAL DRAWING RIGHTS (SDR) AND THE FEDERAL RESERVE

Circulation of SDRs

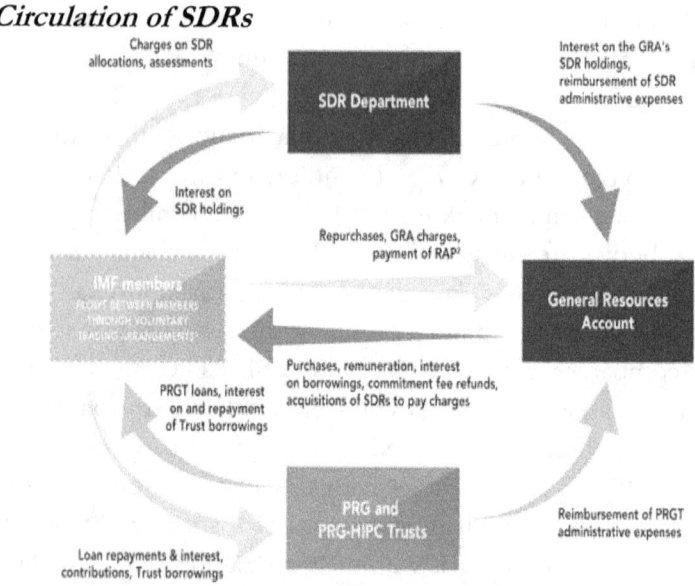

The SDR Department is self-financed, and its fundamental structure is straightforward: it charges interest on members' SDR allocations at the same rate as the interest paid on members' SDR holdings, and it does not charge interest on members' SDR allocations if they do not own SDRs. It is a closed system, with the interest payments and revenues in the SDR Department canceling each other out on a grand scale overall. Similarly, to what was stated earlier, the IMF sets the SDR interest rate on a weekly basis using a weighted average of representative interest rates on three-month debt in the money markets of the SDR basket currencies.

It is widely utilized in transactions and activities between members of the International Monetary Fund (IMF), as well as in the General Resources Account, which plays a key role in the circulation of SDRs.

The following are examples of SDR inflows into the General Resources Account:

(1) repurchases by members in SDRs; (2) payment of the reserve asset share (25 percent) of quota increases. (3) Payments of charges on GRA credit; (4) interest generated on the GRA's own SDR holdings; and (5) assessments for the cost of conducting the operations of the SDR Department.

The following are examples of SDR outflows from the General Resources Account:

(1) payments on members' reserve tranche positions, (2) repayments of GRA borrowing (bilateral loan claims or claims under the New Arrangements to Borrow), (3) interest on IMF borrowing, and (4) sales of SDRs to members for the payment of charges and assessments are all possible uses for the SDR.

The IMF generally offers SDRs as an alternative to currencies in lending operations and transactions with members. In practice, the majority of purchases, repurchases, and loan drawings and repayments tend to be made in currencies, whereas charges, remuneration, interest on loans, and to some extent the reserve asset portion of quota payments tend to be paid in SDRs. Members are not obliged to accept SDRs in any transaction except replenishment, which is a special procedure that the IMF could use to rebuild its holdings of the currency of a participant in the SDR Department. Members who obtain SDRs from the Fund may request to convert these to a freely usable currency in transactions by agreement with other members.

The main flows of SDRs into and out of the General Resources Account are depicted in Figure 4.5, which shows the relative proportions of this flows over the last 10 years and compares them with the level of transactions among participants and prescribed holders.

The IMF recycles the stock of SDRs held in the General Resources Account in two main ways. First, SDRs are channeled directly to debtor members who are making purchases from the

IMF. Second, SDRs are channeled indirectly from the holders of SDRs to other members who need to acquire SDRs to make payments to the IMF (charges and repurchases). The IMF may also assist members in buying or selling SDRs for reserve management purposes. Such transactions are carried out through the voluntary SDR trading arrangements.

Selected SDR Transactions, 2005—15
(Billions of SDRs, as of April 30 each year)
Transactions among Participants and Prescribed Holders
By Agreement Other Prescribed Operations

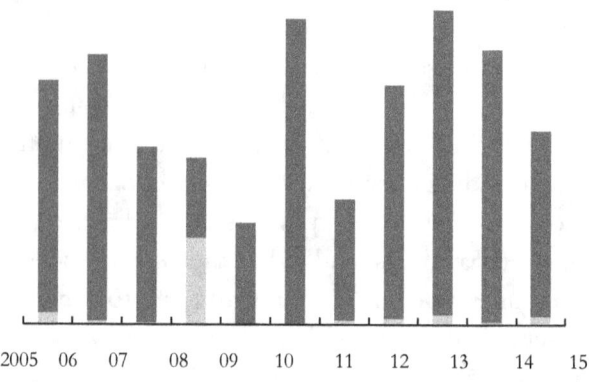

SDR Holdings at the International Monetary Fund

The General Resources Account provides one of the mechanisms for the circulation of SDRs, both to debtor members in connection with their purchases from the IMF and to creditor members through the payment of interest on IMF borrowing and payment on remunerated reserve tranche positions in the GRA. The GRA's holdings of SDRs tend to rise in the wake of reserve asset payments of quota increases for example, following payments of the adhoc quota increases in FY2011 and the quota increase under the Fourteenth General Review in FY2016. The GRA rebalances its SDR holdings mainly through transfers of SDRs for purchases under its quarterly Financial Transactions Plan.

Arrangements for Voluntary SDR Trading

IMF members regularly need to buy SDRs to discharge their obligations to the IMF or to replenish their SDR holdings. They may also wish to sell SDRs in order to adjust the composition of their reserves. A participant or prescribed holder may use SDRs freely, without representing a balance of payments need, to obtain an equivalent amount of currency in a transaction by agreement.

Participants may conduct such transactions bilaterally with any participant or prescribed holder. However, in practice, such transactions are usually made through a market in SDRs coordinated by the IMF through voluntary trading arrangements to buy and sell SDRs with a group of participants and one prescribed holder (so-called market makers). The role of the IMF in transactions by agreement is to act as an intermediary, matching participants in this managed market in a manner that meets, to the greatest extent possible, the requirements and preferences of buyers and sellers of SDRs. The voluntary trading arrangements allow the IMF to facilitate purchases and sales of SDRs on behalf of any participant or prescribed holder in the SDR Department against freely usable currencies, subject to the constraint that all transactions take place at the official SDR exchange rate for the currency involved.

***SDR Sales: Participation by Market-Makers by Region
September 1, 2009—April 30, 2015
(Millions of SDRs)***

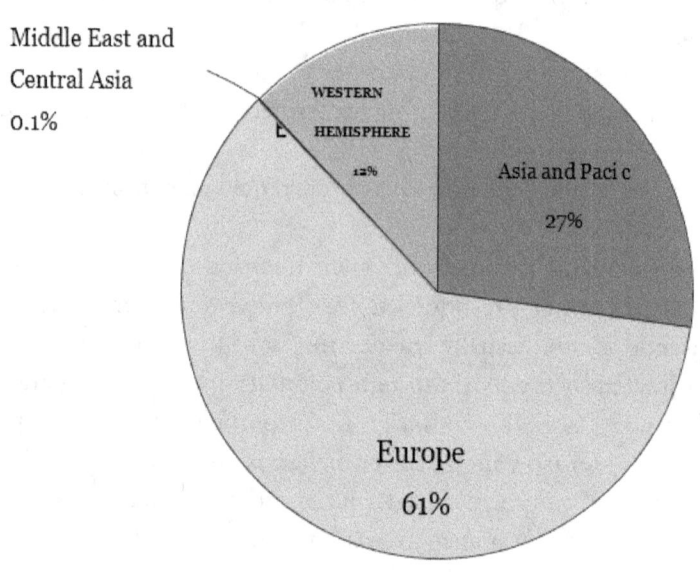

Since the 2009 SDR allocations, the voluntary SDR market has been substantially expanded and has absorbed all sales requests. The number of participants in two-way arrangements has expanded and now stands at 32, including 19 new arrangements since the 2009 SDR allocations and includes both advanced economies and several large emerging market economies.

The IMF staff allocates requests for SDR sales and acquisitions using informal modalities developed to produce equitable bur- den sharing over time. Since the 2009 SDR allocations, sales of SDRs have been allocated among most market makers spanning four major geographical regions. SDR holdings of some market makers are also affected by operations unrelated to their participation in voluntary trading arrangements, including the receipt of remuneration, SDR interest payments, the use of SDRs for Poverty Reduction and Growth Trust (PRGT) lending and subsidy contributions, and the use of SDRs to pay quota increases. In general, market makers with relatively low SDR holdings compared with cumulative allocations have been used more extensively in SDR sales transactions. (Conversely, market makers with higher SDR holdings compared with allocations have been used more in SDR acquisitions.) Consistent with this informal burdensharing modalities, the IMF staff continues to seek the utilization of all arrangements over time.

Each two-way arrangement specifies a range of SDR holdings within which transactions may be initiated, the specific currencies to be exchanged, the minimum and maximum amounts of individual transactions, and the notice period required before initiating a particular transaction.

The ranges of these voluntary trading arrangements have been broadened considerably to ensure increased trading capacity. New trading ranges are now defined as a percent of the net cumulative allocations compared with the nominal amounts used before 2009. Therefore, in the event of future allocations, the absorption capacity will be able to expand correspondingly. As of April 30, 2016, the SDR purchasing capacity of voluntary arrangements was SDR 83 billion and the selling capacity was SDR 24 billion.

Following the general allocation in August 2009 and a special allocation in September 2009, there was an initial surge in SDR sales. During the first 4 months following the allocations, 16 countries sold SDR 2.9 billion. Since then, voluntary SDR trading arrangements have continued to facilitate sales. Most SDR sales have been conducted through the standing voluntary SDR trading arrangements. Many countries have engaged in multiple SDR sales transactions and a few mainly low-income countries have sold more than 80 percent of their 2009 SDR allocations.

Certain operations of the Poverty Reduction and Growth Trust (PRGT) are conducted in SDRs. The PRGT receives part of its loan resources and contributions from members in SDRs. At the request of the borrowing members, the PRGT may also disburse loans in SDRs. In addition, most borrowing members choose to make interest and principal payments on outstanding loans in SDRs. The Bank for International Settlements (BIS) conducts sales on behalf of the PRGT to facilitate the disbursement of loans in currencies funded with resources in SDRs. Eight of fourteen loan and note purchase agreements that were put in place after the 2009 reforms of Facilities for Low-Income Countries provide for disbursements in SDRs and amount to SDR 7.5 billion. The IMF has standing voluntary arrangements with all the member countries (or their financial institutions) that lend SDRs to the PRGT, and most lenders in SDRs have subsequently replenished their SDRs by participating as a market maker in SDR sales during the same period. Sales have also been conducted to convert SDR contributions from members to the PRGT Subsidy Accounts following the two distributions of the general reserve attributable to windfall gold sales profits in October 2012 and October 2013.

Since September 1987, voluntary transactions by agreement have ensured the liquidity of SDRs. However, in the event, that there are not enough voluntary buyers of SDRs, the Articles of Agreement provide for a designation mechanism to guarantee the liquidity of the SDR. Designation plans have been adopted on a precautionary basis and they can be activated if needed to ensure that members with a balance of payments need can exchange SDRs for freely usable currency.

Statements Of Financial Position of the SDR Department

The strict separation of the General Department and the SDR Department implies that their financial accounts are maintained separately. The basic structure of the SDR Department's balance sheet is quite simple. Because interest payments and receipts cancel out for the SDR Department as a whole, it is convenient to keep the accounts on a net basis.

Balance Sheet of the SDR Department

(Millions of SDRs; as of December 31, 2018 - 2019)

As at December 31 (LC 000)	2019	2018
Financial assets		
IMF subscription (quota) (5.1)	1,958,356	1,805,949
Holdings of special drawing rights (SDRs) (5.2)	578,714	531,092
Total claims on the IMF	2,537,070	2,337,041
Financial liabilities		
IMF A/C I (5.3)	4,896	4,515
IMF A/C II (5.3)	20	19
Securities account (5.4)	1,517,022	1,398,961
Loans from the IMF - exogenous shock facility (5.5.a)	–	–
Loans from the IMF - extended fund facility (5.5.b)	–	–
Total local currency liabilities to the IMF	1,521,938	1,403,495
SDR allocations (5.6)	574,975	530,229
Liabilities to the IMF	2,096,913	1,933,724
Net positions with the IMF	440,157	403,318

The asset side of the balance sheet shows the position of debtors to the SDR Department that is, members that have exchanged some of their SDRs for freely usable currency and whose holdings of SDRs therefore fall short of their net cumulative allocations. The accrued interest receivable from these debtor members on the asset side is the mirror image of the accrued interest payable to creditors on the liability side. Participants with holdings above allocations assume a creditor position in the SDR Department, and their SDR holdings in excess of their net cumulative allocations are therefore liabilities of the SDR Department. Interest payable to holders of SDRs is accrued and paid on a quarterly basis.

Income Statement of the SDR Department
(Millions of SDRs; as of April 30, 2015)

Revenue	
Net Charges from Participants with Holdings below Allocations	11
Assessment on SDR Allocations	3
	14
Expenses	
Interest on SDR Holdings	
Net Interest to Participants with Holdings above Allocations	2
General Resources Account	8
Prescribed Holders	1
	11
Administrative Expenses	3
	14
Other Comprehensive Income	—
Total Comprehensive Income	—

The income statement of the SDR Department is equally straightforward. The SDR Department's income consists of net charges from debtors and assessments paid by members for the administrative expenses incurred in operating the SDR Department. The SDR Department's expenses consists of net interest payments to the creditors in the system and the reimbursement to the GRA for the administration of the SDR Department. Because revenue and expenditure are always equal, net income of the SDR Department is always zero.

The establishment of the SDR

Gold was the central reserve asset of the international monetary system created at the Bretton Woods conference in 1944. Under the Bretton Woods system, the value of each currency was expressed in terms of gold (its par value), and member states were obliged to keep their currency's exchange rate within 1 percent of parity. In practice, most countries fulfilled this obligation by observing the par value against the U.S.

dollar and by buying and selling their currencies for U.S. dollars at that time, while the United States undertook to buy and sell gold freely for U.S. dollars at $35 a fine ounce, the par value of the U.S. dollar. This was also the "official" price of gold, at which all IMF transactions in gold were conducted.

In the immediate postwar period, the United States held about 60 percent of the world's official gold reserves. There was widespread concern over a dollar shortage as war-devastated countries sought to buy goods from the United States. These needs were met through the large capital outflows from the United States, which exceeded its current account surplus.

This net transfer of gold and dollars to the rest of the world helped other countries rebuild their reserves. By the end of the 1950s, European countries had largely recovered and many had made their currencies convertible, and the dollar shortage was replaced by what some observers called a "dollar glut." In the 1960s an increasing number of countries sought to exchange dollars for gold with the United States, reflecting their fear that dollars were no longer "as good as gold."

The Bretton Woods par value system had an inherent flaw, the so-called Triffin dilemma. As long as the U.S. dollar was the primary foreign exchange reserve asset, a growing level of world trade and finance required a growing supply of dollars. An ever-increasing stock of dollars, however, required a persistent deficit in the U.S. balance of payments, which itself was a threat to the value of the dollar. Official holders of dollars became concerned that the value of their reserve assets might decrease relative to gold.

To resolve this some countries favored the creation of a new reserve unit. The United States, concerned that such a unit would compete with the dollar, preferred to build on the existing automatic drawing rights (the gold tranche) in the IMF. In the mid-1960s the ministers of the Group of Ten (Belgium, Canada, France, Germany, Italy, Japan, Netherlands, Sweden, the United

Kingdom, and the United States) debated a plan to create "reserve drawing rights" in the IMF. Some European countries feared this mechanism could be interpreted as a replacement for gold and suggested instead the creation of "special" drawing rights. The name stuck. A blueprint for the creation of the new international reserve asset, the SDR, in amounts necessary to supplement supplies of gold and foreign exchange reserves, was agreed at the Rio de Janeiro meeting of the IMF Board of Governors in September 1967, and SDRs were first allocated by the IMF in 1970.

The Fundamental Principles That Guide SDR Valuation Decisions

A number of broad principles have guided decisions by the Executive Board pertaining to the valuation of the SDR since the 1970s. The overall aim has been to enhance the attractiveness of the SDR as a reserve asset.

- The SDR's value should be stable in terms of the major currencies.
- The currencies included in the basket should be representative of those used in international transactions.
- The relative weights of currencies included in the basket should reflect their relative importance in the world's trading and financial system.
- The composition of the SDR currency basket should be stable and change only as a result of significant developments from one review to the next.
- There should be continuity in the method of SDR valuation such that revisions in the method of valuation occur only as a result of major changes in the roles of currencies in the world economy.

Criteria for the SDR Basket's Composition

The current SDR valuation method was adopted by the IMF's Executive Board in 2000, with limited revisions introduced in November 2015. Under the 2000 decision, the SDR valuation method has the following key elements:
(1) Currency selection criteria, (2) currency weighting, and
(3) periodicity of SDR valuation.

Currency Selection: Effective October 1, 2016, the SDR basket comprises the five currencies that are issued by IMF member countries, or by monetary unions that include IMF members, with the largest value of exports of goods, services, and income credits during the 5-year period ending 12 months before the effective date of the revision (the "export criterion") and that the IMF has determined to be freely usable currencies in accordance with Article XXX(f) (the "freely usable criterion"). Article XXX(f) defines a freely usable currency as a member's currency that the IMF determines (1) is, in fact, widely used to make payments for international transactions and (2) is widely traded in the principal exchange markets. Rule O-3 stipulates that the IMF will determine the currencies that are freely usable in accordance with Article XXX(f) and that it will consult a member before placing its currency on, or removing it from, the list of freely usable currencies.

The export criterion is assessed based on balance of payments data. This size-related criterion is meant to reflect countries' relative importance in global commerce, ensure an adequate supply of reserve assets and limit the number of currencies in the basket.

The freely usable criterion was introduced in the SDR valuation method as a second criterion for currency selection in 2000 to recognize the importance of financial transactions for SDR valuation purposes. However, the concept of a "freely usable currency" was developed earlier in the context of the Second Amendment of the Articles in 1978 to ensure that a member purchasing another member's currency from the Fund would be able to use it, directly or indirectly, to meet its balance of payments needs. Specifically, following the definition of a "freely usable currency", adopted the Second Amendment (Article XXX(f)):

- The requirement that a currency be "widely used to make payments for international transactions" is designed to ensure that a currency may be directly used to meet a member's balance of payments need. It has been recognized in past applications that "widely used" would be best assessed by examining the degree to which trade and service payments as well as financial account transactions are undertaken in the currency.
- The requirement that a currency be "widely traded in the principal exchange markets" is designed to ensure that it may be indirectly used, i.e., that it can be exchanged in markets for another currency to meet a member's balance of payments need with reasonable assurances of no substantial adverse exchange rate effect. In past applications, "widely traded" was understood to imply that that there should be "reasonable assurance" that the market for the currency in question has sufficient depth so that no appreciable change in the exchange rate would occur when a member country transacts a sizable amount of that currency.

In 1978, the Executive Board determined that the Deutsche mark, French franc, Japanese yen, pound sterling, and U.S. dollar were freely usable currencies. With effect on January 1, 1999, the euro was added to the list, replacing the Deutsche mark and French franc. More recently, in the context of the 2015 SDR review, the Chinese renminbi was determined to be a freely usable currency and was added to the list, effective October 1, 2016.

Currency Weighting: Effective October 1, 2016, the percent weight of a currency reflects the share (calculated as a percentage of the total of the currencies included in the SDR basket) of exports and a composite financial indicator, each with equal weight, and calculated for the most recent 5-year period for which the required export data are readily available. The variables used in the calculation are as follows:

- Exports (which are meant to reflect currencies' role in global trade): share in the total value of exports of goods and services, and income credits of the member or monetary union issuing that currency.
- Financial indicators (meant to capture currencies' importance in global financial flows) are composed of three parts, each with equal weight: (1) share of the currency held by the monetary authorities of members that are not issuers of the relevant currency (that is, reserves); (2) share of the currency in the total value of foreign exchange turnover; and (3) share of that currency in the total value of international banking liabilities and international debt securities.

Currency weights are used to determine the amounts of each currency in the basket on the last business day of the previous valuation period. These currency amounts remain fixed over the commencing five-year SDR valuation period, while currencies' relative weights can change with exchange rate movements.

Review: The currencies and their weights in the valuation basket must be reviewed every 5 years, unless the Executive Board decides otherwise.

Actual Daily Weights and Currency Values

Currency amounts are calculated on the last business day before the date on which the new basket becomes effective. On that day, currency amounts are derived from the weights decided by the Executive Board using the average exchange rate for each currency over the preceding 3 months. Currency amounts are adjusted proportionally to ensure that the value of the SDR is the same before and after the revision. The currency amounts remain fixed for the subsequent 5-year period. As a result, the actual weight of each currency in the value of the SDR changes daily as a function of changes in exchange rates.

The example below demonstrates this point, showing the calculation of the SDR in terms of the U.S. dollar on April 30, 2016 (before the effectiveness of the inclusion of the Chinese renminbi in the SDR basket), and the corresponding weights. Current valuation can be found on the SDR Valuation page on the IMF's website.

SDR Valuation

(SDR valuation as of January 05, 2011)
Wednesday, January 05, 2011|

Wednesday, January 05, 2011				
Currency	Currency amount under Rule O-1	Exchange rate	U.S. dollar equivalent	% change in exchange rate against U.S. dollar from previous calculation
Euro	0.4230	1.32350	0.559841	-1.084
Japanese yen	12.1000	82.13000	0.147327	0.110
Pound sterling	0.1110	1.55940	0.173093	-0.090
U.S. dollar	0.6600	1.00000	0.660000	
1.540261				
U.S.$1.00 = SDR			0.649241	0.398
SDR1 = US$			1.54026	

Source: www.imf.org

Calculation of SDR Interest Rates

The SDR interest rate is calculated weekly by the IMF as the sum of the yields on the respective financial instruments in the SDR valuation basket in terms of SDRs, using the currency amounts in the valuation basket as weights except if the weighted average falls below the floor of the SDR interest rate of 0.050 percent (5 basis points). If this happens, the rate shall be established at 0.050 percent. The effective weights of the financial instruments representing each component currency therefore reflect the interest rates in each currency as well as the exchange rates and currency amounts in the basket.

As for the valuation of the SDR, the currency amounts remain fixed for the 5-year period following a quinquennial review and revision of the valuation basket. As a result, the actual weight of each financial instrument in the SDR interest rate changes every week as a result of changes in both interest rates and exchange rates, as shown in the example below. Note that these weights can differ from those in the valuation basket on the same date. because the weights in the interest rate basket reflect changes in each currency's interest rates and exchange rates.

The November 2015 decision to include the Chinese renminbi in the SDR basket, along with the new currency weights and inclusion of the representative Chinese renminbi short-term financial instrument in the calculation of the SDR interest rate, took effect on October 1, 2016. Shown below as an example is the calculation of the SDR interest rate on April 30, 2016 (before effectiveness of the inclusion of the Chinese renminbi in the SDR basket). The current rate can be found on the SDR Interest Rate Calculation page on the IMF's website.

Borrowing SDRs To Fill The Reserve Assets Requirement Of A Quota Increase

Members are required to pay 25 percent of their quota increases in SDRs or currencies specified by the IMF, or in a combination of SDRs and currencies. The balance of any such increases are payable in the countries' currencies.

If the gross reserves and SDR holdings of members are low, the IMF, if requested, may make arrangements to assist these members in paying the reserve asset portion of their quota increases. This is done by means of an intra-day SDR bridge loan free of any interest, fee, or commission. The SDR bridge loan mechanism functions as follows:

- The member borrows SDRs from a member willing to lend SDRs.
- The member uses the borrowed SDRs to pay the reserve asset portion of its quota subscription or quota increase.
- The member makes a reserve tranche purchase in the same amount (that is, it pays in domestic currency equal to 25 percent of the increase in its own quota) and receives SDRs.
- The member uses the SDRs received from the reserve tranche purchase to repay the SDR loan to the lending member on the same day.

Arrangements for the Voluntary Trading of Special Drawing Rights

Asia and Pacific: Australia, China, Japan, Korea, and New Zealand

Europe: Austria, Belgium, Cyprus, Denmark, European Central Bank, Finland, France, Germany, Greece, Ireland, Israel, Italy, Malta, Netherlands, Norway, Portugal, Slovak Republic, Slovenia, Spain, Sweden, Switzerland, and United Kingdom

The Middle East and Central Asia: Saudi Arabia Western Hemisphere: Canada, Chile, Mexico, and United States

Timeline to Buy or Sell SDRs under the Voluntary Trading Arrangements

- T — approximately 10 business days: Member notifies the IMF with a request to buy or sell SDRs.
- T — approximately 5—10 business days: IMF arranges trade under a voluntary arrangement.
- T — 5 business days: IMF sends advance notice to SDR seller, including amount and value date.
- T — 2 business days: IMF instructs SDR buyer to pay freely usable currency to seller.

- T — 2 business days: IMF advises SDR seller of expected payment of freely usable currency from buyer.
- T: Value Date for an SDR trade (sale or acquisition).
- T or T+1 business day: SDR seller confirms receipt of currency to IMF.
- T or T+1 business day: IMF confirms debit to SDR seller.
- T or T+1 business day: IMF confirms credit to SDR buyer.

Mechanism of Designation

Article XIX of the Articles of Agreement provides for a designation mechanism under which participants in the SDR Department whose balance of payments and reserve positions are deemed sufficiently strong must, when designated by the IMF, provide freely usable currencies in exchange for SDRs up to specified amounts. The designation mechanism ensures that, in case of a balance of payments needs, participants can use SDRs to obtain freely usable currencies on short notice.

Each designation plan identifies participants subject to designation and sets maximum limits on the amounts of SDRs they can be designated to receive during the next period. Since October 1, 2015, the Executive Board has decided the designation plan on an annual basis (previously, such plans were on a quarterly basis). In practice, the list of SDR Department participants subject to designation is the same as the list of members considered sufficiently strong for inclusion in the Financial Transactions Plan (FTP). If a new participant is added to the FTP, it would not be called upon in a transaction by designation until it has been included in the next designation plan. If a participant's currency is no longer used for transfers under the FTP during a designation period, the participant would also not be selected for a transaction by designation.

The designation amounts for individual countries are determined to promote a balanced distribution of the excess

SDR holdings over time. Specifically, each participant's designation is calculated so that, if all participants were to accept the designated amount, they would all achieve a low, relatively similar "excess holdings ratio." The excess holdings ratio is calculated as the difference between the member's actual SDR holdings and its net cumulative allocation as a percent of its quota.

A participant's obligation to provide currency in exchange for SDRs under a designation plan is subject to a ceiling of SDR holdings of not more than 300 percent of its net cumulative allocation (acceptance limit) unless the participant and the IMF agree to a higher limit.

CHAPTER 2

INVENTION OF THE SPECIAL DRAWING RIGHT IN THE CBDC ERA

On 23 March 2021, Kristalina Georgieva, Managing Director of the International Monetary Fund (IMF) announced a possible Special Drawing Rights (SDR) allocation of US$650 billion, to address the long term global need for reserve assets, benefit all member countries and support the global recovery from the COVID-19 crisis. The formal proposal will be presented to the Executive Board by June. Once the proposal is concurred in by the Executive Board, it would be submitted to the Board of Governors whose decision approving an SDR allocation would require support by members representing 85 percent majority of the total voting power. If passed, this will be the fourth and largest SDR allocation in the history of IMF, increasing the total SDR allocation to 6,628 from 2,041, equivalent to about US$939 billion.

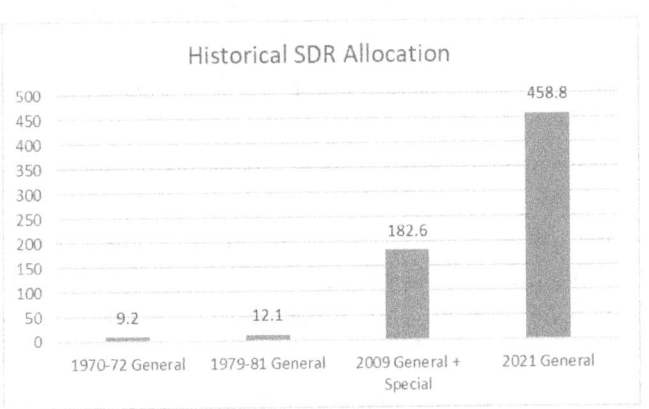

Historical context of SDR Allocation (in Billion SDR)

There have been many discussions on how to enhance the SDR creation and allocation mechanism and how to expand the application of SDR. On 23 March 2009, Mr. Xiaochuan Zhou, Governor of People's Bank of China, published the article "Reform the international monetary system", which drew significant attention inside and outside China. On 1 October 2016, RMB was added to the SDR basket. As of 1 April 2021, the weights assigned to the five constituent currencies are 41.1% for USD, 32.0% for EUR, 10.9% for RMB, 8.4% for GBP, and 7.6% for JPY. IMF will perform a regular check on SDR by mid-2022 (usually once every five years).

In the past five years, the emergence of central bank digital currency (CBDC) is one of the biggest changes in the international monetary system. Bank of England published a working paper on CBDC in 2016. Since April 2020, digital yuan has been piloted in various cities in China and will be applied in the Winter Olympics next year. Federal Reserve Bank of Boston is carrying out research on Digital Dollar with MIT. Jay Powell, Chairman of Federal Reserve, called it a high priority project of Federal Reserve in a U.S. Senate hearing on 23 February 2021. In October 2020, European Central Bank published the first digital Euro report. On 5 April 2021, Bank of Japan announced the launch of the phase 1 proof-of-concept study of CBDC in the coming year.

Some academicians have noticed the relationship between CBDC and SDR innovation. In May 2019, Tobias Adrian, Financial Counsellor and Director of the Monetary and Capital Markets Department of IMF, proposed eSDR or SDR in the IMF-Bank of Switzerland meeting. In December 2019, Mr. Xiaochuan Zhou said, in the second "Asia-Europe Cooperation Dialogue" of the Boao Forum for Asia, that there are opportunities globally to roll out global digital currency such as eSDR and synthetic hegemonic currency (SHC), but it requires a global central bank-like institution. However, neither of them elaborates relevant concepts in detail.

After Covid-19, major countries issuing reserve currency launched unlimited quantitative easing and large-scale fiscal stimulus, which amplifies the deficiency in the international monetary system as Mr. Xiaochuan Zhou pointed out in 2009. With the new round of SDR allocation, SDR will be increasingly important in the international monetary system. In such context, SDR innovation is necessary. This topic can be better studied with the research and experiments conducted in the digital currency field in the last two years.

1. Since 2019, Project Libra (a.k.a. Diem)'s exploration on multi-currency stablecoin deepens the understanding of the design and application of super-sovereign digital currency.
2. In March 2020, with support from BIS Hong Kong Innovation Hub, Hong Kong Monetary Authority, Bank of Thailand, Central Bank of the UAE and Digital Currency Institution of People's Bank of China announced the Multi-CBDC Bridge project to not only explore the application of CBDC in crossborder payments but also enhance the interoperability among different CBDC.

Mr. Xiaochuan Zhou's Recommendations of SDR Reform in 2009

SDR, together with gold and forex, is an international reserve asset. It was created by IMF in 1969 to supplement its member countries' official reserves, in order to support growing international trading and financial activities. SDR was launched in the context of Triffin Dilemma under the Bretton Woods system — US runs current account deficits to provide US dollar liquidity as the international settlement tool, but such deficits have negative impacts on investor confidence on US dollar.

SPECIAL DRAWING RIGHTS (SDR) AND THE FEDERAL RESERVE

SDR is neither a currency nor a claim on IMF. It is a potential claim on freely useable currencies (incl. USD, EUR, RMB, BGP, and JPY currently). SDR can only be held by IMF, members and prescribed holders, not by any private sectors or individuals. SDR is the unit of account for IMF, BIS, African Development Bank, Asian Development Bank, and Islamic Development Bank. SDR has mainly used in transactions between IMF and its members as well as between IMF and international financial organizations, including using SDR to exchange for freely useable currencies, to repay IMF loans, to pay interests, and to pay capital fund in proportion to their quota shares.

At the moment, SDR holders can redeem SDR for freely useable currencies in two ways. One is through the voluntary trading arrangements between IMF members. The other is, when the first one fails, IMF may designate IMF members with strong external positions to buy SDR from IMF members with weak external positions using freely useable currencies.

The value of SDR comes from the promise by IMF members to exchange SDR for freely useable currencies. IMF calculates and publishes SDR exchange rate every day, which is the sum of specific amounts of the five basket currencies valued in US dollars, on the basis of exchange rates quoted at noon each day in the London market. Every Friday, IMF calculates and publishes SDR interest rate, which is a weighted average of representative interest rates on short-term financial debt instruments in the money markets of the SDR basket currencies.

After the collapse of the Bretton Woods system in 1973, major currencies adopted the floating exchange rate system, reducing the reliance on SDR as a global reserve asset. On the other hand, the increase of SDR amount is determined by negotiation with a long decision-making cycle. Hence, there is a decreasing trend of SDR's weight in the global reserve assets. The functions of SDR have not been fully utilized.

Mr. Xiaochuan Zhou expressed the following important views in his article "Reform the international monetary system"

1. Using a national currency as the major international reserve currency is a rare case in the history. It has three key deficiencies. First, Triffin Dilemma still exists in theory. Issuing countries of reserve currencies cannot maintain the value of the reserve currencies while providing liquidity to the world. Second, issuing countries of reserve currencies are constantly confronted with the dilemma between achieving their domestic monetary policy goals and meeting other countries' demand for reserve currencies. They may either fail to adequately meet the demand of a growing global economy for liquidity as they try to ease inflation pressures at home, or create excess liquidity in the global markets by overly stimulating domestic demand (note: the Covid-19 situation magnifies this deficiency). Third, when a national currency is used in pricing primary commodities, trade settlements and is adopted as a reserve currency globally, efforts of the monetary authority issuing such currency to address its economic imbalances by adjusting exchange rate would be made in vain. While benefiting from a widely accepted reserve currency, the globalization also suffers from the flaws of such system. The cost is increasingly higher, not only for the users (e.g. worrying about the depreciation of reserve currencies), but also for the issuers of the reserve currencies (e.g. worrying about the impacts of weak user confidence on the domestic economy and monetary policy).
2. International reserve currencies should be enhanced towards a stable value, rule-based issuance, and manageable supply. A super-sovereign reserve currency managed by a global institution not only eliminates the

inherent risks of sovereign fiat currencies, but also makes it possible to manage global liquidity. This will significantly reduce the risks of a future crisis and enhance crisis management capability, which is the goal of the international monetary system reform. SDR has the features and potential to act as a super-sovereign reserve currency. The scope of SDR application should be broadened, enabling it to fully satisfy members' demand for reserve assets, with following measures.

a. Set up a settlement system between SDR and other currencies, making it a widely accepted means of payment in international trade and financial transactions.

b. Actively promote the use of SDR in international trade, commodities pricing, investment and corporate book-keeping.

c. Create financial assets denominated in SDR (note: World Bank issued SDR-denominated bonds in 2016).

d. The basket of currencies forming the basis for SDR valuation should be expanded to include currencies of all major economies, and GDP may also be included as a weight (note: RMB was added to the SDR currency basket in 2016).

e. The allocation of SDR can be shifted from a purely calculation-based system to a system backed by real assets, such as a reserve pool, to further boost market confidence in its value.

3. Compared with decentralized management of reserves by individual countries, the centralized management of part of the global reserve by IMF will be not only more effective in deterring speculation and stabilizing financial markets, but also promoting a greater role of SDR as a reserve currency. IMF can set up an open-ended SDR-

denominated fund based on the market practice, issuing SDR-denominated assets to member countries, allowing subscription and redemption in the existing reserve currencies as desired. It can even lay a foundation for increasing SDR allocation to gradually replace existing reserve currencies with SDR.

Considering that major issuing countries of reserve currencies launched unlimited quantitative easing and large- scale fiscal stimulus due to covid-19 when they had not exited the quantitative easing and unconventional monetary policy post the global financial crisis, there is no doubt that Mr. Zhou's above recommendations are more meaningful in such context. The development of CBDC provides new mechanisms and technical tools for the implementation of the reform recommendations.

SDR Innovation based on CBDC

SDR innovations are mainly in five areas — 1) payment, clearing and settlement infrastructure, 2) intrinsic value, 3) issuance and redemption mechanism (in the primary market), 4) trading mechanism (in the secondary market) and 5) SDR-denominated assets. Among these, payment, clearing and settlement infrastructure is the most important one as it builds the foundation for extending the scope of SDR application.

Payment, Clearing and Settlement Infrastructure

SDR's ownership and transaction records are now managed by IMF in its account system. There are two ways to extend the holding right to commercial banks and commercial organizations in member countries. One is to allow commercial banks and commercial organizations in member countries to connect into the SDR account system. And the other is to use distributed ledger technology (DLT), which is our preferred approach. First, DLT is highly open, providing more flexibility for commercial banks and organizations to hold and use SDR. Second, DLT better supports SDR's application in international trade and finance. Lastly, DLT is more compatible with CBDC.

SDR adopts a tiered operating model with DLT (Figure 2). The top layer is IMF. Monetary authorities of member countries and prescribed holders are on the second layer. Commercial banks from member countries are on the third and commercial organizations are on the fourth. We do not consider the situation where individuals hold SDR, which means SDR will not enter the retail payment market. From IMF member's perspective, every layer of "IMF-monetary authority-commercial bank-commercial organization" reflects a "wholesale-retail" relationship. Monetary authorities can not only transact SDR directly with IMF, but also trade SDR between each other. Commercial banks and commercial organizations can trade SDR directly across the border. However, they cannot trade directly with overseas monetary authorities or with IMF. Such restriction can be implemented with smart contracts in DLT.

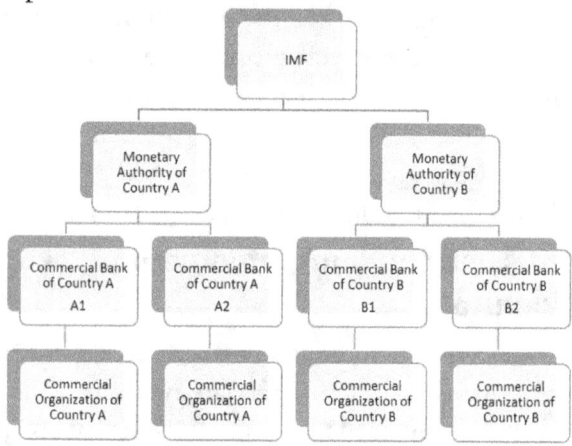

Intrinsic Value

SDR is a claim on freely usable currencies. Members can redeem a basket of freely usable currencies based on the SDR basket composition from IMF using their SDR on hand. IMF

relies on the following two capabilities to respond to SDR redemption requests:
1. SDR reserve, and Unconditional liquidity support from corresponding monetary authorities of the five currencies in the basket.

Under such arrangement, the value of SDR is no longer calculated but is backed by real assets. As members are not likely to redeem SDR at the same time from IMF and they can trade SDR with each other for freely usable currencies via the voluntary trading arrangement, SDR can be issued based on fractional reserve. This reflects the Law of Large Numbers.

Monetary authorities of the five constituent currencies, as liquidity providers of last resort, perform an important role in stabilizing the SDR system, ensuring that a run on SDR will not happen.

The Issuance and Redemption Mechanism

SDR is issued based on fractional reserve which comes from two sources:
1. Initial paid-in capital by monetary authorities of constituent currencies in the SDR basket.
2. When members subscribe for SDR with a set of freely usable currencies, IMF allocates new SDR and injects the received fund into SDR reserve.

SDR can be issued and circulated on DLT, which is the Corridor Network in Multi-CBDC Bridge. The CBDC systems of all constituent currencies (or RTGS if CBDC is not available) are connected to the Corridor Network, and there are depository receipts of the specific currency on the Corridor Network. CBDC and its depository receipts on the Corridor Network are 1:1 interchangeable and the authorities need to ensure that the amount of burnt CBDC is always equal to the amount of depository receipts on the Corridor Network.

SDR, backed by a basket of currencies, is comprised of smart contracts on the Corridor Network and depository receipts.

SDR on the Corridor Network

There are two ways to issue SDR. One is the existing mechanism, where the IMF Executive Board and Board of Governors determine the schedule and amount of new SDR allocation. SDR reserve ratio will also be adjusted with the new allocation. In other word, SDR issuance is based on adjustable fractional reserve. New SDR allocation determined by IMF Executive Board and Board of Governors is not frequent based on historical experience, but the size is likely to be large. New SDR will be distributed to members in proportion to their quota shares (that is, the general allocation). Some portion can also be reserved for IMF's usage or to lower the quota shares of certain key countries.

The other way is market-based issuance where members pay a set of freely usable currencies to subscribe for new SDR from IMF. The subscription time and amount are determined by the member demand. It is highly flexible and calculated based on the respective currency's weights in the basket. This will directly boost the demand of RMB as the international reserve currency. On the contrary, the current general SDR allocation mechanism has little impact in this aspect.

Some academicians proposed to have the endogenous growth and contraction mechanism like the credit currency for SDR, which means SDR owns the feature of "deposit creation from lending". As this proposal gives IMF extremely high decision power, we reserve our views on it. SDR issuance, on the one hand, needs to meet member's demand on reserve assets. On the other hand, it needs to be managed under a comprehensive governance framework. The core is to check and balance member countries and IMF.

When members redeem SDR from IMF, they receive a set of depository receipts of freely usable currencies on the Corridor Network. They can adjust their cash position through the trading mechanism to be discussed in the next sub-section (e.g. sell EUR-DR and buy CNY-DR), and exchange for the freely usable currencies they demand from the respective monetary authorities. IMF first uses the SDR reserve to handle redemption. If it is not sufficient, it will leverage the unconditional liquidity support from respective constituent currencies.

Under this new issuance and redemption mechanism, IMF can continue to calculate and publish the SDR exchange rate every day. This will serve as a reference point (the "reference rate") while the SDR exchange rate will be determined by the market (the "market rate"). However, arbitrage will drive the two rates to converge, due to the following reasons. If the market rate is higher than the reference rate, members can use a set of freely useable currencies to subscribe for new SDR from IMF. The cost of such strategy is determined by the reference rate while the return is driven by the market rate. As a result, there is an excess return. However, the increase in SDR supply, with other conditions held constant, will push down the market rate. Conversely, if the reference rate is higher than the market rate, members can redeem SDR for a set of freely useable currencies from IMF. The cost is determined by the market rate while the return is driven by the reference rate, also resulting in an excess return. But the decrease in SDR supply, with other conditions held constant, will push up the market rate. In a nutshell, SDR market rate will fluctuate around the reference rate with low volatility. This reduces the price fluctuation and associated risks compared to the situation where assets are denominated in fiat currencies, especially for primary commodities globally.

The Trading System

Trading between SDR and constituent currencies (in the form of depository receipts) happen on the Corridor Network

and can achieve Payment vs Payment (PvP) via smart contracts, which is highly efficient. Corresponding to the tiered operating model, SDR's trading mechanism is also tiered:
1. Members and IMF can trade a set of freely useable currencies vs. SDR. This corresponds to the market-based issuance and redemption of SDR, driving the market rate to converge towards the reference rate.
2. Members trade constituent currencies vs. SDR between each other. This helps members to adjust their cash position and implies the SDR exchange rate against different constituent currencies.
3. Within each member country, local currency vs. SDR trade can happen between the monetary authority and commercial banks as well as between commercial banks and commercial organizations. This corresponds to the SDR distribution mechanism within the member country.

In summary, it creates an active market of SDR and various constituent currencies based on the Corridor Network.

SDR-denominated Assets

As the scope of SDR application expands, mismatch between the SDR demand and the SDR amount held by members, commercial banks and commercial organizations may occur frequently. Hence, SDR resources need to be managed from both time and space dimensions. This is the internal driver for SDR denominated assets. It also indicates the underlying reason of current slow development of SDR-denominated assets the scope of SDR application is limited and thus the market-driven demand on SDR resource management is low.

In the long term, a yield curve will be developed by the market to reflect the demand and supply of SDR. SDR is not interest-bearing but SDR-denominated bonds and loans are. SDR interest rate will be determined by the market instead of calculation. However, the existing SDR interest rate is mostly used in self-financing — charge a fee on SDR allocation first and use the fee to pay for SDR interests.

[1] Exchange rate of 1 SDR = US$1.416620 on 1 April 2021 applied, same below.

[2] Another issue pointed by Mr. Chengjun Zhou, Head of PBoC's Financial Research Institute, is that if issuing countries of major international reserve currencies are no longer sitting at the core of the global value chain and supply chain in the global production and trading of commodities, the exchange rate adjustments of major reserve assets and the supply chain as well as industrial structural transformation in different countries are disjoint. Adjusting exchange rates cannot achieve the internal and external balance between the countries where the commodities are produced and the countries along the value chain.

Origins And Guiding Principles For SDR Valuation

The SDR valuation framework aims at supporting the SDR's purpose as an international reserve asset. The SDR was created as a supplemental reserve asset to facilitate the growth of international trade and financial flows and contribute to the stability of the international monetary system. It is a source of unconditional international liquidity, as SDR holders with balance of payments needs can use SDRs without restriction to obtain currency. The SDR is also central to the Fund's operations, used as its unit of account and in transactions between the IMF and its members, such as purchases and repurchases of Fund credit. In adopting SDR valuation decisions, the Executive Board has been guided over the years by several broad principles. These broad principles, whose aim is to enhance the attractiveness of the SDR as a reserve asset, consist of the following:

- The SDR's value should be stable in terms of the major currencies. Wide fluctuations of the SDR exchange rate against the major global currencies, as occurred, for instance, during the period when the SDR was linked to the U.S. dollar, could undermine the SDR's attractiveness as a store of value. Undue influence of a particular currency or group of currencies on the value of the SDR was seen as undesirable. Because of these considerations the Board decided to determine the value of the SDR using a basket of currencies.

- The currencies included in the basket should be representative of those used in international transactions. Representativeness ensures that the component currencies are used by members in international transactions and that the exchange rates that determine the value of the SDR are backed by active foreign exchange markets. A representative set of currencies also provides some degree of diversification.

- The relative weights of the currencies included in the basket should reflect their relative importance in the world's trading and financial system.

- The composition of the SDR basket should be stable in that it should not change easily from one review to the next. The chief argument for stability in the basket composition is to provide certainty to SDR users and thus support the role of the SDR as a reserve asset. Given that international currency use typically evolves slowly as a result of persistent underlying fundamentals, a selection rule should be expected to select the same currencies on the basis of similar data used in consecutive reviews. By the same token, needed changes should be made without delay on the basis of an agreed methodology. Once a needed change becomes apparent, it could be assumed that a delay in making it may mean that a larger change might eventually be needed.

- There should be continuity in the method of SDR valuation such that revisions in the method of valuation occur only as a result of major changes in the roles of currencies in the world economy. In the same way that changes in the composition of the basket should change only as a result of changes in patterns of international currency use, the method of valuation should not be subject to frequent adjustments but rest on how currencies are used in the world economy. For example, as the importance of financial flows in international transactions increased, they were more explicitly accounted for in the SDR valuation method through the adoption of the freely usable criterion.

A LEGAL FRAMEWORK FOR THE VALUATION OF SDR

The role of the SDR as a reserve asset is underpinned by a strong legal framework for the SDR valuation. The Articles of Agreement set the overall parameters for SDR valuation. Within the framework established under the Articles, the specific SDR valuation method is adopted through an Executive Board decision. Unless amended with the required majorities, the approved SDR valuation method has to be applied in determining value of the SDR.

The Articles of Agreement give the Executive Board broad authority to determine the method of valuation of the SDR, subject to special majority requirements. The Articles do not establish any specific substantive requirements or a methodology for SDR valuation. Rather, they only specify the relevant majorities for valuation decisions as follows: as a general rule, the method of valuation for the SDR is determined by a 70 percent majority of the total voting power, provided that an 85 percent majority of the total voting power is required for (i) a change in the principle of valuation, or (b) a fundamental change in the application of the principle in effect. The Articles provide no further guidance as to the type of change that would require an 85 percent majority, and the Executive Board has never developed such a list. The Executive Board, by a decision, adopted by a majority of the votes cast, has the authority to decide which of the two special majorities is applicable. To date, all decisions that have changed the method of SDR valuation have been adopted by the Fund with a 70 percent majority of the total voting power.

The current SDR valuation method was adopted by the Board in 2000. Under the 2000 decision, the SDR valuation method has the following key elements: (i) currency selection criteria, (ii) currency weighting, and (iii) periodicity of SDR valuation.

- Currency Selection Criteria: The SDR basket comprises the four currencies: (a) that are issued by Fund members (or by monetary unions that include Fund members) whose exports of goods and services during the 5-year period ending 12 months before the effective date of the valuation decision had the largest value; and (b) which have been determined by the Fund to be freely usable currencies in accordance with Article XXX(f).
- Currency Weighting: The respective percentage weights of the currencies are based on the relative share of each currency in reserve holdings by monetary authorities and the value of exports of goods and services (see Section VII).
- Periodicity of Valuation: The currency selection and weights are established for 5-year periods, with the current period expiring on December 31, 2015. It has long been recognized that a review can take place earlier if warranted by developments in the international financial system.

The remaining portion of this section provides guidance on the legal framework that is applicable to currency selection criteria, namely: (a) the export or gateway criterion; and (b) the freely usable criterion.

A. Export ("gateway") criterion

Exports have historically played a central role for SDR basket selection. Export shares were originally the sole criterion for currency selection for the SDR basket. This size-related criterion is meant to reflect countries' relative importance in global commerce, ensure an adequate supply of reserve assets, and limit the number of currencies in the basket.

The export criterion is assessed based on balance of payments data. The 2000 decision clarifies that in the case of a monetary union, the determination of the value of exports of goods and services of the union excludes trade of goods and services among members that are part of the union. Under the decision, a currency can only be replaced in the basket by another currency if the value of exports of the member or monetary union whose currency is not included during the relevant period exceeds those of a member or monetary union whose currency is included in the basket by at least 1 percent.

B. Freely usable criterion

The SDR valuation decision requires that in addition to meeting the export criterion, currencies for SDR basket inclusion must "have been determined by the Fund to be freely usable currencies in accordance with Article XXX(f) of the Fund's Articles." This criterion was introduced in the SDR valuation method as a second criterion for currency selection in 2000 to recognize the importance of financial transactions for SDR valuation purposes. It was seen as a way to consider a broad range of measures of the breadth and depth of financial markets to ensure that the SDR contained those currencies that were most representative of use in the world trading and financial systems.

While financial variables had been used to broadly confirm the direction of currency weighting since 1985, they had not been a formal criterion under the SDR valuation method.

The freely usable concept was developed for, and plays a key role in, Fund operations. It was developed in the context of the Second Amendment of the Articles in 1978 to ensure that a member purchasing another member's currency from the Fund would be able to use it, directly or indirectly, to meet its balance of payments needs.12 Thus, freely usable currencies reduce the potential risks and costs for members receiving and using currencies in transactions with the Fund.

In the context of GRA transactions, members that are issuers of freely usable currencies have different legal obligations from those that are not. A member whose currency is not freely usable was is under the legal obligation to ensure that balances of its currency sold by the Fund can be exchanged for a freely usable currency of its choice at the time of purchase (Article V, Section 3(a)). In the context of a repurchase transaction, such member also has to ensure that a repurchasing member can obtain balances of its currency selected by the Fund for repurchase against a freely usable currency of its choice (Article V, Section 7(j)(i)). Both transactions take place at the official Fund exchange rate for the currencies in question. On the other hand, a member whose currency is freely usable is under no legal obligation to convert balances of its currency sold by the Fund into another freely usable currency. Such member is only required to collaborate with the Fund and other members to enable the exchange of its freely usable currency. If the member as part of the cooperation agrees to convert its currency into another currency, the exchange does not have to take place at the official Fund rate. This framework implies that purchasing or repurchasing members might ultimately have to rely on market exchanges if they want to exchange a freely usable currency obtained in the purchase, or if they have to acquire a freely usable currency selected by the Fund for repurchase.

The term "freely usable currency" is defined under the Articles. Specifically, Article XXX(f) defines a freely usable currency as one that "the Fund determines (i) is, in fact, widely used to make payments for international transactions and (ii) is widely traded in the principal exchange markets ". Both elements under this definition, "widely used" and "widely traded," have to be satisfied for a currency to be determined freely usable.

Although the definition of a freely usable currency set forth in the Articles is relatively specific, it is not self-executing. Rather, it requires an interpretation as to what is meant by "in fact, widely used to make payments for international transactions," and "widely traded in the principal exchange markets." In interpreting the Articles of Agreement, the Fund draws principally on public international law principles on the interpretation of international treaties, which require that "a treaty shall be interpreted in good faith in accordance with the ordinary meaning given to the terms of the Treaty in their context and in light of its object and purpose."

Taking into account the above considerations, the interpretation of "freely usable currency" is guided exclusively by the purpose for—and the context within— which it is established under the Articles of Agreement; namely, as an integral element of the framework that enables the Fund to provide temporary balance of payments assistance to members.

Specifically, the requirement that a currency is "in fact, widely used to make payments for international transactions" is designed to ensure that a currency may be directly used to meet a member's balance of payments need, while the requirement that a currency be "widely traded in the principal exchange markets" is designed to ensure that it may be indirectly used, i.e., that it can be exchanged in markets for another currency to meet a member's balance of payments need with reasonable assurances of no substantial adverse exchange rate effect. It has been recognized in past applications that "widely used" would be best assessed by examining the degree to which trade and service payments as well as financial account transactions are undertaken in the currency, and that "widely traded" was understood to imply that that there should be "reasonable assurance" that the market for the currency in question has sufficient depth so that no appreciable change in the exchange rate would occur when a member country transacts a sizable amount of that currency.

Although the Executive Board has decided to "borrow" the freely usable currency concept for purposes of determining the valuation of the SDR, this decision cannot change the meaning and the purpose of freely usable currency as established under the Articles. It is open for the Board to decide to no longer rely on the freely usable currency criterion for purposes of SDR valuation. As long as an alternative criterion is consistent with the "principle of valuation" referred to in Article XV, Section 2, such a decision may be adopted by a 70 percent majority of the total voting power.

In addition, to the above general guidance, the following observations may be made with respect to the legal interpretation of three specific aspects of the "freely usable currency" concept.

- "Principal exchange markets": In order for, a currency to be freely usable it must be widely traded in the principal exchange markets. During the drafting of this provision as part of the Second Amendment process it was recognized that a freely usable currency would not need to be widely traded in all exchange markets, but it had to be traded in more than one principal exchange market. The Fund's identification of the principal exchange markets may evolve over time, taking into account both financial and technological developments.
- Currency convertibility: It was recognized from the outset that full convertibility was neither a necessary nor a

sufficient condition for a currency to be a freely usable currency. A currency may be widely used and widely traded even if the issuing member retains some restrictions. Conversely, a currency that is fully convertible may, not sufficiently in demand to be considered widely used and widely traded. For purposes of identifying those principal exchange markets where the currency in question is widely traded, it will be necessary that there be sufficient liberalization within the market in question to ensure that members who may receive financing from the Fund have adequate access to this market.

- International transactions: It has always been recognized that the transactions that are relevant for an assessment of whether a currency is widely used for "international transactions" include both current and financial account transactions. Moreover, and consistent with the way the term "international transactions" has been interpreted in the context of other provisions of the Articles, the object and purpose of the freely usable definition indicates that transactions should only be considered international for purposes of the freely usable criterion if they take place between members. As discussed further below, it is recognized, however, that some payments made within the territory of a member may be attributable to transactions that are international.

The Executive Board has relied on quantitative indicators as an input in assessing whether a currency is freely usable. While the Board has broad discretion in the selection of indicators to guide its determination, the selection of the indicators should be guided by their ability to provide relevant information for assessing both elements of the freely usable currency definition. Regarding the widely used element, indicators should be selected and constructed to capture use of currency in payments for current and financial account transactions between members, while indicators on widely traded should aim at assessing the depth and liquidity of trading a currency in the principal exchange markets. It has been recognized that these indicators may evolve over time taking into account both financial developments and the evolution in the availability of relevant data.

The final Board determination of what currencies constitute freely usable currencies consistent with the definition in Article XXX(f) ultimately requires judgment on the part of the Executive Board. It has been emphasized on previous occasions that quantitative indicators cannot be applied mechanistically and that ultimately the determination of which currencies are freely usable needs to rely on on a qualitative judgment framed by the definition of freely usable currency set out in the Articles of Agreement, including on the number of currencies. The determination that a currency is freely usable is a decision by the Board, by a majority of the votes cast, but the Fund has to consult with a member before a currency is put on, or removed from, the list of freely usable currencies.

If a currency has not been determined to be freely usable but meets the export criterion at the time of an SDR valuation review, the assessment of whether it is freely usable can take place as part of the review. It is not required, as a legal matter, that in that context the Fund undertake a comprehensive review of all currencies that could potentially meet the requirements under the Articles. If, however, a currency is determined to be freely usable at the time of an SDR valuation review, and other currencies have very similar outcomes on the relevant indicators, for consistency reasons, the same standards would apply if the Executive Board later undertook a broader review of potential new freely usable currencies. As indicated above, inclusion requires consultation with the relevant member and the record indicates that in the past the Fund has taken into account members' preferences to not have their currency included in the list of freely usable currencies.

Currency Selection Criteria
A. Appropriateness of the Current Criteria

The Executive Board undertook a comprehensive review of the SDR currency selection criteria in 2011 and supported maintaining the existing criteria.

- Most Directors agreed on the important role of a size-related criterion and supported maintaining the export gateway criterion. They also agreed that augmenting the export criterion with financial flows would be desirable in principle, but that it would require first that data shortcomings be addressed.
- The Executive Board also supported maintaining the freely usable criterion. A number of Directors were open to exploring alternatives along the lines of a "reserve asset criterion," but most Directors viewed the freely usable criterion as remaining appropriate.

The current selection criteria have remained broadly supportive of the SDR basket's stability and its representativeness of the use of currencies in international transactions.

- Since the current basket took effect on January 1, 2011, the day-to-day volatility of the SDR against its component currencies has remained low. The SDR/U.S. dollar exchange rate has fluctuated in a narrow range, albeit with the dollar appreciating strongly in the second half of 2014, reflecting its appreciation against the three other currencies in the basket
- The currencies identified by the current criteria also remain highly relevant in the global trade and financial systems. As showed further below, the euro area, the

United States, Japan, and the United Kingdom continue to be among the top exporters, along with China. The U.S. dollar, euro, Japanese yen, and the British pound also account for a large share of global financial transactions. Other than the rising share of the RMB, the overall pattern of reserve holdings, foreign exchange turnover, and other financial indicators has not changed substantially since the last review.

In light of the relatively recent review by the Board, staff does not propose to revisit the current currency selection criteria. Developments do not suggest a need for further conceptual work on alternative criteria at this stage. Since the quality and country coverage of data on financial flows has not changed significantly since 2011, staff proposes to maintain exports as the gateway criterion for inclusion, along with the freely usable criterion. However, as discussed above, the criteria for selection are under the broad authority of the Board and can be revisited if Directors wish to do so.

The Export Criterion

Exports provide a first test for the possible inclusion of currencies into the SDR basket. While there have been significant shifts in export shares across the membership since the last SDR valuation review, with many emerging market and developing countries gaining greater importance, the overall picture in terms of leading countries remains broadly unchanged.

- The euro area and the United States remain the largest exporters, accounting for about one-third of the global total. Compared to the last review, their share (measured as 5-year averages) has fallen somewhat.
- China continues to meet the export criterion. China already joined the list of top exporters at the time of the 2010 review. The data suggests that it continues to be the

third-largest exporter, having significantly reduced the gap with the United States and the euro area.
- Japan and the United Kingdom are the fourth- and fifth-largest exporters respectively. Their export shares have fallen somewhat since the last review, with Japan's share now exceeding the share of the United Kingdom by a narrow margin.
- The next-largest exporters are well outside the leading group. The exports of Korea, Singapore, Canada, Switzerland, and Russia are far from the required threshold of exceeding the exports of another member in the SDR basket by 1%.

The Freely Usable Criterion

With China continuing to meet the export gateway criterion, under the current framework for currency selection, the review will focus on determining whether the RMB is a freely usable currency. This section discusses building blocks for such a determination. Under the legal framework for the SDR valuation, the freely usable determination is based on the definition in the Articles of Agreement, ultimately requiring Board judgment with quantitative indicators as inputs. Information is provided on indicators that the Board has endorsed in the past, as well as additional indicators that could usefully complement them. Various conceptual issues related to the underlying data and areas where further work is needed are also discussed.

Indicators: General Considerations

Indicators are an indirect means of assessing whether a currency is widely used and widely traded. Given the interpretation of these concepts described above, ideally, an assessment of widely used would be based on the full currency composition of the balance of payments and international investment position and an assessment of widely traded would compute across a number of foreign exchange (FX) markets a member's costs to convert the currency received in a Fund transaction and the reaction of market prices to such conversions. However, the lack of availability of such data requires the use of summary indicators as indirect proxies in the widely used assessment. Caution must be exercised in interpreting these proxies, also since their information content can change over time.

The Board-endorsed indicators remain relevant for the freely usable assessment. After the initial assessment of freely usable currencies in 1977—78 there was no further comprehensive discussion of the freely usable currency concept until 2011. At that time, the Board considered the indicators to be used for the assessment of the freely usable criterion in the context of the review of alternative SDR valuation criteria. Directors agreed that the shares of currencies in official reserve holdings, international banking liabilities (IBL), and international debt securities (IDS) would be important factors for the assessment of wide use, and the volume of transactions (i.e., turnover) in FX markets for wide trade.

While in many ways these indicators remain useful proxies for wide use and wide trading of a currency, they have some shortcomings. They do not capture some aspects of international currency use, such as the currency composition of balance of payments flows or non-resident investment in domestic debt markets. Moreover, methodological changes after the 2011 discussion changed the information content of the Board-endorsed indicator on IDS. The financial indicators for wide use are all stocks outstanding, tending to respond to changing trends in currency use with inertia, which may understate the importance of dynamic currencies. Definitions of international transactions under the various indicators are not consistent across indicators and are not always aligned with the interpretation of international transactions under Article XXX(f). For example, IBL include all liabilities in foreign currency, including to residents. IDS, meanwhile, include securities issued by residents in foreign currency in the local market where registration is not under local law, and exclude non-resident holdings of domestic currency debt issued in the local market.

There are also gaps in the currency coverage of data on official reserve holdings and IBL, and in the timeliness of the preferred source of FX market turnover data, the BIS Triennial Survey, with the latest data from 2013.

Some additional indicators and data sources, each with their own advantages and disadvantages, could complement the indicators previously endorsed by the Board. The additional indicators are (i) official holdings of foreign currency assets; (ii) the issuance of IDS, to complement the existing indicator on the stock outstanding; (iii) cross-border payments; and (iv) letters of credit for trade finance. Additional data sources are used for FX turnover to provide a more recent picture than the latest BIS survey. The aim is to broaden the currency coverage, capture cross-border flows in addition to stocks in order to better reflect recent trends in the use of currencies, provide more timely data for foreign exchange turnover, and capture some additional aspects of international currency use. That said, the additional indicators and data sources also have some drawbacks, for example incomplete coverage of the relevant transactions, and indicators based on flows are more susceptible to volatility, but staff sees these indicators as useful complements to the assessment nonetheless.

Bid-ask spreads are a possible secondary indicator for assessing widely traded, as discussed by the Board in 2011, though they need to be interpreted with caution. Bid-ask spreads from the New York FX market were included in the 1977—78 freely usable assessment. Even in today's deeper and more interconnected markets, spreads can vary widely throughout the day and across time zones, though most data sources, provide only indicative quotes for a transaction of standard size.

Moreover, spreads can be affected by policies and restrictions on capital flows. Staff is exploring whether a broad sample of transaction-bytransaction data can be obtained to permit analysis across a range of markets, currencies, and trading conditions.

In applying widely traded, a determination is also required as to what constitutes the "principal exchange markets." The rise in prominence of electronic trading has increased the ease and efficiency of trading across physical market locations and the evolution of bids and offers for each currency pair may be continuously monitored, weakening the link between data on FX turnover by market and the actual location of the transacting parties (Annex II). Trading activity now occurs virtually around the clock, with a large share of transactions either through electronic trading platforms or using prices set with reference to them. Nonetheless, market activity and trading volumes remain closely tied to the business hours of major financial centers. In this context, "principal exchange markets" are best understood in terms of three broad time zones corresponding roughly to the Asian, European, and North American market hours—rather than geographical market locations. In light of the requirement for a currency to be widely traded in multiple, but not necessarily all, principal markets, this could lend itself to the interpretation that members need to be reasonably assured of sufficient market depth in at least two of the three time zones.

The widely traded assessment should consider whether a member can transact a sizable amount of the currency at any time with the reasonable assurance that the market for that currency has sufficient depth so that no appreciable change in the exchange rate will occur. While aggregate FX turnover is generally correlated with a market's depth, breadth, and resilience, it does not completely capture these characteristics, and more granular analysis is therefore desirable to ensure that markets can handle sizable transactions in a currency without affecting the exchange rate. A meaningful metric to help answer this question would be to compare a market's depth with the size of Fund-related transactions. In addition, the assessment would have to take account of typical FX trading strategies.

For instance, market participants would split large orders into smaller transactions to keep the exchange rate from moving against them indeed, this practice is becoming increasingly automated in the past few years. Also, risk management practices may limit the size of exposures that agents are willing to take on. This implies that foreign exchange conversions of a size relevant for Fund operations are likely to take place via multiple transactions, typically conducted with a number of agents and over a period of time.

The treatment of Hong Kong SAR, Macao SAR, and Taiwan Province of China presents methodological issues for the computation of some indicators. Interpreting international transactions as "transactions between members" means that RMB transactions within Hong Kong SAR, Macao SAR, and Taiwan Province of China, and between any of those three and the Mainland are not to be considered international transactions for the freely usable assessment.

However, the appropriate treatment may not be so straightforward in the case of all indicators, especially given the status of Hong Kong SAR as a financial center in which business between the Mainland and the rest of the world is conducted. For instance, transactions among Hong Kong SAR residents or between residents of Hong Kong SAR and the Mainland can potentially reflect an underlying international transaction with another member not captured elsewhere. Measuring the proportion of such transactions, however, presents difficulties. In some cases, similar issues may also be relevant for other international financial centers. The presentation of the indicators treats Hong Kong SAR, Macao SAR, and Taiwan Province of

China as domestic where data is available and the text will note these methodological issues where relevant and discuss possible ways to address them where they appear to be quantitatively important.

A broad range of indicators shows where data is available increasing international use of the RMB, albeit from a low base, since the last SDR valuation review.

Official Reserves
(shares in percent of allocated reserves)

	2010:Q2			2015:Q1	
	SDR bn	%		SDR bn	%
USD	2,026	62.5	USD	2,818	64.1
EUR	850	26.2	EUR	911	20.7
JPY	103	3.2	JPY	182	4.2
GBP	135	4.2	GBP	172	3.9
CHF	4	0.1	AUD	83	1.9
AUD 1/		n.a.	CAD	82	1.9
CAD 1/		n.a.	CHF	13	0.3
Other	122	3.8	Other	135	3.1
Unallocated	2,453	43.1	Unallocated	3,893	47.0

Official foreign exchange reserves. Data for this indicator is sourced from the IMF's Currency Composition of Official Foreign Exchange Reserves (COFER) survey. However, the RMB is not separately identified in the survey.

- Official foreign currency assets (OFA). In light of the RMB reporting gap in COFER, staff conducted a survey of members' OFA holdings that includes both reserve assets and other foreign currency- denominated assets not included in reserves. The OFA survey covered 16 currencies, including some not-fully-convertible ones like the RMB, compared to the seven-currency coverage of

COFER. The results closely mirrored COFER data for the currencies covered in both surveys. As for the RMB, 38 respondents reported holding RMB- denominated assets, comprising 1.1 percent of total OFA. This level increased from 2013 to 2014, though it, remains below the Australian dollar and Canadian dollar. The survey was conducted on the same strictly confidential basis as the COFER survey, and any RMB holdings that might have been reported by the Hong Kong Monetary Authority or the Monetary Authority of Macao could not be excluded without revealing confidential information.

Official Foreign Currency Assets
(shares in percent of global total)

	2013				2014		
	SDR bn	%	Reporting countries		SDR bn	%	Reporting countries
USD	2,701	61.3	127	USD	2,961	63.7	127
EUR	1,041	23.7	109	EUR	978	21.0	108
GBP	187	4.2	108	GBP	190	4.1	109
JPY	147	3.3	87	JPY	160	3.4	88
AUD	98	2.2	79	AUD	98	2.1	78
CAD	87	2.0	84	CAD	92	2.0	85
RMB	29	0.7	27	RMB	51	1.1	38
NZD	11	0.2	27	CHF	11	0.2	69
CHF	10	0.2	73	NZD	11	0.2	29
NOK	9	0.2	45	SEK	9	0.2	40
Other	66	1.9		Other	73	1.9	

International banking liabilities (IBL). IBL data for the RMB are not available on a comprehensive basis, since China does not currently report to the BIS, and reporting RMB- denominated positions separately is optional for other countries. The BIS has published an estimate of 1.9 percent for the global share of RMB- denominated international bank deposits by non-banks for end-

2014. However, this does not include the IBL of banks resident in the Mainland and treats Hong Kong SAR, Macao SAR, and Taiwan Province of China as international. The Chinese authorities have recently published data showing non- resident holdings of RMB-denominated bank liabilities in the Mainland amount to the equivalent of $710 billion (this also treats Hong Kong SAR, Macao SAR, and Taiwan Province of China as international). Staff is still in the process of determining to what extent the data is comparable to the BIS data. The information taken at face value, together with information on RMB-denominated liabilities offshore, would suggest that the RMB could be in the range of the Japanese yen and the Swiss franc. Staff is working to obtain the information that would be necessary to treat Hong Kong SAR, Macao SAR, and Taiwan Province of China as domestic.

- International debt securities (IDS) outstanding. RMB-denominated IDS outstanding accounted for 0.6 percent of the total in 2015Q1, up from less than 0.1 percent of the total in 2010. Staff is working to obtain the information that would be necessary to treat Hong Kong SAR, Macao SAR, and Taiwan Province of China as domestic.

- Issuance of IDS. BIS data on the issuance of debt securities points to a rise in the RMB's share to 1.4 percent of the total, from a share of 0.1 percent in 2010. Staff is working to obtain the information that would be necessary to treat Hong Kong SAR, Macao SAR, and Taiwan Province of China as domestic.

- SWIFT cross-border payments. The coverage of this indicator is not universal and staff is examining potential issues on double-counting transactions, but the data provides a direct measure of the use of currencies in making payments for cross-border transactions. The RMB's importance is growing rapidly, with a 1.0 percent share of total payments over the last four quarters (2014Q2 to 2015Q1, compared to a 0.2 percent share two years earlier (2012Q2 to 2013Q1). This measure treats Hong Kong SAR, Macao SAR, and Taiwan Province of China as domestic. However, staff will assess whether some RMB payments between Hong Kong SAR, Macao SAR, and Taiwan Province of China and the Mainland, and also between or within any of the first three reflect transactions undertaken by non-residents and should thus be treated as international. An upper bound of this effect is given by treating as international i) all RMB-denominated transactions between the Mainland and Hong Kong SAR, Macao SAR, and Taiwan Province of China; ii) all RMB-denominated transactions among Hong Kong SAR, Macao SAR, and Taiwan Province of China; and iii) including for all currencies "third- party domestic use," which is when residents within one economy use a currency issued elsewhere. On this basis, the RMB's share would amount to 2.8 percent of total payments, with the RMB behind only the SDR currencies.

- SWIFT trade finance. In the absence of recent data on the currency invoicing of trade, the currency denomination of trade finance can inform how "widely used" currencies are for international trade transactions. SWIFT data on the currency denomination of letters of credit (L/C) cover about one-sixth of total trade. RMB-denominated L/C accounted for 3.8 percent of the total in 2015Q1, treating Hong Kong SAR, Macao SAR, and Taiwan Province of China as domestic.

BIS data available through early 2013 shows that the RMB's share of FX turnover has increased substantially, albeit from a low base. The BIS Triennial Central Bank Survey is the most comprehensive data source for global FX market turnover, being compiled by a number of central banks with extensive coverage of institutions and transactions. The current SDR currencies continued to account for roughly 80 percent of total turnover, with the shares of the U.S. dollar and the Japanese yen rising since the last review and those of the euro and British pound falling. The RMB's total share increased to 1.1 percent (daily average turnover of $120 billion) in 2013, up from 0.4 percent ($34 billion) in 2010.39 The RMB's share of spot turnover was somewhat lower at 0.8 percent ($34 billion). Total RMB turnover in 2013 trailed the Swiss franc, the Australian dollar, the Canadian dollar, and the Mexican peso in addition to the SDR currencies. However, as noted, the latest BIS turnover data (April 2013) is by now considerably outdated.

More recent information, while less comprehensive, suggests a continued rise in the RMB's share of FX turnover:

- Regional and national surveys. Staff obtained data from a number of regional and national sources (Annex V). Based on the latest available data, RMB daily average trading volumes could be around the equivalent of $250 billion on a net-gross basis.
- SWIFT FX transactions. SWIFT data based on inter-bank messages used to confirm foreign exchange transactions shows an increase of 100 percent in total RMB turnover between the first quarter of 2013 and the first quarter of 2015. While the data should be treated with considerable caution given its limited coverage, the rate of growth suggests that RMB turnover is rising rapidly.

Information on FX market activity by region shows RMB trading is most common in Asia, constitutes a small but growing share in Europe, and is still thin in North America. The RMB is one of the most-traded currencies in Asia. The share in London remains relatively low, approaching 1 percent, but is rising fast and has reached already a considerable absolute magnitude (about $35 billion per day). There is very little trading in North American markets.

Data on hourly FX operations from the EBS Market central limit order book platform provides additional detail on the profile of spot trading in the offshore market throughout the day. It confirms that trading is most liquid during the hours the Asian market is open, which also includes the first half of the European trading day. It then becomes more modest in the last few hours of European trading and is very low between the close of the European market and the open of the Asian market. Staff is exploring whether data can be obtained across a number of currencies in order to provide a comparison.

Staff calculations suggest that markets' capacity to absorb potential FX conversions associated with Fund purchases is higher for the current freely usable currencies than for the RMB. The scale of potential currency conversions by Fund members can be estimated using metrics such as the average five largest purchases since 2010 (5 billion SDR) or the largest potential purchase as reflected by FCL commitments (50 billion SDR). The currency composition assumed for these purchases is based on creditor members' shares in the Financial Transactions Plan (FTP). The results of this exercise suggest that transactions resulting from such purchases would amount to a somewhat larger share of FX market turnover for the RMB than for the current freely usable currencies and some other non-freely usable currencies (Table 12). However, there is no clear benchmark for judging the point at which this would affect market pricing, considering also that any conversions would likely be broken up into smaller transactions to minimize price effects. Overall, it is worth noting that even a very large Fund-related transaction would still represent less than 10 percent of a day's worth of RMB turnover.

The preliminary data and analysis presented above suggest that the international use and trading of currencies occurs along a relatively wide spectrum. The U.S. dollar dominates by far, although the euro, also accounts for a sizable share of international transactions. It is likely that all members with a balance of payments need would have a high probability of being able to directly use one of these currencies to meet a balance of payments need or to easily exchange it in the market for another intervention currency. Behind these two dominant currencies, the picture is more mixed, with the Japanese yen and the British pound following for most indicators.

The international use of the RMB is rapidly becoming more common across a range of instruments. The use and trading of the RMB has increased substantially since the 2010 review, from a low base. At the same time, other currencies have not experienced substantial changes in their relative prominence, underscoring that the rise of the RMB is the most significant development in international currency use since the last review. This notion is also supported by other contextual information such as the rising global network of RMB swap lines and the rapid growth in RMB payments from offshore clearing centers to the Mainland. Given that the bulk of policy reforms to support RMB internationalization have occurred since 2010 and the authorities intend to implement further measures, it is likely that their full impact has not yet materialized. These trends suggest that the growing international use and trading of the RMB is part of a durable trend. Further reforms to liberalize onshore markets would also have an impact. Staff will continue work on the issue of how widely used and traded the RMB is, including to address remaining data gaps and to deepen the analysis, which will provide additional input into the Board's future assessment of whether the RMB is freely usable.

Operational Issues

Including the RMB in the SDR basket under current criteria would have important operational implications:

- As an issuer of a non-freely usable currency, China is currently obliged to exchange its currency for a freely usable currency when it provides quota-based or borrowed resources to the Fund in the context of GRA financing operations. By contrast, if the RMB was determined to be freely usable, China could provide balances of its own freely usable currency (RMB) to the Fund and would only be obliged to collaborate with the Fund and other members to enable such balances to be exchanged for the freely usable currencies of other members.

- There would be corresponding implications for other members' transactions with the Fund. Assuming that China would prefer to provide its own currency in purchases after the RMB is determined freely usable, borrowing members would receive RMB and would also need to secure RMB to settle future repurchases. Specifically, repurchases and NAB repayments currently allocated to China, which are currently paid in U.S. dollars, could be required to be repaid in RMB.

Like all currencies in the SDR basket and as a freely usable currency, the RMB would be expected to meet certain key operational requirements. In particular, the current construct of the SDR basket requires identifying suitable representative exchange rates for valuation purposes and a suitable reference interest rate for each of the currencies included in the basket. Fund members, their agents, and other SDR holders would need to have adequate access to RMB-denominated instruments for reserve management purposes and the ability to hedge risks. These elements discussed in more detail below, are essential for the proper functioning of the Fund's financial operations and policies, and for other users of the SDR.

SPECIAL DRAWING RIGHTS (SDR) AND THE FEDERAL RESERVE

Exchange rates for SDR valuation and Fund operations

For SDR valuation purposes, two exchange rates play a key role. The value of the SDR in terms of the U.S. dollar is calculated daily by summing the values in U.S. dollars based on market exchange rates of the SDR basket currencies, currently taken from the same source at the same time. The value of the SDR in terms of all other member currencies is subsequently calculated using "representative" exchange rates of these currencies against the US dollar. For the RMB, this means that:

- Under the current decision, a suitable RMB/USD exchange rate would need to be available in the London (Bank of England) and New York (Federal Reserve Bank of New York) exchange markets, and from the European Central Bank (ECB), to determine the daily value of the SDR in terms of the U.S. dollar. Based on preliminary discussions with the Bank of England, it is expected that such a rate could be made available from the London exchange market. Further inquiries are needed to ascertain the availability of suitable exchange rates from the New York market and the ECB.

- A market-based "representative" RMB rate in terms of the U.S. dollar would be needed to value the RMB against the SDR. The representative rate is currently the onshore fixing rate, i.e., central parity rate, announced daily by the CFETS at 9:15 a.m. However, this rate is not based on actual market trades, and can deviate by up to 2 percent from the onshore market exchange rate. In the event of SDR inclusion, the Fund, in consultation with the Chinese authorities, would need to identify a market-based exchange rate that could be used as a representative rate for the RMB. Based on staffs preliminary assessment, it appears that one of the benchmark exchange rates already calculated daily by the China Foreign Exchange Trading System (CFETS) would be suitable for this purpose. For members not to be disadvantaged in using RMB over another freely usable currency in Fund transactions that are based on the onshore rate, access to the onshore market would have to exist so that members could buy and sell RMB at the prevailing onshore rate.

Deviations between the offshore (CNH) and onshore (CNY) RMB exchange rates raise potential operational issues. Deviations can occur due to remaining capital controls and other restrictions, although the exchange rates have been converging as more investors have gained access to the onshore market. Market participants generally consider the difference at current levels to be small enough to not be material; nevertheless, the divergence has at times been significant. The impact of any divergence on SDR users would be mitigated if SDR users have access to both the onshore and offshore market for conducting spot transactions. Deviations between the two rates imply that the CNH cannot be a perfect hedge for CNY-based exposures. However, members would always have the option of hedging in the onshore market where costs are broadly comparable at maturities up to two or three years.

Renminbi Spot Onshore (CNY) and Offshore (CNH) Daily Exchange Rates (Renminbi per U.S. dollar)

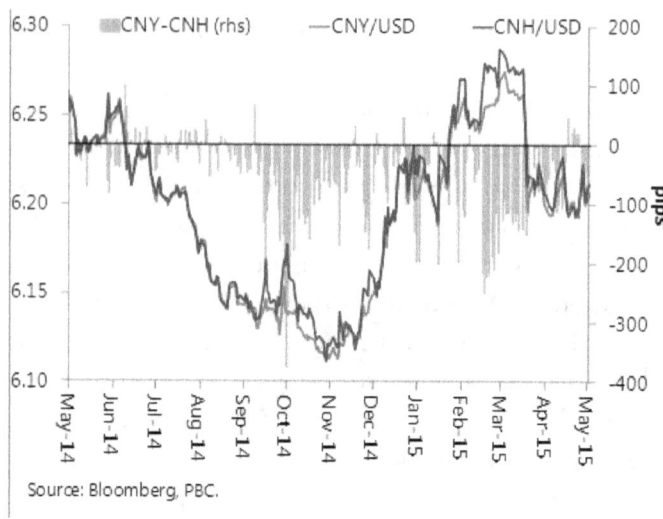

Source: Bloomberg, PBC.

The increasing opening of the capital account should help to further reduce CNY-CNH divergences in the future. In particular, along with other liberalization measures, liquidity support provided to the offshore market via swap lines with other central banks (notably the HKMA) and the plans to allow offshore CNH clearing banks to access repo finance on CFETS should result in CNY and CNH rates trading even closer together going forward.

SDR interest rate

Availability of an appropriate interest rate instrument for the SDR basket is another key operational requirement. The SDR interest rate provides the basis for calculating the interest charged to members on loans from the IMF's general resources, the interest paid to members on their remunerated creditor positions in the IMF (reserve tranche positions and claims under borrowing agreements), and the interest paid to members on their SDR holdings and charged on their SDR allocations. It is also employed in computing interest paid to some Poverty Reduction and Growth Trust (PRGT) lenders and is a benchmark for the Fund's invested resources in the Investment

Account. If a currency is added to the currency basket, it is expected that an instrument in that currency would be added to the interest rate basket, making the availability of such an instrument an important consideration.

The Executive Board has previously agreed that the financial instruments in the SDR interest rate basket should have certain characteristics. They should: (i) be broadly representative of the range of financial instruments that are actually available to investors in a particular currency; (ii) carry an interest rate that is responsive to changes in underlying credit conditions in the corresponding money market; and (iii) have risk characteristics that are similar to the official standing of the SDR itself, i.e., have a credit risk profile of the highest quality, fully comparable to that of government paper available in the market or, in the absence of appropriate official paper, comparable to the credit risk on prime financial instruments. The instruments should also reflect the actual reserve asset choice of reserve managers (for example, as regards the form of the financial instrument, its liquidity, and its maturity), which implies access of members to the instrument. It has been noted in previous discussions that such an instrument is expected to be available for a currency that is determined to be freely usable.

Staff has initiated discussions with the authorities about a possible RMB-based interest rate instrument for inclusion in the SDR interest rate basket. An assessment of a range of money-market interest rates suggests that the three- month sovereign yield, which is published daily by the China Central Depository and Clearing Company (CCDC), could possibly be considered for inclusion in the SDR interest basket. While the secondary market for government securities with three-month residual maturity is relatively thin, market participants indicated that it was not difficult to buy such assets in the market if customers wanted them. A commitment by the Ministry of Finance to regular issuance of three- and six-month treasury bills could help market development by providing more certainty, which could significantly improve liquidity in this tenor and align it more with the guidelines for the SDR interest rate basket. Such issuance could in time is added to the benchmark securities for which the primary dealers must provide quotes. The authorities have recently announced measures to increase the access to the onshore bond market— including government securities—for central banks, other SDR users, and agents acting on their behalf. Staff is assessing whether these measures ensure sufficient access for the operational requirements of these investors.

Hedging

The ability to hedge their SDR-valued positions is important to many members. Borrowing and creditor members may want to hedge their SDR-denominated exposures, and some members may be required by their internal regulations to keep their balance sheets SDR- neutral. The SDR as currently constructed can be replicated in the market, allowing SDR positions to be hedged with reasonable precision and without excessive costs. Borrowers' hedging needs would depend on the repayment schedule of their purchases (up to 5 years for SBA and 10 years for EFF). This would imply a need to have availability of hedging instruments, such as cross-currency swaps, with long durations, or at least have shorter hedges that can be rolled over at a reasonable cost, in order to mitigate exchange rate and interest rate risks.

Likewise, the ability to hedge is important for managing the Fund's Investment Account and Trust assets and for other institutions that may use the SDR for reporting or financial purposes. To mitigate exposure to foreign exchange risk, the Fund's Investment Account as well as the PRGT and other Trust resources are largely held with external managers in amounts proportionate to the share of the four currencies currently in the SDR basket. Introduction of the RMB into the SDR basket would thus require a rebalancing of these resources (i.e., by selling current SDR basket currencies for RMB). The ability to hedge SDR exposures is a key requirement to efficiently conduct transactions to manage these resources. Similarly, the World Bank would be impacted by RMB inclusion as it manages IDA resources in SDRs.

Both the onshore and offshore markets trade interest rate and exchange rate forwards and swaps, repos, crosscurrency swaps, and some options. Liquidity is considerably deeper in the offshore market in Hong Kong SAR at longer maturities, where trades out to 10 years are possible, and pricing for tenors out to 5 years is tight; the offshore market in London is liquid in the shorter maturities. Pricing is typically based on offshore interest rates; but these are increasingly aligned with onshore rates. The shorter tenors available in the onshore market in large part reflect the fact that hitherto most of the onshore market that is allowed access to derivatives is "real economy" trading, and demand does not tend to be much longer-term than 2—3 years, but the lack of on-shore liquidity and activity at longer tenors also reflects capital controls, and could improve with further liberalization.

The authorities have been easing restrictions on access to onshore markets, which should facilitate hedging, and other operations by Fund members and other SDR users. The PBC announced on July 14 a package of reforms that (i) introduced a reporting form for central banks, sovereign wealth funds and international financial institutions requesting access to the onshore bond market; (ii) expanded the authorized investments to a broad range of interest rate instruments including repo, securities lending, and interest rate swaps; (iii) eliminated quotas for these investors; and (iv) allowed these investors to choose their onshore agent for these transactions. However, central banks are still required to use the PBC as their agent for FX transactions, and while the authorities have indicated that further lowering restrictions on access to exchange rate hedging instruments could be contemplated, for now they remain in place. Overall, staff is assessing whether these measures ensure sufficient access to the onshore bond market and related hedging instruments for central banks and other SDR users. As with all steps related to capital account liberalization, further measures will need to be carefully timed and sequenced.

SDR BASKET SIZE

There have been limited changes to the number of currencies in the SDR basket over time. The original SDR basket comprised 16 currencies. The Board reduced the number of currencies to five in 1980, comprising the U.S. dollar, Deutsche mark, French franc, British pound, and Japanese yen. In determining the size of the basket, the Board weighed the tradeoff between the objectives of representativeness and stability of the basket composition. A larger basket was considered more representative of global transactions. On the other hands, a small basket was considered more stable in its composition (as the ranking of currencies and the basket's composition is less likely to change) and easier to replicate (reducing the cost and complexity for SDR users). Also, importantly, aligning the valuation basket with the interest rate basket that was based on these five currencies was deemed an important element to improve the attractiveness of the SDR as a reserve asset. These currencies were also the five that had been declared freely usable in 1978. With the euro replacing, the Deutsche mark and French franc in the basket in 2000, the basket size (as well as the number of freely usable currencies) became four.

At its 2011 discussion, the Board left open the question about the exact number of currencies in the SDR basket. Following the decision in 2000 to set the number of currencies in the SDR basket at four, the size of the basket was confirmed in subsequent reviews. The Board revisited the issue in 2011 and agreed that the number of currencies in the basket should not be prejudged, but should remain relatively small as the SDR evolves, to avoid adding undue costs and complexity for users, while at the same time being sufficiently representative in terms of currencies' use in international transactions.

Staff sees a case for SDR basket enlargement if the Board decided to include the RMB in the basket. In that situation, the Board could in principle decide to either add the RMB to the current SDR currencies, thus enlarging the basket to five currencies, or replace one of the existing currencies with the RMB. In the past, Board decisions on the size of the basket were largely based on "natural breaks in the data," consistent with the stability principle. The export shares of the fourth- (Japan) and fifth-largest (United Kingdom) exporters are close, and their relative ranking has switched over time. At the same time, the gap with the sixth-largest exporter (Korea) is substantial. Thus, mindful of the stability principle discussed above, staff would not see a case to differentiate between the fourth- and fifth- largest exporters at this time. Past experience in operating with a 5-currency basket also suggests that the administrative burden of expanding the basket by one currency should be limited and manageable. This provides a case for maintaining all four current currencies in the SDR basket and adding the RMB as the fifth currency if the Board were to judge that it meets the freely usable criterion. Expanding the basket to five currencies would require a 70 percent majority of Executive Board voting power as it changes the current SDR valuation method on the basket size.

OTHER ISSUES FOR THE REVIEW

The SDR review also provides a potential opportunity to revisit and address other aspects of the valuation framework.

Weighting formula

The current method for determining currency weights dates back to 1978. Each currency's weight is endogenously derived by adding the issuer country's exports and the amount of the currency held in other countries' reserves (from the COFER survey), both expressed in terms of SDR. Exports are meant to reflect currencies' role in global trade, and member holdings of reserves are meant to capture currencies' importance in global financial flows. The relative weights of exports and reserves in the 2010 review were about 67 and 33 percent, respectively, and using latest data, would be about 60 and 40 percent, respectively. Each currency's weight would be broadly unchanged from the last review, with a small increase in the share of USD. Based on latest data, the currency weights would be around 45, 36, 10, and 9 percent for the U.S. dollar, euro, British pound, and the yen, respectively, versus 42, 37, 11, and 9 percent at the time of the 2010 review. Currency weights in the SDR basket are meant to reflect the relative importance of each currency in global trade and finance, and previous reviews have identified significant shortcomings of the current methodology. First, official reserves do not sufficiently reflect currencies' importance in global finance, especially the large increase in private international financial flows. Second, the current formula produces a higher weight for exports even though financial flows are larger and have grown more rapidly. Third, the formula combines export flows with stocks of reserves to endogenously derive weights, mixing incongruous inputs.

Alternative weighting formulas were discussed in reviews since 1980 but never proposed for formal adoption. For example, both the 2005 and the 2010 reviews discussed alternative weighting formulas that gave more weight to financial indicators. Reflecting the problems of the current approach, most Directors during the 2010 review supported further work on improving the weighting, including assessing the role of trade and financial factors, and using supplementary financial variables for calculating currency weights.

Staff will develop proposals for Board consideration, building on work done for the 2010 review. This would seek to better align basket weights with currencies' relative importance in international transactions. The work would build on the extensive analysis undertaken for the 2010 review, which in turn drew on staff work in previous reviews.

SDR interest rate methodology

The SDR interest rate is set weekly, based on 3-month instruments representing the four SDR currencies. These have been the interest rate basket parameters since 1983.

Some technical changes have recently been made to the SDR interest rate basket. In October 2014, a floor of 5 basis points was established for the SDR interest rate to ensure its consistency with the Articles of Agreement in a nearzero interest rate environment, and to address issues related to the functioning of the burden-sharing mechanism. Moreover, as of January 1, 2015, the interest rate representing the euro was changed, when the three-month Europe rate was replaced by an estimated three-month rate for euro area central government bonds, as calculated by the ECB and covering bonds with a rating of AA and above.

Shortcomings identified in the 2010 review could be revisited, but this would not seem to be a priority issue for this review. The 2010 SDR review underlined that the reset frequency being different than instruments' maturity could make it difficult to replicate the SDR interest rate in the market since the remuneration of the SDR functions like a deposit rate that does not include capital gains and losses. Preliminary discussions with some reserve managers also suggest that a daily rather than weekly reset of the SDR interest rate would facilitate hedging, and that interest rate instruments with maturities longer than three months may better reflects assets in which reserve managers typically invest. Given the focus of the current review on the RMB's assessment for inclusion and possibly on alternative weighting formulas, depending on Directors' guidance staff would see a case to revert to issues related to the interest rate basket at a later date.

Extension of the current basket beyond December

The current SDR basket expires on December 31, 2015. Following the 2010 review, the current basket became effective on January 1, 2011 for a 5-year period. In accordance with the 2000 decision, an Executive Board decision is needed before then on a new basket or to extend the current basket (which would require an Executive Board decision with a 70 percent majority of the total voting power).

SDR users and members have indicated that January 1 is not ideal for the inception of a new basket. Most markets are closed on January 1st and trading is relatively thin in the days before and after the New Year. This complicates portfolio rebalancing operations necessary to adjust to the new basket weights every five years.

The possibility of a new currency being included in the basket has also generated a higher-than-usual level of uncertainty for SDR users. Moreover, SDR users have underlined that should a new currency be added to the SDR basket, more lead time than usual would be required to adjust to the new composition. Many have indicated that a lead time of six to nine months would be desirable in such a case. In light of these issues, staff proposes to extend the current basket until September 30, 2016. The extension would not in any way prejudge the outcome of the review or whether the RMB should be included in the basket. Rather, it would address concerns expressed previously by SDR users about introducing a new basket on the first trading date of the New Year. Early guidance on the current basket's duration would also help reduce uncertainty for SDR users and facilitate continued smooth SDR-related operations, while also allowing adequate time to make necessary changes to any contractual agreements, including to the PRGT and the Fund's invested resources. If Directors agree with the proposed extension, a separate decision would be circulated after the informal Board meeting for lapse-of-time approval.

The Discussion Points

This ebook lays out initial considerations for the quinquennial review of the method of valuation of the Special Drawing Right (SDR) currency basket. It takes as a starting point the conclusions of the last review in 2010 and the subsequent Board discussion of currency selection criteria in 2011. In light of the relatively recent review by the Board, staff does not propose to revisit the currency selection criteria at this point. Recent developments suggest that the current selection criteria have remained broadly supportive of the SDR basket's stability and its representativeness of the use of currencies in international transactions. Since China continues to meet the export criterion, under the current framework, a key focus of the review will be the determination of whether the RMB is a freely usable currency. The paper focuses on developing the building blocks to inform such a determination by the Board.

The RMB's international use has been increasing, albeit from a low base, since the last SDR valuation review. The RMB has made substantial progress since the 2010 review notwithstanding the inertia that typifies international currency use, supported by a series of policy measures taken by the Chinese authorities. Across a range of indicators, the RMB is now exhibiting a significant degree of international use, especially in Asia and increasingly in Europe. Preliminary data shows that the RMB generally ranks among the highest of the non-freely usable currencies. At the same time, the RMB generally ranks behind the four freely usable currencies, with trade finance being a notable exception. The standing of the RMB under some indicators will also be affected by data adjustments to address measurement issues involving Hong Kong SAR, Macao SAR, and Taiwan Province of China. The RMB is now one of the most-traded currencies in Asia and the share in Europe is rising but from a low level, while trading in North America remains thin. More granular analysis suggests that the depth of FX markets for the RMB, while lower than that of the four currencies that are currently freely usable, may have reached a magnitude that could allow executing sizable transactions.

Significant work remains outstanding to inform the Board's determination with regard to the RMB's inclusion in the SDR basket. In the area of data analysis, pending issues include clarifying how some indicators will be defined for purposes of the assessment, comparing across multiple data sources for some indicators, and confirming final data.

On the operational side, a number of issues would need to be resolved if the RMB were included in the SDR basket. Suitable exchange rates for SDR valuation and for the RMB/SDR exchange rate for Fund operations appear to be available, and potential operational difficulties arising from divergences between offshore and onshore exchange rates could be gradually mitigated by increasing investor access to the onshore market. Member access to the onshore market is required if CNY rates are used in the context of Fund operations and might be needed to secure adequate depth in FX markets. The three-month sovereign yield could potentially be a suitable interest rate instrument for SDR basket inclusion, but further analysis is needed to verify that it is appropriate for this purpose. Similarly, hedging instruments are becoming increasingly available. The PBC has recently announced a package of reforms in these areas and staff is assessing whether they ensure sufficient access to the onshore markets for members and SDR users. The authorities are working closely with staff on outstanding issues in this area.

The ultimate assessment by the Board will involve a significant element of judgment. The rapidly-changing nature of RMB usage in the world trade and financial system poses challenges for the assessment. Judgment will have to be applied, including on the importance of the various indicators and their proximity to the freely usable concept.

Directors may wish to comment on the following issues:

- Do Directors agree that the current criteria for SDR valuation remain valid?
- Are Directors in agreement with the focus of the current review on assessing the free usability of the RMB to consider its inclusion in the SDR basket?
- Are the suggested new indicators a useful supplement to the previously endorsed indicators?
- Do Directors agree that the current review should discuss proposals for changing the weighting formula?
- Do Directors support an extension of the current valuation basket until September 30, 2016

Annex I. History of SDR Valuation Framework

The SDR valuation was initially linked to gold. Following its creation in 1969, the SDR's value was established in terms of gold with the aim of enhancing its attractiveness as a reserve asset. Although the SDR's value was gold- based, its value in terms of major currencies was expected to be stable based on the assumption that the actual exchange rate of the dollar would remain equal to its par value and there would be no exchange rate realignments between the dollar and other currencies.

However, the devaluations of the dollar in 1971 and 1973 as well as the widespread floating in 1973 revealed that the gold-based valuation did not necessarily imply a stable value of the SDR in terms of major currencies.

In 1974, the SDR's value was redefined in terms of a basket of 16 currencies. After discussing four valuation techniques, the Board approved the standard basket method which determined the SDR's value in terms of the currencies of the 16 countries that had a share in world exports of goods and services over 1 percent. Currency weights were based on export shares; however, the dollar's weight was adjusted upward in order to take into account its dominant role in international transactions. In contrast with the valuation basket, the interest rate basket included only five currencies for which market interest rates were readily available. Specifically, the interest rate was set at around half of a weighted average rate on short-term money market interest rates in the five largest countries in the valuation basket (combined market rate) to accommodate concerns from the United States about potential competition with the dollar from an SDR with a high interest rate, as well as concerns from developing countries on the increased costs of Fund credit.

In 1980, the SDR valuation basket was reduced to five currencies. Although staff proposed to reduce the size of the basket to five currencies in 1976 and 1978, it remained unchanged until 1980. However, the composition of the 16-currency basket changed slightly in 1978 when the analysis of export shares led to the replacement of the Danish krone and the South African rand with the Saudi Arabian riyal and the Iranian rial. Moreover, the SDR interest rate was increased to 60 percent of the combined market rate in 1976 and 80 percent in 1978. In 1979-1980, there was an increasing appetite to align the composition of the SDR valuation and interest rate baskets. As staff showed that nine currencies had well-developed financial markets,

Board discussions focused on whether the unified baskets would include nine or five currencies, with the choice implying a trade-off between a more stable value of the SDR and a more stable composition of the basket. At the same time, a few countries objected to the exclusion of their currencies from the SDR basket, while others argued that the weight of the U.S. dollar be set below the level indicated by the weighting formula (combined export and reserve shares). Staff noted, however, that an artificial adjustment to the dollar's weight would constitute a fundamental change, thereby requiring an 85 percent voting majority. The Board finally approved the five-currency basket proposal without significant adjustments to currency weights as well as increased the SDR interest rate to 100 percent of the combined market rate.

Several changes were made to the SDR's valuation in the period of 1998—2000, including the shift from a member-based to a currency-based approach as well as the introduction of the freely usable selection criterion. In 1998, the Board agreed on an interim approach to automatically substitute the euro for the Deutsche mark and the French franc in the SDR basket. In 2000 the Board decided that the SDR basket should comprise the currencies of the four largest exporting Fund members or monetary unions that have a currency determined by the Fund to be freely usable. Freely usable was added as a second criterion to bring financial considerations into the currency selection process, thus recognizing the growing importance of financial transactions in overall international transactions. It was also seen as a way to consider a broad range of indicators of the breadth and depth of financial markets to ensure that the SDR contained those currencies that were most representative of use in the world trading and financial systems, and also ensure the existence of a short-term interest rate instrument that is in conformance with the guidelines for the inclusion in the SDR interest rate basket. Finally, it was preferred over other alternatives because it allowed the Board to retain flexibility in exercising judgment when determining the currency composition of the SDR basket.

The Board reviewed the composition of the basket and the selection criteria in 2010 and 2011 but did not make any changes. In 2010, the Board concluded that although China had become the third largest exporter of goods and services, and had taken steps to facilitate the international use of its currency, the renminbi did not meet the freely usable currency criterion. In 2011, staff analyzed a number of reform options for the selection criteria, including alternatives to the freely usable criterion; however, the Board decided not to change the valuation method.

Annex II. Electronic Trading Platforms and Principal Exchange Markets

Modern market infrastructure, especially electronic trading, has transformed foreign exchange (FX) trading into a round-the-clock market. This has weakened the link between the market in which a transaction is booked and the location of the transacting parties. Asian FX market infrastructure is less concentrated geographically than in Europe or North America, but the main hubs have become highly integrated and are treated by market participants as a single market. At the same time, trading volumes remain the highest during the business hours of major financial centers. Overall, these developments suggest that, for the purpose of assessing currency-specific market depth and liquidity, principal exchange markets (PEMs) are best understood in terms of three broad time zones— corresponding roughly to the Asian, European, and North American market hours—rather than geographical market locations. 2 In light of the requirement for a currency to be widely traded in multiple, but not necessarily all, PEMs, this could lend itself to the interpretation that members need to be reasonably assured of sufficient market depth in at least two of the three time zones.

The role of electronic trading platforms in FX trading has risen rapidly. According to the 2013 BIS Triennial Survey, these platforms now constitute a majority of global FX turnover, at 57 percent, compared to just 41 percent three years prior (surveys before 2010 did not report electronic trading separately).3 Furthermore, discussions with market participants suggest that trades executed via other methods frequently make reference to quotes from an electronic platform in setting the terms of the transaction.

This has weakened the link between the market in which a transaction is booked and the location of the transacting parties. Electronic trading allows for continuous multilateral interaction by different market participants, rendering less relevant the common physical location of users by allowing users in different locations to connect to the electronic system and interact as if they were in a common location.4 The location where the trade is booked depends on the broker-dealer executing the trade, which does not necessarily correspond with that of either of the participants in the underlying transaction.

The innovations in market infrastructure have helped transform FX trading into a round-the- clock market. At almost any point in time, FX trading is active in at least onetime zone.5 Major market participants pass their trading book to whatever location is active at that time, facilitating liquidity in FX trading. At the same time, trading volumes, liquidity and spreads remain strongly correlated with the operating hours of major financial markets, where many FX dealer desks, the major electronic platforms and other FX market liquidity providers are located, this developments suggest that for the purpose of assessing "widely traded", PEMs could be interpreted to be broad time zones as opposed to specific market locations. In light of the requirement for a currency to be widely traded in multiple, but not necessarily all, PEMs, this could lend itself to the interpretation that members need to be reasonably assured of sufficient market depth in at least two of the three time zones. However, the degree of market depth should be interpreted together with the need for "reasonable assurance". This assurance takes into consideration that the depth and liquidity of any PEM, i.e. market time zone, naturally fluctuates intraday; hence, executing a similar FX transaction at different times may well have a different price impact.

Nowhere is the relevance of the market time zone concept more important than in Asia. In the European and North American time zones markets are more concentrated in London and New York, while in Asia markets are more dispersed, with Singapore, Hong Kong SAR, and Tokyo serving as the leading markets. However, the advent of electronic trading allows market participants to function as if these multiple locations constituted a single market.

Data from the EBS electronic trading platform suggests that RMB trading is most liquid during the hours the Asian market is open, which includes the first half of the European trading day. It then becomes more modest in the last few hours of European trading and is very low from the close of the European market to the open of the Asian market. RMB volumes have increased substantially since 2013 driven by the rising internationalization of the RMB, and also reflecting in part the increasing market share of the EBS platform over this period.

Annex III. The Role of Hong Kong SAR as a Global Financial Center: Implications for Freely Usable Assessment

Hong Kong's status as a special administrative region (SAR) of China and its character as a global financial center (GFC) raise issues for the assessment whether the RMB is a freely usable currency. Under the existing legal framework, RMB transactions within Hong Kong SAR and between Hong Kong SAR and the Mainland are not treated as international transactions for purposes of assessing the international use of the RMB (Box 1).6 However, this could result in an underestimation of the international use of the RMB if a significant part of RMB transactions within Hong Kong SAR are attributable to international transactions as they are either undertaken between non-residents or to settle an international transaction from a third country. The relevance of this issue has to be assessed on an indicator- by-indicator basis and may require further work.

Owing to its unique position as a SAR of China and a GFC, Hong Kong SAR has served as a centerpiece of the Chinese authorities' RMB internationalization strategy. Initial steps included allowing Hong Kong SAR banks to offer RMB-denominated personal accounts to residents in November 2003, followed in December 2003 by the establishment of a clearing bank arrangement to facilitate RMB payments with the Mainland. Subsequent measures included authorization of the offshore use of RMB for cross-border trade invoicing and settlement, the first offshore issuance of RMB-denominated bonds in Hong Kong SAR by the Chinese Ministry of Finance, and permission for mainland financial institutions and corporates to issue RMB-denominated bonds offshore. These initiatives expanded rapidly, and have been complemented more recently by liberalization of RMB use for settling direct investment payments and both inward and outward portfolio investment flows, including through the Shanghai-Hong Kong Stock Connect and other channels.

Several factors lead RMB transactions to be conducted through Hong Kong SAR rather than directly between the rest of the world and the Mainland. The authorities' intentional use of Hong Kong SAR as a platform for RMB internationalization facilitated the development of deep and liquid offshore (CNH) foreign exchange and money markets there. Chinese firms tend to be significant net suppliers to the CNH market, as in the presence of capital controls retaining receipts offshore provides more flexibility than repatriating the funds to the Mainland. This, in turn, leads international firms to obtain RMB in Hong Kong SAR, and many regional corporate treasuries are located there. The pool of CNH market makers is also deep, as the Hong Kong Monetary Authority (HKMA) has designated seven primary liquidity providers that have pledged to expand their market-making activities in Hong Kong SAR for various CNH instruments, and use the Hong Kong SAR platform in promoting their global offshore RMB business.7 Finally, the HKMA has put in place an RMB Real-Time Gross Settlement system, which by its linkage with the Mainland's National Advanced Payment System allows banks from all over the world to handle RMB transactions with the Mainland while eliminating settlement risk.

Payments through the system reached the equivalent of some $140 billion per day by the end of 2014. About 10 percent of these payments were cross- border flows between Hong Kong SAR and the Mainland, while the rest were offshore transactions.

Since RMB transactions involving Hong Kong SAR are so common, their treatment as either domestic or international could have a considerable impact on the assessment of the international use of the RMB. The primary role of Hong Kong SAR reflects its strong economic and cultural ties to the Mainland and first-mover advantages as well as its efficiency as a GFC and the intentions of the Chinese authorities. Despite the establishment of 16 other offshore RMB clearing centers, Hong Kong SAR accounts for over sixty percent of payments between all clearing centers and the Mainland, half of offshore foreign exchange turnover, half of offshore RMB-denominated deposits, and ninety percent of approved investment in the Mainland of offshore RMB under the Renminbi Qualified Foreign Institutional Investor (R-QFII) program. Thus, it is possible that treating transactions involving Hong Kong SAR as domestic could affect the reported international use of the RMB to a greater extent than similar treatment of other GFCs would affect other currencies.

The relevance of these issues will depend on the specific indicator in question. For example, while SWIFT data show that cross-border payments in RMB are fairly modest, including third-party domestic use boosts the RMB's share of total payments (Annex V, Table 1).9 This implies that a significant proportion of RMB-denominated payments are between parties in Hong Kong SAR (or potentially also in Macao SAR or Taiwan Province of China). Including all RMB-denominated payments would certainly overstate the international use of the RMB due to transactions between residents of Hong Kong SAR, Macao SAR, and Taiwan Province of China and residents of the Mainland that are not related to an international transaction. Conversely excluding all these transactions would probably understate the RMB's international use. Unfortunately, it is not possible to distinguish the rationale for each transaction in the crossborder payments data. For foreign exchange turnover, the treatment of Hong Kong SAR, Macao SAR, and Taiwan Province of China would not have any impact on the indicator since foreign exchange transactions in all markets would be considered in the indicator, provided that nonresidents have access.

Overall, the discussion above suggests an indicator-byindicator approach to the treatment of Hong Kong SAR, Macao SAR, and Taiwan Province of China, which will require further analysis. This would include an assessment of the factors driving RMB use between the Mainland and Hong Kong SAR, Macao SAR, and Taiwan Province of China, as well as among these three, and its link to transactions with other members, as well as efforts to improve data availability. Staff will also look at the issue of non-resident use of foreign currency in other financial centers, including London, to examine whether such transactions could have similar links to international transactions.

Annex IV. Renminbi internationalization

The use of RMB in cross-border payments and its status as an actively traded currency in global financial markets have both grown rapidly in recent years, as discussed in the main paper. This annex takes stock of the key developments in the offshore use of the RMB and underlying policy measures that have promoted its internationalization.

A. Offshore use of RMB—key developments

RMB trade settlement. The use of RMB for cross-border trade invoicing and payment has grown rapidly since its introduction in 2009. Close to 20 percent of China's goods trade is now settled in RMB (and almost 25 percent of other current account transactions—services, income and dividend payments). Among factors cited for the rapid rise are the mutual benefits—

better pricing for non-resident buyers, more security against currency risk for Chinese entities, more efficient cash flow management and lower transactions costs for both sides.

RMB direct investment settlement. Since 2011, direct investment payments (inward FDI and outward ODI) have been permitted in RMB. The RMB is rapidly advancing as the currency of choice for settling direct investment payments in both directions. Close to 30 percent of FDI transactions were settled in RMB in 2014, up from 13 percent in 2012. Reflecting a growing willingness of nonresident counterparties to accept RMB in a settlement, close to 16 percent of China's ODI is now settled in RMB, up from just 4 percent in 2012.

Offshore RMB Deposits. Licensed banks in Hong Kong SAR began accepting RMB deposits in February 2004, initially primarily to support Mainland tourism and remittances. The pace of accumulation began to accelerate after cross- border trade settlement in RMB was permitted in 2009, driven by corporate deposit growth.

Offshore RMB deposits have grown close to RMB 2 % trillion (from around RMB 100 billion in 2010), of which just under half is in Hong Kong SAR. Singapore, Taiwan Province of China, and Korea Offshore Deposits in RMB have also seen a build-up of RMB deposits in recent years. The overall offshore deposit base is around just over 1% percent of onshore deposits.

Offshore RMB bonds. The issuance of offshore RMB bonds was initially restricted to Mainland policy and commercial banks, starting with China Development Bank listing in July 2007 in Hong Kong SAR. China's own sovereign issuance in Hong Kong SAR has been an important driver of the market, with the first auction taking place in September 2009. Several corporate issuers have also tapped RMB funds in the offshore market, including foreign companies such McDonald's, Volkswagen and Caterpillar. Issuance activity has since spread, including to centers outside Asia such as London, where the first RMB-denominated bond was issued in April 2012 by HSBC.

- Current size. As of April 2015, outstanding offshore RMB bonds including certificates of deposit stood at RMB 702 billion (around 2% percent of the onshore bond market).
- The bulk of bonds are issued by entities from China and Hong Kong SAR. 65 percent of outstanding bonds are accounted for by issuers incorporated in China and Hong Kong SAR. A further 6 percent is accounted for by other Asian issuers and the remaining 29 percent by non-Asian entities.
- Corporate credits dominate the sectoral breakdown, accounting for 77 percent of outstanding issuance (of which just over half or around 40 percent of total issuance—is by Chinese state-owned banks and enterprises). Chinese government and policy banks comprise about 18 percent of the issuances. The remaining 5 percent of issuances is by supra-national bodies and foreign governments.
- Overseas agencies and governments have also been tapping offshore RMB funds in recent months. In September 2014, the IFC issued what was then the largest London-listed RMB bond worth RMB 1 billion. In October 2014, the UK issued its first RMB-denominated sovereign bond (raising RMB 3 billion) and indicated that the proceeds would be held as FX reserves. A month later, the Canadian province of British Columbia issued in Hong Kong SAR its second RMB-denominated bond for RMB 3 billion.
- Instruments that allow hedging of interest rate and currency risk have accompanied the growth of the offshore debt market. Market participants note rapidly growing volumes in cross currency swaps (CCS) involving

offshore RMB and the emergence of the CCS curve as a key offshore RMB benchmark interest rate curve.

Foreign asset holdings in RMB. Sparse data on central bank holdings of RMB-denominated assets precludes a definitive judgment of how widespread the practice is. As of April 2015, the People's Bank of China (PBC) estimates the total offshore holding of bonds, stocks, deposits and other RMB assets by foreign central banks and monetary authorities amounted to RMB 666.7 billion. just over USD 100 billion.

Overall progress. Most of the progress in RMB internationalization since 2009 has been in its use for trade settlement and direct investment purposes. The use of the RMB as an international funding and reserve currency, while growing, remains in its early stages.

Underlying Policy measures to Promote RMB Internationalization

Policy measures to promote RMB internationalization, particularly its use as a funding and investment currency, have covered three main areas: gradual opening of the capital account, steps to strengthen the domestic financial system, and offshore liquidity support through improvements to cross-border payments infrastructure and central bank swap lines.

Gradual opening of the capital account

Capital account transactions with China are generally subject to restrictions, pre-approvals, and quotas, as summarized in the Fund's 2014 AREAR report. As part of a broader financial reform agenda, however, over time the authorities have been gradually easing restrictions, widening channels of access, and increasing quotas for two-way flows (for example, the USD "Qualified Foreign Institutional Investor—QFII" program, established in 2003, that allows foreign asset managers access to the Mainland securities markets and the USD "Qualified

Domestic Institutional Investor—QDII" program, established in 2006, through which Chinese asset managers can invest in overseas securities markets, both subject to approval and quotas).

Toward a regime of "managed convertibility". More generally, steps have been taken to facilitate cross-border transactions through reducing the costs associated with regulatory approval. For certain direct investment transactions in the capital account, the regulations have already shifted from pre-approvals to registration and expost monitoring. The State Administration of Foreign Exchange (SAFE) tracks each transaction and follows up with banks on aberrant transfers. Recent discussions with the authorities indicate that capital account liberalization will proceed along a path of "managed convertibility". Details have not been announced, but staff understands that the broad rationale is to minimize disruptive short-term capital flows and contain currency and duration mismatches. The approach will likely:

- combine the monitoring system for direct investment transactions with licensing and approvals for securities and loan transactions within an aggregate quota (the eventual goal is to shift all transactions from approvals to monitoring);
- monitor transactions in as real time as possible, and take action if necessary, to contain potentially harmful, destabilizing flows (macro prudential and capital flow measures);
- maintain limits on open foreign positions and shortterm external debt (micro prudential); and
- exercise tight supervision to curb money laundering, terrorist financing, and tax evasion.

In addition to encouraging private flows, the authorities are taking steps to ease access to onshore markets for overseas official institutions. On July 14, the authorities announced that foreign central banks (as well as sovereign wealth funds and international financial institutions) registered with the PBC can choose their own size of investment in the onshore China Interbank Bond Market (CIBM), with access to all instruments including repos, bond lending, bond forwards, interest rate swaps, and forward rate agreements. The guidelines permit these overseas official institutions to select either the PBC or a settlement agent registered with the PBC to conduct trading and settlement on their behalf. Once fully implemented, these measures are likely to ease access to onshore financial markets for overseas official institutions. As outlined in the guidelines, however, these institutions shall act as long-term investors and the PBC will regulate their trading behavior in accordance with reciprocity principles and macroprudential requirements.

Against the backdrop of a gradual opening of the capital account, non-resident interest in RMB as a funding and investment currency has been helped by specific steps to allow RMB funds to flow onshore.

- The 'Renminbi Qualified Foreign Institutional Investor (R-QFII)' program, introduced in 2011, allows foreign asset managers to channel offshore RMB funds into the Mainland securities markets, subject to approval from two agencies: a license from the China Securities Regulatory Commission (CSRC) and a quota from SAFE. Market participants note that restrictions on remittances of dividends, minimum holding periods, and 'soft' barriers to holding cash onshore deter entry (around 50 percent of overall approved quotas have been used). Nevertheless, familiarity with market conditions seem to mitigate these obstacles in some cases (the Hong Kong SAR R-QFII quota has been fully taken up).
- Since November 2014, individuals and institutional investors with a brokerage account in Hong Kong SAR can trade stocks on the Shanghai stock exchange under the North-bound corridor of the 'Shanghai-Hong Kong

Stock Connect' scheme, while a South-bound corridor permits trades in the reverse direction (Hong Kong SAR stocks traded via a Shanghai brokerage account). Although take-up from Hong Kong SAR has been significant (around 50 percent of the RMB 300bn Northbound quota has been used as of May 2015), lack of clarity on the legal framework governing ownership and voting rights for onshore stock appears to have so far deterred participation by large international institutional investors. Plans are underway, however, to expand the Connect program to cover Shenzhen by the end of the year.

- More recently, in May 2015, the PBC announced that offshore clearing banks as well as nonresident banks with quotas to access the CIBM can borrow in the onshore interbank repo market to fund offshore RMB business. The limit on financing secured through repos will be tied to the bonds held onshore. Greater access to the onshore market should enhance the efficiency of offshore RMB liquidity management, facilitate participation in Stock Connect schemes and offshore issuance of RMB securities, and advance the cross- border use of RMB more generally.
- In July 2015, a new channel for two-way flows between Hong Kong SAR and the Mainland ("Mutual Recognition of Funds") will open with mutual funds in either location permitted to mobilize investments from the other jurisdiction, subject to regulatory approval and within an overall quota.
- Measures to facilitate regional corporate treasury operations. Since February 2014, corporations registered in the Shanghai Free Trade Zone have been allowed onshore-offshore RMB and USD cash transfers between the parent company, subsidiaries, and affiliates. In November 2014, the program was extended to

corporations registered in pilot cities across the country. These 'cash pooling' or 'cash sweeping' arrangements are intended to help corporations centralize and standardize risk management, debt service, and working capital transfers.

Domestic Financial Reforms

The international appeal of RMB securities ultimately rests on the stability of the domestic financial system (along with other attributes such as overall macroeconomic performance and access to information on corporate issuers). As part of their broader structural reform agenda to transition China to a safe and sustainable growth path, the authorities have initiated financial reforms aimed at achieving more market-based pricing, better alignment of risks with returns, and greater efficiency of credit allocation. Key elements include:

- Interest rate liberalization. Over the last decade, the PBC has gradually dismantled controls over commercial bank interest rate settings. Lending rates were completely liberalized in 2013. Deposit rates are still guided by a benchmark set by the PBC, but since 2012 commercial banks have been given greater control over pricing deposits through an increasingly wider band of flexibility above the benchmark (currently set at 1.5x). In June, 9 large banks were permitted to issue negotiable certificates of deposits to households and nonfinancial corporations at 'market rates', subject to an annual target balance quota.

- Deposit insurance. A nation-wide deposit insurance program was established on May 1. It covers all deposit-taking banking institutions, excluding branches of foreign banks. Deposits up to RMB 500,000 ($80,600) per depositor per bank are insured, which covers 99.6 percent of depositors.

- Measures to rein in shadow banking. Over the last two years, the authorities have taken steps to tighten regulation and supervision of securities and trust companies, activity in the interbank market, issuance of high yield 'wealth management products', and lending to high risk sectors of the economy. These measures appear to have had an impact on the composition of credit: the share of intermediation that has been brought back on to bank balance sheets (and is therefore subject to capital and provisioning requirements) has increased significantly in recent months, while off-balance sheet activity has decelerated sharply.

Cross-Border Payments Infrastructure and Offshore Liquidity

Since 2003, the PBC has designated 17 overseas subsidiaries or branches (hereafter referred to as "clearing banks" of the Chinese banks in the Mainland to provide RMB settlement services (Table 1). The settlement institutions of their clearing systems are participants in China's real-time gross settlement system and intermediate the exchange of RMB against foreign currencies, between offshore and onshore banks.

Clearing banks have a settlement account with the PBC and have access to RMB liquidity from the PBC or through their headquarters in China. In addition, they have access to the onshore inter-bank lending and bond market, and the foreign exchange market. They thus provide liquidity to the offshore markets, while also allowing the PBC to monitor the RMB flows.

A new RMB Cross-border Interbank Payment System (CIPS) is expected to be launched later this year. The system will adopt real-time gross settlement for cross-border trade, cross-border direct investment and other cross-border RMB business settlements. The new payment system is intended to improve the efficiency of RMB clearing and settlement and thereby support wider international use of the currency.

Bilateral swap lines provide a liquidity backstop to counterpart central banks. Since 2008, the PBC has signed bilateral swap lines with over 30 foreign central banks, cumulatively worth over RMB 3 trillion (Table 2). The PBC notes that the purposes of each bilateral currency swap arrangement include promoting bilateral trade and direct investment for economic development of the two countries, supporting domestic financial market stability, and other purposes agreed upon by both parties. Though the purpose of foreign exchange intervention is not explicitly included, a counterpart can convert RMB into other currencies in the offshore market and use the funds for purposes it deems appropriate. Swap agreements are effective for a three-year period from the effective date of agreement and the drawing / usage period is up to 12 months. The RMB leg of the swap is priced off SHIBOR as the benchmark rate, with the spread over the benchmark priced according to the counterpart's credit rating, credit default swap spread, and other factors. The PBC does not provide an implicit agreement to convert RMB into a major reserve currency.

RMB internationalization began to accelerate in 2009, principally through the offshore market in Hong Kong SAR. The status of the RMB as a payment currency for settling China's cross-border trade and direct investment transactions has advanced rapidly. However, its use as an international funding and reserve currency remain in the early stages. As part of broader reforms aimed at moving China onto a sustainable growth path, the authorities have gradually opened the capital account and introduced measures to strengthen the domestic financial system. Together with efforts to expand cross-border payments infrastructure, the reforms are also aimed at enhancing the international appeal of RMB securities

Annex V. Data Issues Pertaining to the Freely Usable Currency Assessment

This annex presents definitions, data sources, and methodological issues relating to indicators used in the assessment of "Freely Usable". The first section recounts the four indicators endorsed by the Executive Board in 2011. International bank liabilities and international debt securities, two of the three Board-endorsed indicators for widely used, have undergone methodological changes in definition since then. It also describes complementary sources of data for foreign exchange turnover, the Board endorsed indicator for widely traded. In the second section, data sources and issues relating new indicators proposed by staff for assessing free usability are discussed.

Board-endorsed Indicators (2011)

Official foreign exchange reserves: The Currency Composition of Official Foreign Exchange Reserves (COFER) database provides data on the currency composition of official foreign exchange reserves on a quarterly basis. COFER provides break-downs for seven currencies representing 97 percent of allocated global reserves but it does not separately identify the RMB.

International banking liabilities (IBL): They are defined by the BIS as liability positions denominated in any currency to non-residents (Locational Banking Statistics, Table 5A, external positions vis-à-vis all sectors) plus liabilities denominated in foreign currency to domestic residents (Locational Banking Statistics, Table 5D, local position in foreign currency vis-à-vis all sectors and vis-à-vis the nonbank sector). Currently the BIS require reporting the currency breakdown into local currency, each of the SDR currencies, the Swiss franc and the residual. The full breakdown is encouraged but not required. The BIS, on its part, is assessing whether information on the RMB- denominated liabilities of banks resident in Hong Kong SAR, Macao SAR, and Taiwan Province of China to residents of mainland China can be provided.

IBL statistics from BIS was endorsed as an indicator for freely usable by the Executive Board in 2011.

In December 2012, the BIS changed its methodology for compiling data on international banking positions. Previously, reporting banks' positions, denominated in either foreign or local currency, for which the counterparty was unknown had been treated as "external or crossborder". After the revision, a new category "unallocated by counterparty country" captured unallocated positions denominated in foreign currency. Positions unallocated by counterparty country in local currency were removed from external positions.

The difference in external banking liabilities resulting from the methodological change is measurable, reflecting the removal of positions in local currency for which the country counterparty was unknown, mainly debt securities issued by banks (hence affecting liability positions more greatly than assets). As compared to the BIS data from 2010 included in the 2010 review, the value of liability positions declined on average by about 10 percent over the period with the revised data in 2013. Importantly, the distribution of the change between currencies was relatively even, with the US dollar and euro gaining some share.

International debt securities (IDS): BIS international debt securities are defined as bonds and notes and money market instruments issued in a market other than the local market of the country where the borrower resides (Securities Statistics, Tables 13A and 13B). They encompass what market participants have traditionally referred to as foreign bonds and Eurobonds. Foreign bonds are issued by nonresidents under the registration rules of a local market. Eurobonds, also known as offshore bonds, are issued outside the registration rules of any local market, usually in a foreign currency. The BIS compiles data on international debt securities from various national, market, and institutional data sources such as DEA logic, Thomson Financial Securities Data International Capital Market Association, the Bank of England, and Euroclear. The BIS is exploring whether it would be possible to consolidate Hong Kong SAR, Macao SAR, and Taiwan Province of China with mainland China in compilation of RMB- denominated IDS.

Prior to 2012, the BIS definition of an international debt security was based on targeted investor rather than the primary market i.e. the market where securities are issued for the first time. It covered debt securities placed with international investors, including securities issued, in the local market by local residents but targeted at international investors. Therefore, they reflected an estimate for the external indebtedness of a country.

The methodological revision meant a significant reduction in the outstanding stock of international debt securities and significant reallocation of currency shares. The value of the outstanding issuances fell by 27 percent at end-September 2012 and on average 20 percent in 2005—09, the period covered by the 2010 review. Almost all of this reduction is explained by the reclassification as domestic bonds of local currency bonds issued by residents in the local market but underwritten by a syndicate that included at least one foreign bank. A small amount is also explained by the reclassification as domestic of debt securities issued by residents in the local market but denominated in foreign currencies. The redistribution of the currency shares is more significant, with the share of issuances denominated in US dollar experiencing a large downward revision while other currencies—particularly the euro and pound gaining.

Foreign exchange turnover: This is defined as the gross value of all deals concluded during the month, and is measured in terms of the nominal or notional amount of the contracts based on the location of the sales desk. The BIS Triennial Central

Bank Survey is the only comprehensive and reliable data source for global foreign exchange market turnover. The survey compiles the nominal or notional amounts of executed spot and derivative foreign exchange transactions from about 1300 reporting financial institutions from 53 jurisdictions. However, it is conducted only once every three years for the month of April. The latest available one dates back to April 2013, failing to capture most recent market developments, including the continued increase in Chinese RMB turnover. Furthermore, the survey covering only a one-month snapshot may affect cross-currency comparisons by capturing any exceptional currency-specific volatility.

Higher frequency local surveys by regional foreign exchange committees and monetary authorities may complement the BIS Triennial Survey with more up-to-date information. Six regional committees (London, New York, Singapore, Tokyo, Australia and Canada) covering roughly 75 percent of global market turnover publish survey results on a semi-annual basis, while the Hong Kong Monetary Authority and People's Bank of China have provided the IMF with local foreign exchange turnover on a monthly basis for the purpose of the SDR review. These surveys are broadly underpinned by similar methodology as used for the Triennial Survey, but are not as comprehensive and typically have limitations to the currency pairs covered. In absence of coordination by the BIS, turnover statistics from local surveys cannot be adjusted for double-counting of cross-border trades reported by dealers in different jurisdictions (data is compiled on net-gross basis).

Data compiled by Society for Worldwide Interbank Financial Telecommunication (SWIFT) provides a potential complementary high-frequency source for foreign exchange volumes. The turnover data is based on interinstitution back office messages for confirming details of a foreign exchange transaction in SWIFT's FIN messaging service network (Message

Type 300) from SWIFT's FIN network. Unlike survey-based data, SWIFT data is based on actual interaction between market participants and can be obtained at a high (monthly) frequency. However, SWIFT data broken down by instrument or by the market where the trade was booked are not available, which would have been relevant for the purposes of the freely usable assessment. The data records both legs of FX swaps as separate spot transactions, which exaggerates the actual market depth for each currency involved in swaps. Importantly, the data covers only part of the global FX market. Some FX trades are confirmed outside the SWIFT network (through smaller alternative networks or nonautomated processes) and a significant portion of trades in the 17 currencies settled by the CLS are confirmed through an alternative SWIFT messaging service (InterAct), which is separate from the FIN network and is not included in the data. This, in turn, significantly skews cross-currency turnover comparisons in favor of non-CLS currencies. There may be further data quality issues related to the degree of "noise": for example, messages with no underlying foreign exchange transactions or typos cannot be filtered out in compiling the data set. Staff will explore possible remedies to some of these issues and assess feasibility of using SWIFT data for purposes of the free usability assessment.

Additional Surveys Conducted By Specific Markets

Market size 1/ 2/ Financial center Data Latest data			Data availability (total and by currency) 3/								
			USD bn	% Total	USD	EUR	JPY	GBP	RMB	AUD	CHF CAD
London	Public	Oct 14	2667	41%							
New York	Public	Oct 14	1095	17%							
Singapore	Public	Oct 14	481	7%							
Tokyo	Public	Oct 14	363	6%							
Hong Kong SAR 4/	Bilateral	Apr 15	275	4%							
Sydney	Public	Oct 14	150	2%							
Toronto	Public	Oct 14	60	1%							

Mainland China	Bilateral	Apr 15	44	1%	

New proposed indicators

Survey on the use of Currencies in Official Foreign Currency Assets: The IMF conducted an adhoc survey of member countries on the use of currencies in official foreign currency assets. The survey asked for a by-currency breakdown for a selected set of currencies. Official Foreign Currency Assets include Monetary Authorities' holdings of both Official Reserve Assets and other foreign currency assets (both claims on non-residents and residents) not included in official reserve assets. The ad-hoc survey was conducted during April—May 2015, and requested end position data for end-2013 and end-2014.

Monetary Authorities encompasses the central bank and certain operations usually attributed to the central bank but sometimes carried out by other government institutions or commercial banks. In cases where monetary authorities included institutions other than the central bank, the survey was sent to both the central bank and the agency managing reserves. The broader definition of official foreign currency assets allowed members to report the currency composition of all assets denominated in foreign currencies.

The ad-hoc survey targeted the full membership of the Fund, and it was reported on a voluntary and confidential basis by 130 jurisdictions. Following the guidelines of the quarterly survey of the Currency Composition of Official Foreign Exchange Reserves (COFER), the ad-hoc survey information was treated as strictly confidential, as only four staff at the Fund had access to individual country data. The information on individual members is not disseminated or published. The names of the jurisdictions that reported are also confidential, consistent with the COFER guidelines.

Gross issuance of international debt securities: Gross issuance of international debt securities from BIS covers same markets, instruments and methodology as outstanding international debt securities, a 2011 Board-endorsed indicator. As for IDS, the BIS data currently does not allow for consolidating issuance of Hong Kong SAR, Macao SAR, and Taiwan Province of China with that of mainland China.

Trade finance: Trade finance comprises financial transactions aimed at supporting international trade, involving credit, insurance or guarantees. The financing can be accorded directly between importers and exporters (commonly referred to as trade credit), or intermediated by banks. SWIFT provides data on letter of credits (L/C) underlying their interbank message code MT 700, which is estimated to be about half of total trade finance. The main drawback of using trade finance (based on L/Cs) as an indicator for the freely usable assessment is that growth in trade finance has lagged the growth in nominal trade-in many countries for the past 10—15 years, and trade finance figures may not reflect correctly the developments in the "wide use" of currencies in international trade payments. Although the series from SWIFT are very comprehensive in terms of country coverage, as an indicator the L/Cs has a more regional rather than a global representation since the advanced economies and global banks account for a very limited share in total L/Cs, whereas emerging Asian economies account for a large share. SWIFT data allows Hong Kong SAR, Macao SAR, and Taiwan Province of China to be treated as domestic.

International Payments: SWIFT is a unique source of high frequency data on global payments that could potentially be useful for the assessment of currencies free usability if a number of issues can be addressed. SWIFT publishes a ranking of currencies used in global payments based on monthly data collected from the use of its standardized inter-bank messages, MT 103 and MT 202, for transfer of funds instructions. MT 103 covers payment instructions sent by or on behalf of the financial institution of the ordering customer to the financial institution of the beneficiary customer. MT 202 covers payments instructions sent by or on behalf of the ordering institutions directly or indirectly to the beneficiary financial institution. Besides being high-frequency, SWIFT's data on payments offer granularity that allows for assessing the use of currencies from different vantage points. For instance, with the breakdown of payments between cross-border and domestic available, domestic payments that SWIFT uses in its ranking can be eliminated from the assessment of currency use in international transactions. Furthermore, intra-euro area payments and transactions within and between mainland China and Hong Kong SAR, Macao SAR, and Taiwan Province of China can be excluded.

MT103 and MT202 cover different underlying businesses and differ significantly in magnitudes. MT103 reflects single customer transfers related to transactions directly relevant for freely usable assessment. MT202, however, includes payments relevant for freely usable assessment as well as account transfers between financial institutions for book keeping purposes that are not relevant for the freely usable assessment. Payment transactions for which MT202 is used include purchase of securities, commodities, and foreign exchange. MT202 payments are about four to ten times as large as MT103 payments as transactions between financial institutions are generally much larger than transactions on behalf of banks' customers.

There are some issues with SWIFT payment data relevant for the context in which it is used worth noting. First, payments related to a single economic transaction can be captured multiple times if several banks are involved in the payment chain, which could potentially overestimate currency use in this context. Second, while SWIFT's financial messaging system is used in most countries; coverage can vary across countries, as some domestic payment messages may be exchanged through countries' own payments networks. This is less of an issue if only cross-border payments are counted as international transactions, where except for messages transmitted through some major banks' systems, SWIFT estimates its coverage at 90 to 95 percent of global transactions. Third, and specifically related to 202 messages, it is not possible to single out MT202 transactions driven solely by account transfers for book keeping purposes that are not relevant for the freely usable assessment. While including MT202 transactions would simply capturing some transactions not directly relevant for freely usable assessment, discarding them would mean removing relevant international transactions, particularly given the large magnitude of MT202 relative to MT103 transactions. Therefore, both 103-only and 103+202 are presented below to inform judgment on the global role of currencies in cross border transactions.

CHAPTER 3

SDR: RESERVE CURRENCIES AND THE INTERNATIONAL MONETARY SYSTEM'S FUTURE

Much as the strength of the Bretton Woods institutions h as always been their adaptability, the same can be said of the SDR. The instrument was created in the 1960s to avert the prospect of a liquidity shortage that threatened the stability of the Bretton Woods System. But by the time two SDR allocations had taken place in the 1970s, circumstances had been transformed. The price of gold had risen, inadequate liquidity had become excessive liquidity, and pegged-but- adjustable exchange rates had given way to floating. After initially being defined in terms of the gold, the SDR was redefined in terms of 16 currencies in 1974 and in terms of five currencies in 1981. Yet despite these adaptations and changing circumstances, the instrument is still very much with us.

The SDR competes with national monies that are possible candidates for international use, including the dollar, the mark, and the yen. It competes most directly with these currencies (and also with gold) as a reserve asset held and traded by central banks. The question therefore arises whether there will be a role for the SDR in the changed circumstances of the future and if so whether it can be justified in terms similar to those of the past. Our topic in this paper is whether the future of the international monetary system will provide such a justification.

Answering this question requires a forecast of how the international monetary system will evolve from here. We construct our forecast using economic logic and by extrapolating historical trends, and distinguish three phases in the likely future evolution of the international monetary system. The first, the immediate future, will extend the movement toward exchange rate flexibility and capital mobility. Neither of these trends, we argue, will significantly enhance the role of the SDR; if anything, the opposite will be the case. The second phase, what we call the intermediate future, adds to this picture the possibility of monetary union in Europe. EMU, if and when it occurs, will have significant effects on the demand and supply of international reserves. Several of this work in opposite directions, however. On balance, they are therefore unlikely to create a significant demand for SDRs.

Any analysis of the third phase, the distant future, is necessarily the most conjectural. In the spirit of "social science fiction," we hazard a glance fifty years ahead and ask whether a world of monetary blocs or a single world currency will create a role for the SDR. Again, our conclusion is largely negative.

Essentially, we conclude that the dollar will remain the leading international currency. Assisted by newcomer currencies, particularly the mark and the yen, it will satisfy the needs of the international monetary system.

What might the SDR supply that the others cannot? There are two possible answers: an adequate total supply of reserves and an attractive, stable unit of account.

If the supply of reserves were inadequate under a system where international reserves were created only by individual countries -- a modern Triffin dilemma -- new issues of SDRs could make up the difference. But we think that the Triffin dilemma is obsolete under the multiple reserve currency system. If dollar liabilities or mark or yen liabilities ever become so great in relation to the gold or other international reserves held by the issuing country (or the exports, or GDP, or net international investment position) as to bring their value in question, central banks could simply switch to the currencies of new rising countries in which they have confidence. The multiple reserve currency system may not make for stable exchange rates, but it does not want for reserves.

The story is somewhat different as regards a unit of account to use for pegging, invoicing trade, denominating debt and so forth. Economies of scale tend to make a one-currency system more efficient than a multiple-currency system in these functions. The SDR, computed as a basket, is in some ways an intrinsically more attractive unit of account than the dollar or other single currencies. But a review of the attributes that make for a successful international currency suggests that the SDR is an unlikely candidate, even if the dollar were to fall from the number-one slot over the next 50 years. The SDR simply does not have a natural constituency, which is a prerequisite for a currency to come into widespread use.

We start with a section on analytical issues. We then analyze the bases for an international currency, with particular reference to the SDR but also considering its rivals. With this material in hand, we consider the likely future role of the instrument in the operation of the international monetary system. The paper closes with a conclusion and two appendices: one on institutional arrangements and one on the history of the SDR.

II. Analytical Issues

The SDR was originally created as a form of international reserves. Our discussion of its past and future therefore begins with countries' motives for holding reserves. We analyze how changes in the structure of the international macroeconomic environment toward greater exchange rate flexibility and international capital mobility affect the demand for reserves. We seek to clarify several confusions: whether capital mobility and floating exchange rates obviate the need for reserves, whether all countries can accumulate reserves simultaneously, and whether the advent of exchange rate flexibility and capital-account convertibility has removed instability in the reserve-supply process of which Robert Triffin warned.

1. Capital Mobility and the Demand for International Reserves

According to traditional wisdom, countries hold reserves to smooth the time profile of production and consumption and to insulate their economies from balance-of-payments shocks. Consider, for example, a country linked to the rest of the world by merchandise trade alone (financial capital is immobile internationally). An adverse shock to its terms of trade will cut its capacity to import. If the country reduces imports of intermediate inputs, domestic production will be disrupted. A lower-cost strategy may be to maintain the flow of imported inputs, financing them out of reserves until the terms of trade recover or domestic sources of supply can be developed. Similarly, it will not be efficient for a country suffering a temporary disturbance to cut consumption when the shock hits, only to raise it once the shock passes. Rather, its government will wish to smooth consumption, using reserves to finance the deficit in the country's trade.

This thought experiment assumes no international capital mobility. It is sometimes asserted that capital mobility removes the motive for holding reserves. It eliminates the need to hold reserves in order to smooth the time profile of production and consumption insofar as countries can accomplish this by borrowing or lending in the private market. The proposition that capital mobility renders reserve-holding obsolete is correct strictly within the confines of certain models. In practice, however, it is incorrect.

Obstfeld (1993) constructs a model of a world of perfect capital mobility in which the demand for reserves is zero. Some authors have taken the implications of such models quite literally. Thus, Schroder (1990) argues strongly that capital mobility reduces the demand for reserves and eliminates the rationale for

SDRs. To quote, "as long as the international capital markets continue to function, there is no danger of a shortage in international liquidity and therefore no convincing economic reason for creating SDRs."

But Obstfeld's result depends on the assumption that countries can borrow without limit at the world interest rate. In reality, even when statutory and technological barriers to international capital mobility are absent, countries cannot borrow in unlimited amounts at that interest rate. Default risk is a problem, particularly because of the absence at the international level of any sort of bankruptcy court.

Asymmetric information and adverse selection therefore cause lenders to charge higher interest rates as the borrowers' indebtedness grows (Stiglitz and Weiss, 1981; Eaton and Gersovitz, 1981). In other words, governments must allow the domestic interest rate to rise to attract foreign capital. Periods when they especially need reserves namely, balance of payments crises are precisely when they cannot borrow at the going interest rate. They may be able to borrow, at least to an extent, at higher interest rates. But higher interest rates have costs; like lower supplies of intermediate inputs, they can disrupt production. Governments may find it intolerable to raise rates to whatever level is needed to finance balance-of-payments shocks. They may find it prudent to finance a portion of transitional payments deficits out of international reserves.

Ultimately the argument is an empirical one. Countries continue to hold reserves; therefore, they must find them useful.

One might think that the advent of capital mobility would nonetheless reduce the demand for reserves since countries can finance at least a portion of their external deficits by borrowing abroad. But this assumes that the capital account is not itself a source of financial instability. Even countries with floating currencies continue to hold reserves with which to intervene in the foreign exchange market and dampen variability in the exchange rate. But a high degree of capital mobility can increase the variability of the exchange rate, thereby increasing the demand for reserves. Countries with pegged exchange rates may suffer larger balance-of- payments shocks when capital mobility is high. Sudden changes in the price or availability of external finance such as Mexico experienced in 1994 can destabilize balances of payments in general and those of heavily- indebted countries in particular. The existence of this additional source of disturbances may heighten the need for insulation. Hence, there can be no presumption that the advent of capital mobility either raises or lowers the demand for reserves. Which effect dominates is again an empirical question.

2. Exchange Rate Flexibility and the Demand for International Reserves

Similar statements regarding the obsolescence of reserves accompanied the move toward floating exchange rates in 1971-73. It was anticipated that more frequent exchange rate adjustments would enhance the scope for using relative prices to adjust to balance of payments shocks. Countries with payments deficits could simply depreciate their currencies, improving their export competitiveness and the attractiveness of their assets. This mechanism would eliminate the need for reserves.

While the use of exchange-rate changes to offset shocks is a staple of international economics textbooks, governments are reluctant to make full use of the instrument. That exchange rates continued to be managed following the breakdown of Bretton Woods is no coincidence in our view. Large exchange-rate changes have economic costs that render governments reluctant to undertake them. Depreciations can lead to inflation, depress output by raising the prices of imported inputs, increase the burden of servicing foreign- currency-denominated debts, and threaten the solvency of banks with foreign-currency-denominated liabilities. Exchange rate volatility per say is undesirable because it can discourage international trade and investment.

In fact, with the demise of the Bretton Woods System, the demand for reserves did not decline, let alone disappear. Even the demand for reserves on the part of the industrial countries, most of which adopted some form of floating exchange rates, continued to grow in nominal terms, though some studies found a modest decline relative to appropriate benchmarks. And there was continued growth in the demand for reserves on the part of developing countries, the vast majority of which continued to peg in the short-run and used reserves to accommodate fluctuations in the availability of debt finance (Heller and Khan, 1978; Frenkel, 1980). This difference in behavior was predicted by the literature on choice of exchange rate regime (e.g. Heller, 1978), in which it was argued that relatively large countries with diversified exports and well- developed financial markets can afford to float, while their smaller, less-diversified, less-developed counterparts will prefer to peg. Insofar as the former rely more on exchange rate changes for adjustment, they may have a lower demand for reserves.

Even for countries prepared to float, there can be no general presumption that this automatically reduces their demands for reserves. Just as with international capital mobility, this conclusion assumes that foreign exchange markets were not themselves a source of disturbances. Authors like Rose (1994) document that the increased volatility of exchange rates after 1973 has not been associated with increased volatility of fundamentals, suggesting that at least some shocks are indigenous to the foreign exchange market. Authors like Woodford (1991) model these shocks in terms of extrinsic (sunspot) noise. The increased volatility of exchange rates for any given level of intervention, or the increased amount of intervention necessary to accomplish any given level of volatility, can then imply an augmented demand for international reserves.

3. Understanding the Triffrn Dilemma

After World War II, the U.S. dollar was the only major currency that was freely convertible, even just for current account transactions. Aside from gold, whose supply was relatively inelastic and which did not pay interest, this made dollars the only form of reserves. Under these circumstances, not all countries could accumulate net reserves simultaneously. As a group, other countries could accumulate net reserves only by importing gold or dollars from the United States. Collectively, they had to run balance-of-payments surpluses. But since the global balance of payments must sum to zero, the United States had to run deficits. In other words, the rest of the world could increase its claims on the United States only if the U.S. increased its liabilities to the rest of the world: the U.S. net reserve position had to fall for that of the rest of the world to rise.

In a world without capital mobility, foreign central banks and governments could not borrow on the private U.S. market to obtain reserves; they could accumulate reserves only by acquiring claims against the U.S. authorities, implying a decline in the net reserve position of the latter.

This accounting identity is the source of the Triffin Dilemma.[8] If the U.S. allowed its balance of payments to remain in deficit, accommodating the demands of the rest of the world for additional foreign exchange reserves, U.S. international monetary liabilities would rise relative to U.S. reserves. Because this meant that net U.S. reserves declined (rather than rising with the growth of the American economy), the system would have been in long-run disequilibrium. The ratio of dollar liabilities to U.S. gold reserves (or to American export capacity) would rise without limit.

Eventually the ability of the U.S. to convert dollars into gold at the statutory price of $35 an ounce would be called into doubt. Other countries would rush to convert their foreign exchange into gold before the U.S. gold window was closed, liquidating the gold-dollar system. On the other hand, if the U.S. raised interest rates and deflated to eliminate its balance-of-payments deficit, other countries would have been collectively unable to augment their dollar balances. In their desperate scramble for reserves, those other countries would have been tempted to deflate even more than the United States, subjecting the world economy to intense deflationary pressure.

4. Does International Capital Mobility Remove the Triffin Dilemma?

In the post-World War II world of controls to suppress international capital movements, the only way for governments and central banks outside the United States to obtain additional reserves was by running balance-of- payments surpluses against the U.S. and importing gold or obtaining claims against the U.S. government. An increase in the net reserves of the rest of the world had as its counterpart a decline in the net reserves of the United States (an increase in its net monetary obligations to foreigners). Reserve distribution was a zero-sum game, creating an argument for an SDR allocation to allow all countries to obtain additional reserves simultaneously to match the growth of their economies. With the recovery and liberalization of international capital markets, this constraint has been removed. The Fed can now borrow or buy foreign currencies from private traders on foreign capital markets (and even in its own financial markets) at the same time foreign central banks borrow or buy dollars on the U.S. Market (or in the Euromarkets). For every asset there is still a corresponding liability; international capital mobility does not remove the constraint that the global balance of payments must sum to zero. If the Fed sells treasury bonds (or dollars) to private foreign investors in order to augment its foreign exchange reserves, it incurs an additional financial liability to foreigners. But it does not follow that the Fed has failed to augment its stock of reserves. The name "reserves" is bestowed on the foreign- currency-denominated assets of the authorities precisely because they are in official hands. Compare the situation in which the authorities have foreign exchange in hand with one in which they hold treasury bonds of their own issue which they can sell for foreign exchange. While in the first situation we say they possess reserves, we don't say the same about the second precisely because there may be circumstances in which the market is unwilling to buy those treasury bills, or similar domestic-currency assets, at any price. These circumstances, of course, are precisely those times when reserves are most valuable. In short, the world? s central banks can indeed take advantage of international financial markets to create reserves.

This is not to deny that short-term dollar liabilities in the hands of foreigners (to continue with the example of the Fed) are a possible source of dollar instability. A measure of the dollar liabilities in the hands of foreign central banks has a place on the long list of variables that might influence the probability of adverse speculation or the probability of successfully withstanding it. Other possible variables on this list include the dollar liabilities in the hand of foreign private citizens, dollar liabilities in the hands of domestic citizens, aggregate short-term liabilities of domestic residents vis-avis foreigners (regardless of currency of denomination), domestic holdings of foreign short-term assets, net dollar indebtedness to foreigners (whether long-term or shortterm), net foreign-currency indebtedness to foreigners (whether long-term or short- term), and the rate of change of some of these variables, especially of net overall indebtedness to foreigners (i.e., the current account). But even if all these things may matter, there is still a distinct role for reserves per se as suggested by the observed continued desire of all central banks to continue holding them. Thus, there seems to us no particular argument for netting out foreign holdings of domestic currency from the measure of domestic reserves. If anything, liquid dollars held by private citizens are a greater possible threat to the Federal Reserve than those held by other central banks.

Hence, the advent of highly developed and integrated international financial markets has removed the zero-sum nature of reserve distribution. This is why the official statistics, reported in Table 1, show total foreign exchange reserves increasing year after year by 3 1/2-fold between 1978 and 1995. Indeed, so far as the authors are aware, no official source reports figures for the net balance of payments, or net holdings of reserves, with net defined as netting out foreign central bank holdings of the domestic currency. A system in which the Fed, the Bundesbank and the Bank of Japan can all transact in one another's private markets simultaneously has eliminated one traditional argument for the creation of a synthetic reserve asset like the SDR.

But if the foreign monetary liabilities of the U.S., Germany and Japan as a group continue growing relative to the size of their national economies (reflecting, presumably, the relatively rapid economic growth and incremental demand for reserves on the part of the developing world, though it could also reflect excessive money creation by the reserve- currency countries themselves), there might come a time when the ability of these countries to convert their liabilities into goods or other assets of value to those countries that hold their currencies as reserves would be called into doubt. The Triffin Dilemma could be resurrected in a new guise.

Competition among prospective reserve currencies might conceivably help stabilize the system, however. As additional countries develop and remove their exchange and capital controls, they will become candidates for supplying international reserves. This would simply be a repeat of the evolution of the system in the 1970s and 1980s, when Germany and Japan liberalized their financial markets and acquired reserve-currency status for the mark and yen. One can imagine Singapore, for example, gradually acquiring reserve-currency status (especially within East Asia). Countries that supply international reserves earn seigniorage. The advantages of seignories encourage those that meet the preconditions for supplying reserves to do so, holding constant other considerations. If the supply of reserves provided by the traditional reserve-currency countries appear to be approaching unsustainable levels, there will be a demand for the newcomers to do so.

The elasticity of these alternative reserve supplies will be greater in the long than the short run; Le Chatelier's principle should apply in this context like any other. But our point still stands: the dilemma created by the fact that there are only a limited number of national sources of international reserves will be removed by the elimination of controls on international transactions in other countries and the emergence of alternative sources of supply. There may be an argument for an SDR allocation to permit countries to obtain international reserves without expending real resources (without having to service the debts they incur when borrowing on foreign markets, in other words), as suggested in Michael Mussa's paper in this volume. (This assumes, of course, that difficult issues of distributive equity can be finessed, and that the recipient governments will actually use their SDR allocations to acquire and maintain reserves, assumptions which should not be taken for granted.) But it does not alter our conclusion that open international capital markets remove the specter of a global reserve shortage and therefore eliminate one of the most powerful of the traditional arguments for an SDR allocation.

III. International Currencies: The SDR and its Rivals

In this section we consider the extent to which different currencies are used internationally, both by governments and by private agents. Informed by the results of this "market test," we then describe the conditions that seem to make a unit suitable for international use. This leads us to a judgment on the international role of the SDR.

It is worth flagging one theme from the start: while our discussion of the aggregate supply of reserves in Part II concluded that a multiple-reserve currency system might be more stable than the old dollar standard, Part III points to powerful forces (economies of scale and scope) encouraging actors to specialize in the use of a single international currency (Krugman, 1984; Matsuyama, Kiyotaki, and Matsui 1991). What is efficient at a point in time may not be stable over time and vice versa.

1. The Choice of Currency in Which to Hold Reserves
   International uses of currencies can be categorized according to whether the decision is made by public monetary authorities or by private actors. They can also be distinguished according to such traditional functions of money as store of value, unit of account, and medium of exchange (Kenen, 1983). We begin by considering the actual composition of reserve holdings of central banks (the subject of the preceding part of the paper), before proceding to the authorities' choice of a pegging currency, and then to the various uses in private markets.

As known, the levels of reserve holdings in the form of various currencies, including the SDR, as it has evolved over the last two decades. It is presented the same information as percentage shares.

The figures show that the share of the dollar fell steadily in the 1970s and 1980s, as it made way for the increase in the mark and the yen. The rate of increase in the use of the latter currencies looks particularly rapid because they started from relatively low levels (especially in the case of the yen).

This trend reversed in the early 1990s, though one would never know it listening to popular commentary on the declining role of the dollar. Contrary to widespread belief, the figures show that the dollar's share in reserve holdings was virtually flat in 1994, and substantially up relative to 1990.

The yen share, again contrary to expectations, was down slightly in 1994. The mark's share, while approximately flat in 1994, is down since 1990. In short, data for the 1990s show no acceleration of the downward trend in the dollar's share. If anything, they show the reverse.

What is going on in a short-term sense is that the Bank of Japan and major European central banks have in the 1990s bought the dollar on foreign exchange markets in order to prevent its value from falling more against their own currencies. They may not be happy with this situation, but they find it preferable to the alternative. In a longer-term sense, the dollar remains the leading reserve currency.

Figures for 1995 may turn out to show a switch away from dollar holdings toward yen and marks, particularly among East Asian central banks. But it is unlikely that such a switch, when viewed in the historical perspective, and would constitute an abrupt acceleration of the gentle downward trend of the 1970 and 1980s.

The share of the SDR peaked at 6 per cent in 1982, which put it in third place, after the mark but before the yen.

(The denominator is the total foreign exchange reserves including SDRs, but excluding countries' reserve position in the IMF and excluding gold.) The SDR share has declined since then, leveling off at 2 per cent in the 1990s. The yen surpassed the SDR in 1984, and even the pound and French franc did so in 1992. This is not entirely a fair contest, since SDRs enter the system when the members of the IMF vote to create them, which they have not been doing. The other currencies become reserves when central banks choose to acquire them.

Perhaps the ECU is a more appropriate competitor for the SDR than are the national currencies. The ECU like the SDR is defined in value as a basket of currencies, and like the SDR is created by a collective body of national governments.

There is a private market in ECUs, unlike SDRs, so any central banks could in principle create ECU reserves by purchasing them on the private market. But most ECUs came into existence when the European Monetary System was established in 1979, and are backed by international reserves (dollars), so that they are not as yet fiat money to the extent that SDRs are.

Indeed, although ECUs are reported as constituting the third largest share of international reserves (approximately tied with the yen), one point of view is that they are simply dollars in disguise. (This point of view is favored by the authors, until such time as EMU successfully, takes place.).

2. The Choice of Currency to Which to Peg The other major arena in which countries' monetary authorities must choose among major international currencies is the choice of which currency to peg to, among those countries who choose to peg. A country will tend to hold more of its reserves in the form of a given currency, other things equal, if it also pegs to it. Conversely, it is more likely to peg to a given currency, other things equal, if it is already using that currency in international dealings.

There are a prior reasons to think that the SDR should be a popular peggers unit. The dollar is the natural peg for Latin American countries which undertake much of their trade with the United States (and with other countries linked to the dollar). Similarly, the DM (or a prospective new EMU currency) is the natural peg for a typical European country, which undertakes much of its trade with other European countries. But in Asia, Africa, the Mideast and elsewhere, countries tend to distribute their trade more equally among

Japan, Europe, and North America. Pegger to any single major currency exposes them to the risk of large fluctuations relative to other currencies. An obvious solution is a basket peg, with the weights, determined so as to suit the country in question. To be sure, 31 countries are currently classified as pegging to a composite of their own design. But this basket pagers tend to lose one of the principle advantages of a fixed exchange rate policy (after the first advantage, reducing exchange rate uncertainty). They lose the credibility of the nominal anchor to monetary policy. Basket-pagers tends to keep the weights secret, to change the parity secretly and frequently, or to change the weights secretly and frequently. (Keeping the weights secret to begin with, of course, facilitates making the changes in policy in secret.) As a result, the public is unable to ascertain on a day-to-day basis, or even a month - to- month basis, whether the central bank is abiding by its officially stated policy of pegging the currency. Logically, this should undermine the credibility argument in favor of a currency peg. One would think that the SDR would solve this problem.

Its value is computed as a weighted average of five major currencies: the U.S. dollar, Japanese yen, deutschemark, pound sterling, and French franc. While the weights are unlikely to match exactly the trade weights on a country in Asia, Africa, or elsewhere, they come reasonably close. A country that pegs to the SDR will not experience the large changes in effective exchange rates that have discouraged East Asian countries, for example, from pegging to the yen.

3. The Choice of the SDR as a Peg

The use of the SDR as a currency peg showed the unit to its best advantage 15 years ago. Now, this measure also shows its stagnation. It is presented in the statistics. The number of countries pegging to the SDR stood at 12 in 1979, and then peaked at 16 in 1982. Many of them were in Africa or the Mideast. As a percentage of peggers, this was a rise from 16.4 per cent in 1979 to 22.5 percent in 1982. But by 1995 (including up to the third quarter), the number had declined to only three -- Libya, Myanmar, and Seychelles -- countries hardly at the frontier of international trade and finance. As a percentage of peggers, they constitute a mere 6.4 per cent. (As a percentage of all members of the IMF, the SDR peggers rose from 8.9 per cent in 1979 to 11.0 per cent in 1982, only to sink to 1.7 per cent in 1995.) Despite a decline, the dollar remains the leading currency peg. In 1995, 23 currencies pegged to the dollar. This represented 49 per cent of peggers, down from 55 per cent in 1979 (=40/73) or 57 percent in 1975 (=46/80). The French franc has remained steady, in second place, with 14 clients; this is 30 per cent of 1995 peggers, up from 19 per cent of 1979 peggers and 16 percent of 1975 peggers. The pound and the peseta each lost its last pegger in 1986. The pound's fall was from a grace of 9 percent of peggers in 1975. It is still the case that no currencies anywhere are pegged to the yen. One currency (the Estonian kroon) pegged to the mark in 1990. The mark, of course, also plays a central, if unofficial, role in the European Monetary System. If one broadens the test to include countries that peg to a weighted basket, whether tightly or loosely, one again concludes that the dollar remains dominant within the baskets. Even among East Asian countries, where the yen occasionally has a statistically significant weight, the weight placed on the dollar is always for higher.

4. The Choice of an International Currency in Private Use
Measures of international currency status in private use, for 1990 and 1994, are discussed. These measures are relevant to a consideration of the international monetary system for two reasons. First, one attribute of an international monetary system (along with the exchange rate regime and issues of reserves and liquidity) is which currency or currencies are in international use generally. Second, even if we are only interested in the question of which currencies are used as a form in which to hold reserves, the answer is correlated with the question of which currencies are in international use privately. An Asian central bank, for example, is more likely to hold reserves in the form of yen, if the yen comes into use in foreign exchange trading (as opposed to the present system, where the dollar is almost always used as the vehicle currency in Asia) and if private financial markets are otherwise well-developed in yen.

The share of the SDR in private markets is small, generally negligible. The dollar is still on top, despite a gradual decline by some measures in its use versus the mark and yen over the last twenty years. The trend is so gradual that is hard to detect it over the four-year gap between the two tables.

A. Vehicle currencies in foreign exchange trading. In the past, almost all trades in the foreign exchange market involved the dollar as the currency bought or sold. As recently as the mid-1980s, if a firm wanted to exchange pound sterling for deutschmarks, it had to trade pounds for dollars, and then dollars for marks. These days the firm would be more likely to be able to go directly from pounds to marks. Largely as a result, only 83 per cent of foreign exchange transactions in April 1995 involved the dollar, as opposed to 90 per cent only six years earlier. Yet this is still twice the share of the DM. The dollar's share is equal to that of the next four competitors (the DM, yen, pound and Swiss franc) combined. (When reported in the third column of tables they have been divided by two so that the total does not exceed 100 per cent and they are comparable with the other measures).

B. Denomination of financing. Various measures of use of currencies to denominate private international financial transactions -- loans, bonds, and deposits -- show the dollar as the dominant currency. The yen has gained a bit in terms of external bank loans and the mark in terms of external bond issues.

The yen's share of long-term external financing is particularly high among developing countries. This is especially true in East Asia, where the Japanese government lent freely in the 1980s. Among five major East Asian debtors, the yen's share doubled in the 1980s.23 The fraction of long-term debt denominated in yen crossed the 50 percent mark in Thailand in 1993, with Indonesia, the Philippines, Malaysia and Korea also above 30 percent. In East Asia and the Pacific overall, however, the yen's share has not yet surpassed the dollar's (at 30.0 percent in 1993, versus 31.1 percent).

Among long-term debt of developing countries in the aggregate, the yen remains a distant second to the dollar.

As reported in the mark is in third place, followed by the French franc, pound sterling, and Swiss franc. In the mid- 1980s, the SDR broke into these rankings, but its share has been steady at a paltry 0.2 percent. SDR- denominated debt is heavily concentrated among low-income countries (where it constitutes 0.6 percent of debt), particularly countries in South Asia and Africa (and to a lesser extent the Middle East and North Africa).

C. Currency of invoice in international trade. An important function of major currencies is as a unit of account and medium of exchange in international trade. Unfortunately, up-to-date global figures on the currency of invoicing and payment are not available. Calculations pertaining to 1987 show the dollar in first place, at 38 percent, followed by the mark at 21 percent, the yen at 13 percent, the French franc at11 percent, and the pound at 10 percent.

Among the largest countries, only the governments of Japan and Germany maintain more up-to-date figures. The share of yen invoicing in Japan's imports rose from 2.4 per cent in 1979 to 14.4 percent in 1990 and 20.9 percent in September 1993 (with a larger increase in the case of imports from Southeast Asia). The share of the yen in Japan's exports rose from 25 per cent in 1979 to 39 percent in 1983 (again, with a concentration in Southeast Asia). It declined subsequently, and then recovered (to 37 percent in 1990 and 39.9 percent in September 1993). The dollar remains the dominant invoicing currency, even in Japan's exports.

The currency pattern of invoicing of Germany's exports was more stable in the 1980s, at about 82 percent marks, 710 percent dollars, and 5 per cent pounds, French francs, and Swiss francs combined. German imports, however, saw a shift from 43 per cent in marks in 1980 to 53 percent in 1988, at the expense of the dollar (from 32 percent to 22 percent).

The other currencies were steady at a combined 8 percent, and the yen rose from negligible to 2.5 percent of German imports.28 Occasionally OPEC discusses abandoning its policy of setting the price of oil in dollars, and perhaps switching to the SDR. These discussions generally begin when the dollar has undergone a large drop in value, and end when the dollar stabilizes or reverses.

D. Currency substitution in cash transactions. Figures on the use of international currencies as substitutes in local cash transactions are not available. The two leaders are certainly the dollar, for which internationally-circulating cash has been estimated by the Fed at roughly 60 percent of U.S. currency outstanding, and the mark, for which international circulation has been estimated by the Bundesbank at 35-40 percent of German paper currency outstanding. Thus, there were about 240 billion dollars and 66.8 billion marks, in cash, circulating in third countries in 1995.29 At the October exchange rate, the dollar's share of this market works out to 78.2% and the marks to 21.8%, counting other entries at zero.

Wherever hyperinflation or social disorder undermines the public's faith in the local currency, the American dollar is the preferred alternative. (The drug trade and other illegal activities are another source of demand, of course.) The United States profits whenever people in Argentina or Russia hold dollars that do not pay interest. Seignorage is a growing source of effective revenue for the United States. A simple calculation -- multiplying the interest rate times foreign-held dollars -- suggests that the United States now derives about $12 billion a year in seignorage from foreign holdings of U.S. currency.

IV.   Implications for the Future

In this section, we draw out the implications of the preceding analysis for future competition among aspiring international currencies.

1. Conditions for an International Currency

Having seen how the various candidates for international currency status currently rank, we now ask what are the attributes that make a currency suitable for this role. Four major sorts of conditions determine whether a currency is used internationally.

A. Patterns of output and trade. The currency of a country that has a large share in international output, trade and finance has a natural advantage. By such measures, Japan should clearly be number two, ahead of Germany. The U.S. economy is still the world's largest, however, in terms of output and trade. Alarmist fears notwithstanding, it is not very likely that Japan, a country with half the population and far less land area or natural resources, will surpass the United States in sheer economic size.

If the measure of being a vehicle currency is how often it is used in the invoicing and financing of international trade, then other aspects of the pattern of trade may also be relevant. The fact that much of Japan's imports are oil and other raw materials and that much of its exports go to the Western Hemisphere, for example, helps explain why a disproportionately small share of trade is invoiced in yen as opposed to dollars. Raw materials still tend to be priced in dollars.

B. History. There is a strong inertial bias in favor of using whatever currency has been the vehicle currency in the past. An individual (exporter, importer, borrower, lender, or currency trader) is more likely to use a given currency in his or her transactions if everyone else is doing so. For this reason, the world's choice of international currency is characterized by multiple stable equilibria. The pound remained an important international currency even after the United Kingdom lost its position as an economic superpower early in the century. In the present context, the inertial bias favors the continued central role of the dollar.

C. The country's financial markets. Capital and money markets must be not only open and free of controls but also deep and well-developed. The large financial marketplaces of New York and London clearly benefit the dollar and pound relative to the deutschmark and the yen. The controls on international financial transactions that Germany and Japan only began to dismantle in the 1970s (1974 and 1979, respectively) and the domestic regulations that they continued to retain, made their currencies less attractive candidates for international use. This is the basis for our view that capital controls were one component of the Triffin Dilemma and for the argument for the SDR as a reserve currency. It is true that Japanese financial markets came a long way in the 1980s. But Tokyo still lags behind New York and London as a financial center, while Singapore and Hong Kong has been gaining.

It has also been argued that a strong central bank, and large financial sector to counterbalance the political influence of the trade sector, are important. The point is to be able to resist political pressure in favor of depreciating the currency to help sell goods.

D. Confidence in the value of the currency. Even if a key currency were used only as a unit of account, a necessary qualification would be that its value not fluctuate erratically. As it is, key currencies are also used as a form in which to hold assets (firms hold working balances of the currencies in which they invoice, investors hold bonds issued internationally, and central banks hold currency reserves). Confidence that the currency will be stable and particularly that its value will not be inflated away in the future is critical. The monetary authorities in Japan, Germany and Switzerland established a better track record of low inflation in the 1970s than did the United States, which strengthened their bids for international currency status.

Given good U.S. inflation performance over the last ten years, this is no longer the concern it was formerly. A more important negative for the dollar is the fact that the United States is now a debtor country. Indeed, 1994 and 1995 were the first two years when the country actually paid out more in interest, dividends, and repatriated profits to foreigners, on their past U.S. investments, than it received on its own past investments abroad. Even if the Federal Reserve never succumbs to the temptation to inflate away the U.S. debt, the continuing U.S. current account deficit is always a possible source of downward pressure on the dollar. Such fears make dollars less attractive.

2. The Prognosis for the Dollar, Mark, Yen and SDR in light of these desiderata for an international currency, what is the prognosis for the aspirants to the top slot? It is unlikely that some other currency will supplant the dollar as the world's premier currency by, say, the year 2020. The dollar will still be the world's favorite currency for holding reserves, pegging minor currencies,

invoicing imports and exports, and denominating bonds and lending.

There is no plausible alternative for the number-one position.

This is not to suggest that the dollar is ideally suited for this role. It has characteristics that mar its appeal: most importantly the United States is a debtor country with a large current account deficit. But an international currency is one that people use because everyone else is using it. Three of the four determinants of reserve currency status - - economic size, developed financial markets, and historical inertia -- support the dollar. The fourth determinant could in principle disqualify the dollar if the Federal Reserve produced a high-inflation strategy, but this is unlikely to happen.

The SDR lacks a natural constituency. While the mark and the yen have natural constituencies, they have three drawbacks relative to the dollar that have already been noted: their financial markets are not as liberalized or well- developed as those of the United States, their natural constituency is not as large, and a challenger is always at an inertial disadvantage relative to an incumbent.

Over the period 1970-1992, U.S. GDP fell from 24 percent of Gross World Product, evaluated at purchasing-power- parity rates, to 20 per cent. It is possible that one can explain much of the downward trend in the dollar's share of world reserves over the last 25 years, and the upward trends in the yen and mark shares, by the falling share of U.S. GDP in the world economy and the rising share of the Japanese and German GDPs. A careful econometric study of the determinants of central bank reserve holdings is beyond the scope of this article. But a crude analysis of the role of relative growth rates may be worthwhile.

We have estimated econometrically that for every one percentage point of economic growth increase that one of the G-3 major countries experiences as a share of Gross World Product (measured at purchasing-power-parity rates), its currency experiences a 1.33 percentage point increase in its share of central bank reserve holdings.36 In a statistical sense, one can explain a decline of the dollar share over the period 1970-1992 of 5 percentage points by the shift in GDPs.

One can also explain increases in the mark and yen shares of 1 percentage point and 5 percentage points, respectively.

The tests described here are crude. A careful analysis of a well-specified equation would require access to data on foreign exchange holdings broken down by central bank, rather than aggregated. Most central banks report their holdings to the International Monetary Fund, but under conditions of secrecy. The responsible department in the Fund does not analyze the data itself, nor, normally, will it even let researchers in other parts of the Fund do so. (Shockingly, there is no way for a reader of the aggregated tables that are reported each year in the IMF Annual Report even to know whether the currency composition has been drastically affected in a particular year by a change in the list of countries that have dutifully reported their holdings.)

The only exception, to our knowledge, is the study by Dooley, Lizondo, and Mathieson (1989), who had blind access to the data (i.e., access without identification of the individual central banks). They estimated the responsiveness of country central bank holdings of dollars, marks, yen, pounds and French francs to the trade undertaken by the country in question with each of the five large countries.

One could in principle combine these estimates with projections of rates of growth in income and trade to make forecasts of reserve demand for the five currencies. However, the equation estimated by Dooley, Lizondo and Mathieson includes also among its explanatory variables dummy variables indicating choice of peg (or other exchange rate regimes), and the proportion of interest payments on external debt in the five currencies. These decisions regarding currency-pegging and debt- denomination are ones that we would wish to regard as determined simultaneously with the reserve-holding decision.

If rapid growth of Japan's trade or an increase in confidence in the yen, for example, is making the yen a more attractive international currency than the dollar, this would show up in pegging and debt policies as well as in reserve policies.

Thus, we are unable to use their equation for forecasting. What does our crude regression equation predict for the future? (The following calculation should be regarded as merely illustrative.) The United States is estimated to have a permanently higher intercept term than the mark or yen.

This difference is presumably attributable to the openness and development of its financial markets and inertial bias. At current exchange rates, the aggregate GDP of the EC 12 is approximately equal to that of the United States (which is 26.1 per cent of Gross World Product). At purchasing- power- parity exchange rates, EC GDP is slightly smaller than that of the U.S. (which has a share of 22.5). Japan's share is smaller, but it has been gaining on the U.S. rapidly, when evaluated at current exchange rates. To take an extremely pessimistic scenario from the viewpoint of the dollar, imagine that by the start of the next century, the Japanese economy is as large as the United States, and the mark has become the common currency throughout a Western Europe of the same size.

If the aggregate size of the three regions together, evaluated at purchasing power parity, remains the same (one half of gross world product in 1992), then each becomes one- sixth of the world economy. Our equation predicts that the dollar's share of world reserves would in that case fall only to 62 per cent (from 63 per cent currently), the mark's share would rise to 28 per cent (from 16 percent), and the yen's share to 17 per cent (from 9 per cent). This would indeed be a continuation of the trend of the 1970s and 1980s. Yet the dollar would remain number one by a large margin.

This calculation rules out a priori a sudden "tipping" that would render the old constant terms obsolete. But why should the world equilibrium converge on a non-dollar currency? This would only happen in the event of a drastic change in some of the conditions enumerated above, such as either Japan or a deutschmark-dominated area actually surpassing the United States in economic size, which is unlikely. (The possibility of a single currency coming into use throughout Europe, which would indeed pose a challenge to the supremacy of the dollar if it were to happen, is discussed below.)

Why is the dollar the world's lingua franca, while the SDR is not? There is an analogy with the international use of the English language. Nobody would claim that English is particularly well-suited to be the world's lingua franca by virtue of its intrinsic beauty, simplicity, or utility. Yet it is the language in which citizens of different countries most often converse and do business, and increasingly so. One chooses to use a lingua franca, as one chooses a currency, in the belief that it is the one that others are most likely to use.

If the dollar is the world monetary system's version of the English language, the SDR is the system's version of Esperanto. The SDR was created by the IMF to be an ideal international currency. Its definition makes it intrinsically more useful than the dollar, just as Esperanto is intrinsically superior to English. The reason that the SDR is even less widely used today than it was ten years ago is that, like Esperanto, it lacks a natural base of constituents who would use it even if it were, not in international use.

V. Implications of the Evolution of the International Monetary System

The crucial characteristics of the international monetary system in the immediate future will be three: the movement of additional countries toward flexible exchange rates, continued high capital mobility, and the gradual diversification of reserve portfolios. Over the intermediate run, a European monetary union may be established.

Peering very far into the future, one can envisage the possibility of a world of three currency blocs, centered on the United States, Western Europe and Japan, or even a single world currency. What would be the role of the SDR in these scenarios?

1. The Immediate Future

As late as 1984 fewer than a quarter of IMF member countries had adopted floating rates. But by the end of 1994 the proportion operating systems of managed and independent floating rates had risen to more than 50 per cent. There is good reason to think that the trend will continue. The existence of large, highly liquid international financial markets increases the difficulty of operating currency pegs.

While exceptional circumstances, such as a recent history of very high inflation (as in Argentina), political threat to confidence (as in Hong Kong) or close links with foreign governments (CFA franc zone), may induce a few developing countries to peg their currencies, the prevalent view, especially in the wake of the Mexican crisis, is that few developing countries are well advised to peg.

We noted in Section II that following the breakdown of Bretton Woods, there was some decline in the demand for reserves on the part of large, industrialized countries, but little change, and even an increase, in the reserve demands of smaller developing countries. We attributed this contrast to the reluctance of small, highly-specialized commodity exporters with underdeveloped financial markets to allow their currencies to float freely, as suggested by the literature on the choice of exchange-rate regime. As developing countries continue to grow, their exports diversify, and their financial markets deepen, their exchange-rate and financial arrangements will increasingly resemble those of the industrial economies, and so too will their demands for international reserves.

This points to some decline in the global demand for reserves.

As we saw in Section II above, there is some empirical support for this view, although it suggests that the decline in reserve demand will be modest. This suggests no pressing role for the SDR to augment the supply of global liquidity.

Another common rationale for the SDR is to provide a unit of account that fluctuates less against each component currency than that currency fluctuates against the other component currencies. This enables national governments, international institutions, and private parties to maintain accounts and denominate contracts in a more stable unit than would be available otherwise. As more currencies begin to fluctuate, this rationale would appear to acquire additional force.

But this argument was formulated before the development of today's highly liquid, low-cost foreign exchange markets.

If governments and private agents find it attractive to hold assets in the form of a composite basket of five currencies, they can do so without the IMF's help by undertaking foreign exchange transactions that replicate the SDR basket. With spreads on foreign exchange markets as low as five basis points, the relevant transactions can be undertaken at minimal cost. This would not obviate the need for the Fund to define, calculate and publish the value of the SDR, since services such as these would create the focal point encouraging basket peggers, for whom the attractions of a particular basket peg are likely to increase with the number of countries that also peg to that basket, to peg to the SDR rather than to another currency composite. But it would not create an immediate rationale for additional SDR allocations.

Another direction in which the international system will evolve is toward still higher capital mobility. As explained in Section II, we see this as blunting the Triffin Dilemma and weakening associated arguments for an SDR allocation. Capital mobility allows all governments and central banks to augment their reserves simultaneously by borrowing on private foreign markets. It removes the danger that the foreign monetary liabilities of the reserve currency countries will grow at an unsustainably faster rate than their domestic economies, calling into question their ability to convert their liabilities into other assets or commodities at prevailing prices by allowing - indeed encouraging -- the emergence of alternative national sources of reserve supply.

Along with higher capital mobility will come greater access to and reliance on foreign bond and equity finance for developing economies. The role of the SDR, in the view of its founders, was to "permit the Fund to assure an appropriate level of international reserves." Is this role obviated by this ability to borrow? While some have argued that ability to borrow diminishes the demand for reserves because it makes their supply more elastic, the volatility of the supply of commercial capital may actually increase the need for official reserves to smooth fluctuations in the external accounts. As illustrated by the Mexican crisis of 1994-95, countries in need may find themselves unable to obtain borrowed reserves at any price. To prevent a meltdown of the Mexican financial system, the IMF provided the government nearly $20 billion of credit as part of a $50 billion assistance program. The largest single transaction in the history of the IMF's SDR department was the sale of SDR 3.5 billion by Mexico from its stand-by purchase in February 1995.

The idea that an SDR allocation could provide the resources needed to head off national financial crises with global repercussions goes back at least to Group of Ten (1985). But the growth of international financial markets renders existing Fund resources increasingly inadequate. Rather than being allocated to member countries in proportion to their quotas, the SDR issue could be allocated to the Fund itself to underwrite loans by a special financial-crisis facility targeted to where they are most needed. (For further discussion of this idea, see the paper in this volume by Marcello de Cecco and Francesco Giavazzi.)

But there are also other ways of financing international-lender-of-last-resort intervention. The relevant finance can be provided by national governments, as in the case of U.S. and European loans to Mexico in 1995. Still, it can be difficult, as that experience illustrates, to provide the needed resources with the speed required by the operation of modern financial markets, for political as much as economic reasons. Alternatively, resources can be mobilized by increasing IMF quotas. Members would pay in SDRs and reserve currencies in the amount of their quota increases, thereby providing the Fund the requisite resources. But there would be political resistance to the substantial quota increases that would be necessary to enable countries to draw automatically on the Fund in the amounts required to cope with modern financial crises. Mexico, for example, was allowed to draw five times its quota, in an exception to IMF rules.

Another option is to increase the General Arrangements to Borrow, under which the governments and central banks of the G-10 countries and Saudi Arabia provide lines of credit which allow the Fund to borrow up to $28 billion at market interest rates if its resources are sufficient to deal with an emergency. At the Halifax Summit, the leaders of the G-7 countries agreed that the GAB should be doubled through a combination of increased contributions from existing members and the participation of new countries. But if the GAB is doubled by leaving the G-10 and its $28 billion of credit lines intact and creating a parallel grouping comprised of the G-10 plus a number of smaller countries responsible for an additional $28 billion of credits (a proposal which finds favor among the smaller G-10 members who fear that simple expansion would erode their influence), this two-tier arrangement might not be appealing to potential new members and might not attract their participation. And while

GAB members can receive money "to forestall or cope with impairment of the international monetary system," the terms under which GAB credits can be extended to non-members are more restrictive. These requires an "exceptional situation of a character or aggregate size that could threaten the stability of the international monetary system." Some would say that this would have been difficult to claim of the Mexican crisis, for example. Would Mexico therefore have been eligible to draw from the GAB?

Thus, there is a second-best (really, a third- or fourth- best) case for an SDR allocation -- with the SDRs being allocated to the Fund itself rather than to member countries -to finance a facility for dealing with Mexico-style crises, if and only if it proves impossible to expand Fund quotas and the GAB and to liberalize the provisions for drawing on either of them.

The final direction in which the international monetary system will evolve is toward some diversification of reserve portfolios. As argued above, we believe that the dollar will remain the dominant reserve currency for the foreseeable future. But there is some evidence that Asian countries, which hold an increasing share of global reserves, have been substituting yen for dollars in their reserves because their debts are increasingly denominated in yen. Japan, Taiwan, China, Singapore and Hong Kong are five of the six largest holders of international reserves, reflecting their rapid economic growth and the magnitude of the capital inflows they have received. It is sometimes inferred that, if these trends continue, the yen could supplant the dollar as a reserve currency. But this argument overlooks two facts. First, Japan itself cannot hold yen as reserves. Second, there is reason to think that Asian economic growth in the future will not outstrip growth in other parts of the world to the same extent that it has in the past.

All this suggests that reserve portfolios may become slightly more balanced among currencies in the short run.

None of it provides an obvious rationale for an SDR allocation to supplant national currencies in international reserve.

2. The intermediate Future

In this subsection we assume, for sake of argument, that a European monetary union (EMU), encompassing some but not necessarily all members of the European Union, will come into existence in the intermediate run. That event, assuming it occurs, will have important effects on supplies and demands for international reserves. Because several of these work in opposite directions, however, they are unlikely to give rise to a significant excess demand for reserves and to create an argument for an SDR allocation.

Because EMU members will no longer have to stabilize their exchange rates vis-a-vis one another, their demands for reserves will decline. Gros and Thygesen (1991) put the decline at $100 billion, European Commission at $200 billion.

But a further short-run impact of EMU is likely to be some increase in the demand for dollars as reserves and additional ability of the United States to provide them. The introduction of the Euro would reduce the fraction of reserves denominated in European currencies, compared with the fraction held in EU currencies before the Euro is introduced because European central banks' holdings of one another's national currencies will be transformed into domestic-currency claims.

Unlike the Bundesbank, which could hold francs, and the Bank of France, which could hold marks, the European Central Bank would only be able to hold its reserves in the form of non-European currencies like the dollar. The dollar will account for an even larger share of global reserves. To the extent that a larger share of world reserves is denominated in dollars, network-externality effects may encourage countries to accumulate even more.

With time, the creation of a single European currency would lead to a concentration of foreign exchange transactions in that asset compared to the volume of transactions that take place currently in, inter alia, the French franc, and the deutschmark. With both Frenchmen and Germans transacting in Euros, bid-ask spreads in the single currency would decline, since spreads are a decreasing function of the volume of transactions. In turn, this will attract other currency traders to the Euro market. Prominent among them will be those holding the currencies of countries in Southern and Eastern Europe who are not among the founding members of the monetary union but wish to join subsequently; their currencies are likely to shadow the Euro, encouraging foreign exchange transactions to pass through it rather than the dollar. And as the Euro becomes more important as a vehicle currency, it is likely to gain use as an intervention currency and to become an increasingly popular form in which other countries hold their reserves. Ultimately, the creation of the Euro would mean a new and increasingly powerful rival for the dollar as the international monetary system's leading reserve currency.

One can imagine two ways in which this transition might take place. The first one gives rise to an argument for an SDR allocation to avert an incipient reserve shortage, but we find it far-fetched.

Assume that central banks around the world decide all at once to switch their holdings from dollars to Euros. This could imply considerable exchange rate instability between the major currencies, strains on the international monetary relations of smaller countries, and a rise in the demand for international reserves. The instability of a major reserve currency like the dollar could spook its major institutional holders, who might then dump their holdings, reducing the effective supply of international reserves. The consequent scramble for Euros and yen, and appreciation of those currencies relative to the dollar, could place significant deflationary pressure on the European and Japanese economies.

In this scenario there might be a case for an SDR allocation to avert the incipient reserve shortage and a substitution account to absorb redundant dollars without destabilizing foreign exchange markets, as suggested by Kenen (1995). But this sudden switch from dollars to Euros is unlikely.

Central banks will be aware that they face a collective action problem; if they all scramble to sell dollars, they will depress the value of the claim they are attempting to sell. In the same way that they hesitated to liquidate their gold reserves at once in the 1970s, they are likely to adopt a similar attitude toward the management of their excess dollars, and to rebalance their portfolios by gradually acquiring other currencies as their need for reserves continues to grow. Even Kenen agrees that the disaster scenario that motivates his call for the creation of a substitution account is a low- probability event.

3. The Distant Future

Wyplosz (1995) envisages the emergence of a world of three currency blocs, organized around the dollar, the yen, and the European currency, respectively, sometime in the next century. The members of these blocs will be inclined to make their own monetary arrangements and organize them around a dominant national currency or a regional reserve unit like the Euro. Imagine, for example, that Canada, the United States, and Mexico form a monetary union or a pegged rate system in which the members agree to extend unlimited intervention on behalf of one another's currencies. The dollar or an asset analogous to the Euro, not the SDR, would serve as this bloc's common unit of account. Intervention, in the event that the separate national currencies are maintained, would take place through purchases and sales of U.S. dollars for their Canadian and Mexican counterparts, leaving little obvious role for the SDR.

Because the three blocs will be larger and collectively less open to the rest of the world than today's nation states, they will be more inclined to float their common currencies against one another. Wyplosz predicts that the three blocs will tend to follow policies of benign neglect with regard to inter-bloc exchange rate fluctuations. Hence, there will be less need for international reserves than today if this three- bloc world comes about.

Cooper (1990) and Bergsten (1993), peering far into the future, suggest that there is an efficiency argument for the development of a single world currency to complement an increasingly integrated global trading system. In a world of a single currency, there is no need for international reserves to smooth balance of payments disturbances, any more than there is a need for Federal Reserve districts to hold international reserves to deal with disturbances to regional balances of payments. Some, following Gurley and Shaw, would argue that successful management of any financial system requires an "outside asset," and that in a world of a single international currency the SDR could play this part. The IMF would assume the role of world central bank and vary the volume of SDRs it supplied to commercial banks and other financial intermediaries that used the instrument as backing for their own liabilities, thereby controlling the money supply. The alternative, anti-Gurley and Shaw view, is that the entity vested with responsibility for controlling the volume of currency could simply hold, and operate through markets in, the debt instruments of national governments and other issuers.

Could greater reliance on SDRs in the intermediate run encourage the emergence of such a currency, along the lines of the competing-currency arguments of some architects of EMU?

If governments and the Fund concentrated a greater share of their transactions in the form of SDRs, this argument goes, private agents might find it convenient to do the same, and the world might gravitate, without direction by national governments, toward a situation where a single world currency effectively prevailed.

We are skeptical of the relevance of this argument. Very large quantities of SDR transactions would have to be undertaken before the network externalities they threw off dominated those associated with the dollar. The Yen and the mark, and even the French franc, Swiss franc and British pound, remain far ahead of the SDR in terms of natural constituency, as we showed in Section III. And if denominating assets in a composite basket is attractive to private agents, they themselves can do so by undertaking low-cost foreign exchange market transactions. It is not clear to us that additional SDR allocations will add significantly to the momentum for the development of a single world currency.

In attempting to forecast the role of the SDR in the future of the international monetary system, we began by putting to rest many misunderstandings about the supply and demand for reserves. The rise of international capital mobility and exchange rate flexibility does not remove the need for international reserves. To the extent that capital mobility allows countries to borrow reserves and exchangerate flexibility provides an instrument of adjustment that can supplement reserve financing of balance-of-payments deficits, there could be some modest decline in the demand for reserves as capital controls are removed and additional countries gravitate toward exchange rate flexibility. But in so far as international capital markets are themselves the source of shocks, greater exposure to these markets implies a greater demand for reserves.

In any case, contrary to the view that not all countries can obtain international reserves simultaneously, an argument that arose in the control-ridden 1950s and 1960s, international capital mobility goes a long way toward removing this Triffin Dilemma. All central banks and governments can simultaneously obtain additional reserves on private markets.

To the extent that any single country or group of countries begins to incur foreign monetary liabilities that grow alarmingly large relative to the size of its economy, new sources of reserve supply can spring up, in a world of convertible currencies.

Thus, neither the total supply nor the total demand for reserves is likely to change dramatically as the world moves further in the direction of international capital mobility and exchange rate flexibility. There is no compelling argument for an SDR allocation to avert a pending global liquidity shortage or to remove an intrinsic instability in the reserve- supply process, as was the case in the control-ridden world of the 1960s. There is a consistent argument for an SDR allocation to provide the resources needed to manage national financial crises with international implications crises of a sort that may grow more prevalent with the globalization of markets -- but there are more direct and desirable means of underwriting the relevant facility. European monetary unification, if and when it occurs, will have major implications for the demand and supply of reserves, but several of these work in offsetting directions; there is little reason to think that they will create a significant excess demand for international reserves or destabilize the reserve-supply process. In a future world with a single world currency or three relatively self- contained currency blocs floating against one another, the demand for international reserves would decline or disappear. While there would be a role for the SDR or an instrument like it if the IMF is the world central bank that issues the single world currency, any such scenario is so remote as to have no significant implications for short- or medium-term policy planning.

Our conclusion, for better or for worse, is that the future of the international monetary system is unlikely to entail a significantly expanded role for the SDR.

What is the Future of the SDR as an International Reserve Asset? The Financial System.

The Special Drawing Right (SDR) is an unconditional claim to the hard-currency reserves of other International Monetary Fund (IMF) members and certain other prescribed holders. After the large IMF allocations of August-September 2009, SDRs still account for only 2 percent of lower-income country reserves and less than 4 percent of global reserves.

At present the SDR mechanism functions largely as a reserve-pooling arrangement, useful in reallocating global liquidity from countries with ample liquidity to those with higher needs. But the mechanism does not create new liquidity, in the form of higher supplies of high-powered reserve currencies, as might be needed during a global crisis. The SDR's value is linked to that of a basket of the four principal reserve currencies, so as to stabilize the value of IMF members' claims on the reserve pool. But the SDR is not itself a currency that can be bought and sold in private markets.

In light of the small scale and conditionality of the international liquidity safety net, including IMF resources, many lower-income countries have chosen self-insurance through accumulation of substantial international reserves, mostly U.S. dollars and euros. The resulting insurance system has numerous drawbacks, however, some at the country level, some systemic. At the country level, reserve holders may earn low returns on their balances of the "privileged" reserve currencies. At the system level, official shifts between reserve currencies could destabilize exchange markets. And there are other potential problems.

If countries held more SDRs and fewer reserve currencies, these problems might be mitigated. The main proposal for large scale replacement of currency reserves with SDRs is through a substitution account, under which countries deposit currency reserves with the IMF in return for SDRs. This scheme, however, merely transfers any financial burden to the IMF, which itself could earn low returns on its currency balances and would bear the risk of exchange rate changes. How can IMF members share the cost? Plans for a substitution account foundered on this rock in 19791980; the scale of the problem is even greater now. As has been true in the euro zone, absence of a centralized fiscal power hobbles the provision of public goods that might enhance systemic financial stability. (Of course, individual counties are free now to choose reserve portfolios that reproduce the SDR basket, though most hold a higher weight of U.S. dollars.)

If SDRs can be created only through the allocation process and not through substitution, then under current arrangements, the extent to which they can replace currency reserves is self-limiting. Roughly speaking, because SDRs are merely claims on hard-currency reserves and cannot be used in private markets, their emission has no further value once the value of outstanding SDR claims is sufficient to purchase the outstanding stock of gross currency reserves.

The situation would be different if SDR claims could be presented directly to central banks in return for their own currencies, as some have suggested, because this change would make the outside supply of reserve currencies elastic in a crisis. Such a system would reproduce the stabilizing properties of the network of central bank swap facilities set up during the recent global financial crisis, but it would be predictable rather than ad hoc and all countries, not just a select few, would have access.

An equivalent mechanism could be set up without reference to the SDR at all, simply by instituting lines of credit from central banks and administered by the IMF. The IMF could extend the facilities directly to national central banks meeting specified standards of supervisory diligence and independence from political interference. Such credit lines would complement expanded flexible IMF loan facilities for sovereigns. Likewise, even the current SDR-based reservepooling arrangements could be accomplished, perhaps in a more flexible and need-based way, by explicit reserve pooling. An advantage of this approach is that countries would not need to offset the currency risk taken on through SDR transactions with opposite, possibly costly, forwardmarket transactions. The costs of these could become significant were SDRs to become more important as a reserve category.

Denominating more global reserves in SDR would affect exchange rate volatility among the main reserve currencies primarily to the extent that it reduced potential official demand shifts among those currencies. Were more countries to peg to the SDR as a result, however, their effective nominal (and probably real) exchange rate volatility would fall. Adding China's yuan to the SDR basket, given its current policy of heavy management against the U.S. dollar, would effectively increase the dollar's weight in the SDR basket. Since the yuan is not an international reserve currency, the rationale for tying the SDR's value to the yuan at the present time is unclear.

An enhanced international liquidity safety net, whether based on the SDR or on some system of credit lines centered on the IMF, would enhance the IMF's power and thus calls for complementary reforms in governance structure. These should be aimed at increasing the voice of emerging and developing countries, in line with their growing weight in the world economy. An enhanced safety net also could worsen moral hazard on the part of market participants or governments, so the IMF's macroeconomic and financial surveillance powers would likewise have to be upgraded. That change would greatly add to the need for reformed governance.

This paper reviews the history and performance of the Special Drawing Right (SDR) and examines the prospects for expanding its role in the international monetary system. Key questions include: Can the SDR enhance international liquidity, especially that of emerging market economies (EMEs), under the current IMF rules for its management? Is the current SDR mechanism an efficient and effective way of doing so? What changes in the institutional structure for SDR allocation and use could benefit EMEs and the world economy? Are there collateral benefits, aside from liquidity enhancement, to expanding the SDR's role? Are there more effective ways toward these goals? A key point to keep in mind is that the SDR asset is not now, and is highly unlikely ever to become, a currency. Thus, its potential role in supplanting true national currencies as a source of international liquidity is inherently derivative.

Efficient means of allocating and creating global liquidity need not involve the SDR at all.

1. The roles of international reserves and problems of selfinsurance through large reserve holdings. International reserve holdings provide a country with unconditional liquidity in case of need. A need can arise due to a sudden stop in private capital inflows, problems of sovereign borrowing or refinance, depreciation pressure on the exchange rate, or banking system illiquidity. This last set of issues loomed large in the 2007-09 global financial crisis, as banks, notably European banks, found themselves unable to roll over big volumes of short-term liabilities denominated in foreign currencies.

After the financial crises of the late 1990s (in East Asia and elsewhere), many poorer countries embarked on programs of self-insurance through unprecedented accumulation of international reserves. At the end of 2010, the aggregate foreign exchange reserves of emerging and developing countries stood at over USD 4 trillion. Rich countries have held much lower reserve levels, relying in the past on dependable credit market access. In the recent crisis, however, many rich countries relied on ad hoc central bank swap lines to channel foreign-currency liquidity to credit- constrained domestic banks. Thus, the Federal Reserve, for example, became the last-resort lender of dollars to the world, including several emerging economies. The need for such international support of advanced countries, on so large a scale, was unprecedented. Now that the fiscal solvency even of some richer countries has been questioned, the need for international liquidity in several key currencies has been recognized as universal, cutting across income levels.

The global scope of the recent crisis was unusual in light of past history, but the rapid progress of financial globalization suggests that global rises could well recur in the future.

As a response to the resulting liquidity needs, gross reserve accumulation has many drawbacks. At the individual- country level it is expensive. In a sterilized purchase of euros or dollars, the Reserve Bank of India would pay interest of 5.75 percent (the RBI's reverse repo rate) on domestic borrowing but earn far less on the foreign exchange it acquired, implying a substantial quasi-fiscal cost (apart from possible changes in the rupee's exchange rate). But the systemic issues raised by large-scale self-insurance are even more worrisome. Reserve transactions can affect interest rates, and shifts in reserve portfolios between currencies could cause large and destabilizing exchange rate movements. Central-bank reserve withdrawals could impair liquidity elsewhere during a global crisis. There may be an "arms race" in reserves as countries seek to appear financially strong compared to their neighbors. And if reserves are accumulated through policy-induced current account surpluses, the resulting global imbalances could have adverse effects abroad.

In light of these drawbacks of self-insurance through reserves, the international community is seeking alternatives (in addition to the very helpful actions already taken to strengthen the IMF). The SDR was designed in the late 1960s precisely to augment international liquidity and ameliorate some of the disadvantages of a system based on U.S. dollar reserves. Thus, the SDR — long viewed as an arcane relic of an earlier international monetary system — has been advanced as a potential basis for global reform.

2. History of the SDR and its issuance. The SDR currently is a synthetic unit of value that may be transferred by a holder to other International Monetary Fund (IMF) members (or to prescribed holders such as the Bank for International Settlements) in return for needed national currencies. The SDR was launched on January 1, 1970 following passage of the First Amendment to the IMF Articles of Agreement the year before. The SDR provided an unconditional supplement to other financial resources that might be obtained through the IMF — unconditional because, unlike in standby arrangements, a country's use of its SDRs was not subject to IMF policy conditionality (only to the payment of interest to the IMF).

Until the recent big allocation of August and September 2009 following the onset of the global crisis, SDR allocations were infrequent, taking place only over 1970-72 and 1979-81. None of these allocations, not even the most recent one, has pushed the total stock of SDRs to be a large fraction of global foreign exchange reserves. Figure 1 illustrates the numbers, based on data in the IMF's International Financial Statistics. The stock of SDRs has never exceeded 6 percent of global reserves and that global figure declined steadily until 2009 following the 1979-81 allocation. On the eve of the crisis SDRs were less than 0.5 percent of global reserves, and an even smaller percentage of EME reserves, which themselves had expanded rapidly over the years since the late 1990s. In April 2009 the IMF allocated USD 250 billion worth of SDRs as a response to the global crisis, and a further USD 34 billion in a September 2009 special allocation to endow members that had never received allocations. Except for such extraordinary allocations, SDR allocations are proportional to IMF quotas, so as to achieve an internationally balanced increase in world reserves. Thus, the bulk goes to the advanced economies (which also hold much lower stocks of foreign exchange reserves). Even the nominally large 2009 allocations restored the SDR share in global and EME reserves only to the levels of the late 1980s (about 2 percent for EMEs). Replacement of existing reserves by SDRs, especially for the EMEs, would require a huge emission.

3. Original rationale for the SDR. Gold formed the fundamental basis of the Bretton Woods gold-exchange standard. In practice countries held gold or U.S. dollars as foreign exchange reserves (outside the sterling area), exchange rates against the dollar were fixed (but adjustable on occasion), and the dollar price of gold was supposed to be fixed at USD 35 per ounce. With world monetary gold supplies growing more slowly than the world economy, however, U.S. dollars made up a growing fraction of world reserves. The following dilemma motivated the creation of the "paper gold" SDR: Dollar reserves, along with gold, might grow too slowly to fulfill global demand. The gap could be filled by SDRs allocated by the IMF. On the other hand, if global dollar reserve holdings did grow rapidly enough, the Triffin problem — the U.S. inability to redeem all dollar reserves for gold at USD 35 per ounce — would worsen, creating the possibility that central banks would run the dollar-gold link. Transforming dollar claims on the U.S. into SDR claims on the IMF could lessen or eliminate that likelihood. Even though SDRs are not money, they could be used, like demonetized gold, to settle international claims between central banks. Furthermore, it was argued, SDR issuance by the IMF could reduce the world's dependence on U.S. balance of payments deficits to fulfill international liquidity needs.

4. Basket valuation of the SDR. Currently the SDR's value is defined to be that of a specific basket of U.S. dollars, euros, British pounds, and yen. The basket composition reflects basket members' importance in global trade and the shares of their currencies in other countries' global foreign exchange reserves. The basket's membership comprises the four largest countries on

those measures, and membership presupposes that the included currencies are "freely usable" — defined as "widely used to make payments for international transactions" and "widely traded in the principal exchange markets" [IMF Articles of Agreement XXX(f)]. For now, this criterion would seem to preclude China's membership in the SDR despite its large share in global trade.

Official SDR basket weights (and components) are subject to re-evaluation and readjustment by the IMF every five years. The current official weights came into effect on January 1, 2011. The new (old) weights are USD, 41.9 (44) percent; EUR, 37.4 (34) percent; JPY, 9.4 (11) percent; GBP, 11.3 (11) percent.1 These shares down weight the dollar compared to its share in global international reserves (over 60 percent, insofar as IMF and other data are available). According to Treasurer's Department, IMF (1995, p. 3), changes in basket weights must be accompanied by changes in the absolute amounts of currencies in the basket ensuring that the value of the new basket equals the value of the old one "on the last business day preceding the day the new basket becomes effective." Thus, there is no risk of capital gains or losses due to re- weighting, and the same principle applies as well to changes in the currencies that the basket includes.

Such changes have occurred on several occasions. Originally the SDR was not linked to a basket at all, as noted above, but instead was a gold substitute intended to reduce dependence on dollars. In 1970 the unit was equivalent to the gold content of 1 U.S. dollar at a gold price of USD 35 per ounce. The demise of the par value system in 1973 and the sharp run-up in the market price of gold called into question the practicality of defining the SDR as equivalent in value to a fixed amount of gold. On July 1, 1974, therefore, the SDR became a basket of 16 currencies, and in January 1981, five. The current composition dates from the euro's launch on January 1, 1999.

Conceptually, the basket denomination of the SDR is distinct from its operation, but this denomination does determine the currency resources that can be obtained by exchanging SDRs with other holders or the IMF. The primary rationale for the basket numeraire is that it stabilizes the weighted-average value of each country's SDR assets in terms of the reserve currencies that are most likely to be needed — based on those currencies' importance in world trade and finance. In principle, this stabilization could be accomplished in other ways, without reference to a basket, but the basket approach is convenient for administrative and political reasons. Unfortunately, it can give rise to the misconception that the SDR itself is a basket of currencies. It is not.

5. How SDRs are actually used: A reserve-pooling arrangement. The main utility of an SDR to its holder is that the SDR can be exchanged with another IMF member (or a prescribed holder) for a needed currency — euros for exchange intervention purchases, for example, or dollars for on-lending to a domestic bank unable to roll over shortterm dollar liabilities. The country offering SDRs reduces its SDR balance and increases its balance of the foreign currency it desires; the country that receives the SDR has the mirror-image balance sheet change, gaining SDRs but losing an equivalent amount of currency reserves.

Crucially, the SDR is not itself a true currency. SDRs are not traded in private markets and cannot be used to make private payments.[3] They are useful (aside from limited official purposes, such as official transactions with the IMF) only insofar as they can be transformed into true, usable currencies. Moreover, the IMF does not function as a central bank, nor has it the fiscal backing to do so. There is no world government obliged to re-capitalize the IMF should its assets fall below its liabilities. The SDR is simply a claim to another official entity's foreign reserves. Evolution of the SDR into a true global currency would require a global central bank with fiscal backup from governments and an incursion into national monetary autonomy. At this juncture, these developments seem politically out of the question. Even a country that pegs its exchange rate to the SDR basket, as some have done, cannot directly intervene in markets using SDRs.

Most exchanges of SDRs are voluntary. However, there exists also a "designation mechanism" through which the IMF may oblige members with sufficiently strong balance of payments and/or reserve positions to accept SDRs in exchange for currency reserves from another member. Designation has been deployed infrequently, but it has been used for example, during the developing country debt-crisis period of the 1980s.

The SDR mechanism can thus best be thought of as a reserve-pooling arrangement. By using its SDRs, a country needing hard-currency reserves can get them from another country that either has them in abundance or can easily procure them by borrowing. This mechanism is potentially very useful (and has proven so in the past) it enhances the effectiveness of a given level of global liquidity by getting reserves from those who value them less to those who value them more highly but it does not generally create additional global liquidity (as would also be true if the IMF were to borrow reserve currencies in private markets in order to augment its loanable resources).

An SDR allocation creates offsetting claims on and liabilities to the IMF. When a country exchanges SDRs for currencies, it pays the IMF interest on those SDRs, while the country that accepts them receives interest from the IMF. The nominal interest earned on an SDR is based on short-term riskless nominal interest paid by the basket components.

6. Role in the international system so far. The initial rationale for the SDR collapsed soon after its introduction: Dollar reserves exploded, the dollar-gold link was scrapped, and richer, creditworthy countries both flexed their exchange rates and took advantage of growing world capital markets, where

reserves could be borrowed. SDRs remained more useful for the less-developed countries, which did make use of them. But between 1981 and 2009, no further SDR allocation occurred, and even the 1997 IMF decision to equip newer IMF members with SDRs on the same terms as the others languished for many years due to U.S. inaction. The result was the decline shown in Figure 1 — a decline reversed only by the global crisis.

7. The substitution account proposal. The Second Amendment to the IMF's Articles in 1978 set the ambitious goal of making the SDR the "principal reserve asset in the international monetary system." This obviously has not happened, but proposals for a "substitution account" are designed to replace currency reserves with SDRs on a large scale. Such ideas were debated in 1979-80, ultimately to no avail, but they have resurfaced recently (for example, Kenen 2010) as critics of the dollar's privileged reserve-currency role have sought to dislodge it. Figure 1 shows that substitution would have to be on a huge scale to displace a substantial portion of currency reserves.

Under a substitution scheme, a country such as India might transfer some of its dollar reserves to the IMF, receiving SDRs of equal current value in return. (These SDRs would be created outside the usual allocation process.) Two portfolio shifts occur as a result.

India is now long SDRS, and might (or might not) want to readjust its portfolio in private markets. Presumably, its degree of participation in the scheme will already reflect its diversification goals. More importantly, the IMF is short SDRs and long on U.S. dollars, and the substitution account's solvency is at risk if the dollar depreciates.

Which countries will compensate the IMF for portfolio losses if the dollar declines against the SDR? How will the IMF finance discrepancies between the interest earned on its dollars and that paid on its new SDR liabilities? In the last discussions of

1979-80, some countries involved thought the U.S. should bear the bulk of the costs, but the U.S. was unwilling and others refused to step in. Poorer countries, including India, were reluctant to see the IMF use its gold holdings to support the account — they hoped gold sales might instead subsidize borrowing by poorer countries. So, the negotiations failed. It is unlikely that the U.S. would be more willing today, and even less so that the eurozone countries — which lack a centralized fiscal organ — would be willing to underwrite a euro/SDR substitution account. Once again, the absence of a fiscal authority at the global level creates a difficult coordination problem for a centralized and coordinated move to an SDR-based system. That problem remains today.

8. Advantages of substitution of SDRs for currency reserves. Notwithstanding the practical obstacles to a substitution account, a reserve system largely based on the SDR would have some advantages. Through allocating new SDRs (or canceling old ones), the IMF could influence aggregate world reserve growth and perhaps make it less erratic. In addition, central banks would have less incentive for possibly abrupt shifts between reserve currencies and the SDR would have a more stable value than its components.

Of course, any "exorbitant privilege" of lower interest on dollar reserves would be at the expense of the IMF, which would become the large-scale holder of dollars. This is perhaps why many feel the U.S. should provide any fiscal support needed to keep an IMF substitution account solvent — an idea the U.S. rejected in the past. Similarly, the insurance provided to reserve holders through the basket denomination of their reserves would likewise be an expense of the IMF, and the international community would have to devise some mechanism to share the expense of this global public good.

Even if the SDR displaced the dollar as the main reserve currency, the dollar's dominant vehicle currency position something like 85 percent of all foreign exchange transactions involve the dollar wouldn't necessarily decline.

9. Outside liquidity and the SDR. As noted above, if the SDR functions merely as an "admission ticket" to a pool of extant national reserve stocks, no additional (or outside) liquidity is routinely created when SDRs are used there is merely a reallocation of existing liquidity, which generally will improve the allocation of that liquidity, but will not change the aggregate amount of liquidity available to all countries.

This fact raises a Triffin-like paradox. Suppose the IMF were to allocate more SDRs over time, leading countries to economize on currency reserves. Eventually, there would be more SDR claims to reserves than gross reserves themselves. Absent a private SDR market, more SDRs would have no value at that point. In summary, the extent to which SDRs can replace currency reserves would be selflimiting if the SDR system is exclusively a reserve pooling arrangement, with SDRs created exclusively through allocation. This is not necessarily true when SDRs are issued through a substitution account, because those SDRs could be traded back for the reserve currencies that the IMF holds in the account. Even so, redemption of SDRs for currencies held by the IMF would not create new liquidity — as might be desirable in a global crisis.

The situation is very different if SDR claims can be sold directly to the central banks that issue reserve currencies in return for issuing new high-powered deposits. Under that scenario, there is no natural limit to the reserve currency stocks SDRs can purchase, and those stocks would represent outside liquidity for the international system. Truman (2010) suggests that the IMF could be authorized in emergencies to "exchange specially allocated SDR to the central banks issuing international currencies in the SDR basket in return for their own currencies." Such schemes would allow SDR exchanges to increase outside liquidity. Even if the issuing central banks sterilized their SDR acquisitions, as they normally would do absent a global crisis, the scheme would still improve the global allocation of liquidity. Truman's proposal is designed to allow the IMF to act as an international last-resort lender in multiple currencies, much as central banks did collectively through the network of swap lines initiated by the Federal Reserve in 2007. The swap network had big net benefits by preventing a more severe meltdown of the advanced economies' banking systems, as well as by mitigating exchange volatility (especially against the dollar) in the most intense phases of the global crisis.

10. Equivalent arrangements that do not involve the SDR. Explicit reserve pooling would allow the IMF to capture the main substantive benefits of SDRs — but to reproduce the unconditional nature of SDR liquidity, some tranche of access to the reserve pool would have to be unconditional as well. Ideally, access could be relaxed in crisis situations — with due attention to the moral hazard such expectations could generate among government actors and market participants. For example, China could lend some of its copious dollar reserves to the IMF for relending to countries that need liquidity. (This is also the idea of the regional Chiang Mai initiative.) This direct approach has an advantage. After exchanging dollars for SDRs. China might want to restore its original portfolio by shorting the SDR basket components. The need for such costly transactions could be avoided by adopting a currency pooling arrangement tout court, in which China's dollar reserves, if added to the IMF pool, simply become a dollar claim on the IMF. A further drawback of the SDR mechanism is that its capacity to redistribute liquidity among IMF members is limited by the size of SDR holdings — the "admission tickets" to the reserve-pooling club. An explicit reserve pool could be augmented by IMF market borrowing, and it would be useful to allocate access in a need-based way through a formula more flexible than the quota-based rule used for SDR allocations. Because assessments of "need" are discretionary, and

thus politically charged, it is important that voting rights in the IMF, as well as decision-making processes, are reassessed to enhance the perceived legitimacy of IMF decisions throughout the international community. Of course, proposals to enhance the international role of the SDR — thereby conferring more power on the IMF — likewise make reforms in IMF governance more pressing.

As noted above, reserve pooling does not create outside liquidity, which is particularly important during systemic crises. Furthermore, in financial crises, foreign- currency liquidity may need to be deployed rapidly and directly to financial institutions, not governments. Central bank swap lines in multiple key currencies could be run through the IMF.8 These would mimic the very useful network of central bank swap lines set up during the crisis. Indeed, the IMF might lend directly to central banks that have met specified standards of independence from political interference and supervisory diligence. SDRs might usefully supplement such a system, but they would play no essential role. The system would be symmetric in form and avoid many of the problems implied by large gross reserve positions — for example, there would be no scope for official portfolio shifts between different reserve currencies. But, like the reserve-pooling scheme above, a system of swap lines would require complementary initiatives in IMF governance and in control of moral hazard. Credit lines would have an advantage over reserve pooling in greater elasticity, as well as the creation of outside liquidity. By managing the size of credit lines, the IMF could control the growth of world liquidity.

11. Would an SDR regime reduce exchange-rate volatility? Were the SDR to become more important as a reserve asset, individual countries might be inclined to peg to it, thereby reducing the volatility of their multilateral effective exchange rates. The choice to peg to the SDR is, however, logically independent from the choice of a portfolio of reserve assets;

countries can peg to the SDR now, although this has not been widespread.

A systemic trend of pegging to the SDR by lower-income countries would cause a greater reduction in effective exchange rate volatility for those countries, all the more so as trade continues to expand among them. Only to the extent that exchange rate shifts outside the high-income affect rich countries, however, might there be an impact on the bilateral exchange rates of the four major currencies presently in the SDR basket.

Adoption of an SDR reserve system, even without any increase in pegging to the SDR, might reduce volatility among the SDR basket currencies by reducing fears of shifts among reserve currencies by official holders. Again, however, other equivalent arrangements that do not rest on the SDR could accomplish the same goal.

Some have suggested that in view of China's growing global role, its yuan should become a component of the SDR. Because the yuan is not fully convertible, however, its path into the SDR is murky. Furthermore, and related to the last point, the yuan is not (yet) an international reserve currency, so the rationale for indexing the SDR basket partially to the yuan is unclear. Were the yuan to enter the SDR, though, and if China were still controlling the yuan's nominal dollar exchange rate, one effect would be to reduce the SDRs variability against the U.S. dollar, as well as the variability against the dollar of any currency pegged to the SDR. With widespread pegging to the SDR among poorer countries, the yuan's effective exchange rate would become more rigid. India's sizes in world exports and (even more so) reserves are too small for it to aspire to SDR membership any time soon.

Hypothetically speaking, however, what consequences would follow? Were India to join, a tendency for other countries to peg to the SDR would then reduce the effective flexibility of the rupee. In that case, bigger changes in rupee nominal exchange rates against the other SDR basket currencies would be needed to bring about a given change in the rupee's multilateral effective exchange rate. The consequent reduction in medium-term exchange volatility might, however, be viewed as an advantage.

12. International adjustment. The preceding system would enhance global liquidity but would not mitigate the asymmetric current-account adjustment pressures as between surplus and deficit countries.

Could a system base on the SDR further that goal?

As noted earlier, Truman (2010) proposes allowing countries to trade SDRs to central banks for their currencies. In such a system, countries might do the reverse transaction as well: trading currencies back to the issuing central banks for SDRs. If so, the system would contain a symmetric Hume-type adjustment mechanism. A country with a balance of payments deficit might see its central bank buying back money with SDRs, thereby reducing its monetary base. The surplus country buying the SDRs would have increased its base at the time it bought the foreign currency. At present, in contrast, a central bank that issues a reserve currency is not obliged to redeem that currency.

Two obstacles to symmetric adjustment arise. First, the reserve-currency issuer could sterilize the SDR loss, a feasible strategy because it is not pegging its exchange rate. Second, unlike under a gold standard, the reserve-issuing central bank could simply stop buying back its currency with SDRs once it runs out of them. This suspension of convertibility has no consequence. It is hard to envision a politically viable mechanism for forcing a central bank to change course simply because it is running out of SDRs.

Another strategy, similar to schemes that have been unsuccessfully proposed in the past, would be to restrict countries from holding reserves other than SDRs and then to tax excessively positive SDR balances. Such a regime also seems politically unfeasible.

It is worth noting that if SDRs are gained via substitution rather than allocation, the incentives some countries might have to run current account surpluses for reserve growth remain in place. Allocation of SDRs by the IMF, or creation of swap lines such as those discussed above, would be more effective in discouraging precautionary current account surpluses, and thus in discouraging global imbalances.

Conclusion. As currently conceived, SDRs constitute a system for giving countries limited unconditional access to other countries' currency reserves. The SDR itself is not a currency; it is not used in private markets. The basket valuation of the SDR is motivated by denominational convenience, and can be argued to be quite incidental (and inessential) to the main purposes of the SDR. Large-scale substitution of currency reserves for SDRs would have advantages — for example, there would be no danger of official portfolio shifts between reserve currencies — but those advantages would come at a fiscal cost, and disagreement about the sharing of that cost among countries has defeated the substitution account idea in the past. The SDR would be more effective if, as some have suggested, it could be traded directly for reserve currencies with the issuing central banks, thereby resulting in the rapid creation of outside liquidity. Such a system could be affected, without being based on SDRs, simply though a system of central bank swap lines centered on the IMF. Were such a system instituted, however, the IMF's surveillance capabilities would need to be extended and its governance structure reformed.

The Evolution Of Special Drawing Rights (SDRs)

SDRs is a special reserve asset allocated to IMF member countries participating in the SDR Department proportionate to their IMF quotas. The SDR is not a claim on the IMF but is 'potentially a claim on the freely usable currencies of IMF members, in those holders of SDRs can exchange their SDRs for these currencies' (IMF 2002). Its value as a reserve asset comes from the commitments of members to hold and accept it. The IMF members have indeed undertaken to honor all obligations related to the SDR system. The Fund ensures that the SDR's claim on freely usable currencies is honored by first 'designating IMF members with a strong external position to purchase SDRs from members with weak external positions, and through the arrangement of voluntary exchanges between participating members in a managed market' (IMF 2002). The least developed countries (LDCs) may use the SDRs (i) to repay the IMF; (ii) to repay Paris Club debt; (iii) to help countries in foreign exchange crisis get hard currency from IMF by exchanging at the Fund their SDRs for US dollars with the IMF matching them up with a source of dollars, and (iv) to release hard currency reserves for use in such transactions as importing and servicing foreign private debt.

Indeed, in its basic form, the SDR is a promissory note issued by the IMF to member states on the basis of a quota that is related to their relative strength in the world economy. Members that receive these notes may either hold them or exchange a part of them over time for hard currency, through the Fund itself and their central banks. In a regular sense SDRs may be perceived as liquid assets that are created by the IMF in the same manner that national monetary authorities issue their currencies as liabilities against themselves and can affect the supply of money. In this limited context, the Fund may behave like a central bank so long as it commands sufficient credibility. On the other hand, however, because of the peculiar treatment that SDRs are given, such as the fact that they are allocated by quota and only central banks can hold them while no other asset has to be exchanged for them, they cannot be treated as money. If countries received their allocations of SDR and held them, there is no interest cost to them. But they actually receive interest income from the Fund for their SDR holdings. They only pay interest at the same rate on their total cumulative allocations. When countries seek to exchange SDRs for hard currencies, the new holders then earn the accompanying interest from the Fund. In effect, it is only when a country's holdings of SDR are less than its cumulative allocation that it becomes a net payer of interest. So, obviously when poor countries give them up in exchange for hard currency, they have to pay the interest on these. It is this interest cost that serves as the tool for regulating international stabilization; and so long as the interest rates are effective, international stabilization should not be affected in any dramatic manner.

1 The SDR interest rate provides the basis for calculating the interest charges on regular (that is to say, nonconcessional) IMF financing and the interest paid to members that are creditors to the IMF. The SDR interest rate is determined weekly and is based on a weighted average of representative interest rates on short-term debt in the money markets of the SDR basket countries. The yields on three- month treasury bills serve as the representative interest rates for the United States and the United Kingdom. In keeping with the changes introduced to the SDR basket on January 1, 2001, the three- month Euribor (Euro Interbank Offered Rate) became the representative rate for the euro area, replacing the national financial instruments of France and Germany. The representative interest rate for the Japanese yen was changed from the three-month rate on certificates of deposit to the yield on Japanese government thirteen-week financing bills.

In addition to the general allocations of SDRs for the purpose of supplementing existing official reserve assets of member countries, there is currently a proposal to create a special one-time allocation of SDRs that would enable all members of the IMF to receive such SDR on an equitable basis, making amends for the fact that a fifth of the membership have never received any SDR allocation. The proposal followed the fourth amendment of the Articles of Agreement by the IMF board of governors in 1997, and will be effective only when the US gives its backing to what 73.34 per cent of the total voting power already supports.

Even though the original intention behind the creation of SDRs was the provision of international liquidity, Clark and Polak (2002) argue that that rationale is no longer relevant. They maintain that if international liquidity were simply an aggregation of all the economies of the world, then there was adequate liquidity and this had been growing as fast as the world's economies, if not faster. Hence the concept of international liquidity was no longer relevant for creating SDRs. They also point out that the conditions in the global economy that necessitated the creation of SDRs changed shortly after these reserves were created. This included the adoption of flexible exchange rate regimes which may have reduced the size of the reserves needed, compared to what was required to maintain a fixed exchange rate regime. But they argue that, this situation notwithstanding, there were still good enough reasons to create SDRs in view of efficiency gains resulting from the low-cost access to reserves and the reduction in systemic risk.

Trends in SDR allocation and the global reserve system

There have so far been only two rounds of creation of SDRs, each spread over three years. The first allocation was in 1970, for a total amount of SDR 9.3 billion, which was distributed in three equal annual instalments. The most recent allocation, made on 1 January 1981, brought the cumulative total of SDR allocations to SDR 21.4 billion. The IMF executive board discussed the possibility of an SDR allocation during the fourth, fifth, sixth, and seventh basic periods, that is up to 31 December 2001, but there has not been enough support for an allocation.

A major reason for no SDR being allocated since 1981 is that industrial countries no longer see clear benefits from receiving such allocations, particularly in the presence of thriving capital markets with full capital mobility. Also, as the SDR interest rate, has increased in relation to the average short-term interest rate in the five largest industrial countries, this has made SDRs even less attractive to industrial economies. They currently borrow on the international capital market under similar terms as prevailing with the SDR allocations. For low-income developing countries that have considerably far less stable international earnings, SDR allocations according to their quotas provide rather little opportunity for their stabilization and growth needs.2 But any allocation that is not in accordance with IMF quotas would require amendment of the Articles of Agreement. It is this need to amend the Articles of Agreement that has left the 1997 agreement to make a special one-time allocation of SDRs, which would equalize the ratio of cumulative allocations to current quotas for all member countries not ratified, six years on.

Hence the refusal of developing countries to support a regular allocation in 1972.

The situation has extensively reduced the role of SDRs as a reserve asset. By April 2002, SDRs accounted for less than 1.25 per cent of IMF members' non-gold reserves, even though the holding of reserves was growing worldwide. Indeed, the developing countries added little to reserves between 1980 and 1995, but then added SDR 37 billion in five years. When the Zedillo Panel called for the resumption of the issue of SDR, the panel members argued that, 'the cessation of allocations has severely prejudiced the interests of developing countries. They suggested that developing countries were not in a position to borrow additional reserves in the market on terms similar to SDR. But many of them were trying to build up their reserves in order to reduce their vulnerability to crises. They were estimated to hold reserves of over US$850 billion, which was almost

US$300 billion more than they did before the Asian crisis broke. That additional reserves had has been borrowed largely on terms that were more difficult than SDR issues. At the time, emerging markets paid an average premium of about 8 per cent more than the US Treasury bond rates.

The panel noted that 'the result is a large flow of what is sometimes called "reverse aid", which in the aggregate is not far short of the flow of conventional aid from the DAC countries'.

Stiglitz (2003) estimates that there are currently US$2.4 trillion held in reserves around the world, held in a variety of forms including US Treasury Bills for most developing countries:

While the United States may benefit from the resulting increased demand for US Treasury Bills, the cost to the developing countries is high. Today they receive a return of 1.25 per cent a negative real return rate even though investments yield high returns in their own countries. This is the price developing states have to pay to insure against unpredictable market events.

There are a limited number of private financial instruments that are denominated in SDRs. Because of the limited use of SDRs 'the SDRs' main function is to serve as the unit of account of the IMF and some other international organizations' (IMF 2002). It is thus used almost exclusively in transactions between the IMF and its members.

The IMF, developing countries and SDR creation

The creation of SDR has always been seen in developing countries as an inadequate but necessary tool for countering the usual problem of low reserves. It has been perceived as inadequate in relation to the financing needs arising from increasing volatility in exchange rate instability and foreign exchange earnings. While inadequate, its creation has sometimes been seen as an attempt by developed or industrial economies to cover their reluctance to deal with the real financing issues confronting developing countries through an IMF that has been seen for long as a rich men's club. Aboyade (1983) notes strongly that, The Fund has always related its (foreign) currency sales and stand-by facilities for member countries to their respective quotas. This means the richer countries, which have (and have always had) the highest quotas, can also borrow the most.

... It is generally unsympathetic to exchange rate policies, which offer any strong prospect of affecting the existing pattern and structure of international economic power, with the excuse that they may hurt international trade. Most of its innovations over the last decade (for example, the creation of SDRs and the establishment of a Substitution Account) are more to help the currencies of the rich nations and preserve international stability, than as direct answers to the clamor of the poor countries Aboyade (1983: 30).

Wade (2002) comments on similar sentiments expressed by Triffin (1968) who had suggested that since the allocation went strictly proportionally to the countries' quotas, it was 'as indefensible economically as it (was) morally'. At the time, the two biggest economies received one-third of the total. In Triffin's (1968) view, 'the SDR designers had created an asset that made the rich even better off.

The role that the Fund's board plays is crucial in understanding some of the sentiments often expressed about the issue of SDRs. The board of governors of the IMF (in which all member governments are represented) has to approve each issue of SDR by an 85 per cent majority.3 The voting system is weighted so that a small number of industrial countries can veto any new creation. This allows the US alone to do the same.

A decision to make a general allocation has to be based on the finding that there is a long-term global need to supplement existing reserve assets. The decision of the Board of Governors is on the basis of a proposal by the Managing Director with the concurrence of the Executive Board, with an 85 percent majority of the total voting power. Decisions on general allocations are made in the context of five- year basic periods lack of interest of the industrial economies, for reasons already provided, that has ensured that there was no new approval between 1978 and 1997. Opposition from Germany, Japan, the UK and the US effectively made new allocations impossible in the period. The status quo is that any changes in the quota arrangements would require an amendment to the IMF's Articles of Agreement.

It is interesting that in 1997 when an attempt was made to make new allocations in order to make the cumulative proportions of SDRs received up to that time equal to the various member-countries' current quotas, this received a negative response only outside of the Fund itself. Indeed, the necessary changes to bring about the Fourth Amendment to the Articles of Agreement, which would allow an allocation other than in proportion to current quotas, had been made, but the amendment failed year after year to reach the required level of ratification by 110 members with 85 per cent of voting power. By the end of April 2001, only 107 members had ratified it. The main obstacle has been that the US Congress remains opposed to it, despite the support of the administration.

The US Congress and other industrial country governments believe that there are a number of good reasons why they should worry about changes in the power structure that pertains at the IMF, particularly if that change means an increasing use of SDR for reserve holdings in many countries. Increasing the stock of SDR would mean a likely reduction in the holding for reserves of US bonds among the smaller nations.

Certainly, expansion of the SDR stock touches America closely because of the prominence of US dollar holdings among existing reserves. Cutting the world's dependence on dollar reserves would reduce Americans' access to a deepening well of cheap credit (Clunies-Ross 2002: 30).

But economists at the Fund have made some of the strongest arguments for the resumption of regular SDRs. Clark and Polak (2002) provide an interesting argument for allocating new SDR. After indicating that the original justifications for creating SDRs were no longer relevant as the concept of international liquidity lost its meaning in the post-Bretton Woods era, they argue strongly that the individual developing countries' need for reserves was still significant, and this was important for improving the operation of the international monetary system. Considering that most countries still needed to increase their reserve holdings in view of expanding current and capital account fluctuations, if countries were to attempt doing this by generating a balance-of-payments surplus this would be costly in terms of foregone consumption and investment. On the other hand, attempting to borrow such reserves on the international capital markets is very costly for poor countries, while some countries have no access to such markets. They also indicate that while borrowed reserves may substitute, to some extent, for owned reserves, 'volatile capital flows demonstrate that undue reliance on international capital markets for (the) purpose (of holding reserves) can be risky' (Clark and Polak 2002: 11). Their main argument is that, (following an earlier point of Mussa 1996), SDRs offer a costless reserve asset, which if properly managed as required by the Articles of Agreement, lead to enormous efficiency gains for the world economy compared to the cost of foregoing consumption and investment, and the cost of borrowing from the capital markets. The risk involved in increasing SDR allocations to developing countries can also be shown to not worsen. They observe that:

A number of considerations suggest that the provision of reserves in the form of SDRs would in fact reduce credit risk. Allocations of SDRs make more external resources available to a country, enabling it to weather potential balance of payments crises without undue reliance on import compression or the imposition of trade and other restrictions' (Clark and Polak 2002: 19).

Clark and Polak (2002) additionally argue that SDR allocations would contribute to reducing systemic risk and this is because they are a permanent addition to the world's stock of reserves since the Fund is unlikely to cancel any stock of SDR holdings. They contrast this with reserves acquired from borrowing on the capital market, which may be 'withdrawn under inauspicious circumstances. The example from the crises of the 1990s that made it difficult for countries to refinance their debt is given to support this point.

In the Zedillo report, the panel members argue that resuming allocations now will be a good time, 'in that the original concern was not just with the cost to a typical country of having to earn or borrow a secular increase in its reserve holding, but also with the impact on the financial fragility of the country issuing reserves'.

They argue that the financial fragility of the countries that issued the reserves was not much of a concern before, but it is now. This they attributed to the unprecedented size of the US current account deficit. This is partly a consequence of the desire all over to build up dollar reserves, and these have become too large for comfort and a source of discomfort in the financial markets. 'Substantial SDR allocations might help to shrink the US deficit while allowing other countries to continue to build up the reserves they feel they need to guard against financial crises' (UNDP 2001).

Proposals for an SDR geared toward development

As already mentioned, there is a long history of proposals to resume allocations of SDRs for specific purposes, often development, or to redistribute holdings of SDRs. Indeed it would appear that the campaign for SDR to support development is being pushed along two complementary lines. The first is for the resumption of the regular SDR to deal with what has become the frequent shortage of liquidity in developing countries (Stiglitz 2003), while the second looks at the occasional injection that mainly targets the developing countries (Soros 2002). The second is intended to be an allocation beyond the scope of the regular SDR. It might have elements of a regular SDR (allocation by quota) with a modification coming by way of donations to other users. Further extensions of this might take the form of alterations to the agreed quota as was indeed negotiated in 1997. It might therefore favor some countries and institutions, namely those that may be assessed to be in need of development assistance well beyond what traditional assistance packages may afford.

The IMF, as an institution, however, has tended over the years to view proposals to finance specific development initiatives with SDRs more cautiously, suggesting that the use of SDR for such purposes would generally require a change in the Articles of Agreement, except if industrialized countries voluntarily transferred their SDRs to other countries. The Fund has always observed that there was nothing preventing countries from engaging in such voluntary transfers. On the proposals to supplement fund resources, the Fund has responded that:

To the extent that these proposals involve balance-of-payments financing with conditionality, they can be viewed as essentially substituting for an increase in IMF quotas or IMF borrowing. The key difference among them is the degree of IMF involvement in intermediating redistributed SDRs and the implications of this for conditionality and the assumption of credit risk (IMF 2002).

The IMF places SDR proposals into two broad categories as follows:

- Proposals to supplement Fund resources. These proposals seek to direct SDRs allocated to industrial

countries to countries with more severe international liquidity needs.
- Proposals to finance development. These are generally of two types, those that may involve voluntary donations to a prescribed holder or another country and not requiring a change in the Articles of Agreement; and those that call for a redistribution of quotas.

These proposals may be further classified as those requiring mild reforms in the international financial system or no change to the status quo and those requiring more radical or substantial reforms that would imply changes to the governance arrangements of the IMF. While the proposals from the Zedillo Panel seemed to call for both broad categories of change in the way SDRs were allocated, it may be noted that most of the calls over the years have been related to the first category of change. A slight departure from the category of mild reforms is the Soros proposal, the best known of them. A central part of the proposal from his book George Soros on Globalization (2002), is that there should be periodic creations of SDRs and that the rich countries should agree to make their allocations available for global public goods and aid to development in individual countries. He would like to see the process started with the activation of the proposed allocation of 1997. The Soros proposal was intended to achieve additional aid resources in a manner that was more or less automatic. The pooling of funds was also expected to engender proper coordination. In this proposal, SDR donations from the industrial economies would first be paid into an escrow account, and there would be no budgetary cost to them until the SDRs were withdrawn from the account in order to pay for the approved development projects.

Stiglitz (2003) has suggested clearly there is a need for more than just one-time issuance of SDR. He calls for a complete overhaul of the global reserve system which he blames for being at the center of the failures of the global financial system. His argument is also based on the fact that developing countries' reserves are growing much faster than they can afford to, as they set aside huge reserves against a variety of contingencies, including decreases in foreign investor confidence and declines in export demand. With imports growing at 10 per cent per annum, about US$160 billion has to be set aside each year for reserves, and a part of this could easily have been made available for health and education. In advocating more frequent issues of SDR to finance development, Stiglitz (2003: 54-9) writes that:

Keynes, during the founding of the IMF, envisaged the issuance of 'global greenbacks', more familiarly known as special drawing rights (SDR) Global greenbacks could be used to finance global public goods, such as improving the environment, preventing the spread of diseases like AIDS, increasing literacy in the developing world, and providing humanitarian and broader development assistance.

Some countries may receive more than they put into reserves, which they can exchange for conventional currencies, while countries receiving less than they put into reserves may supplement these reserves, freeing up money that would otherwise have been set aside.

Richard Cooper (2002) has proposed an amendment of the Articles of Agreement to allow the IMF to create SDRs on a large enough and temporary basis to counter financial crises and to forestall creditor panic. Interestingly, while the Monterrey Conference on Financing Development discussed the various proposals for using SDRs among other schemes, it did not provide support for any particular scheme.

Analysis of proposals for development SDR

The discussion here focuses on the perceived role of SDR within the context of the cases for and against the issuance of such development focused SDR. Noting the general concern about what development SDRs might do to international stabilization, Clunies-Ross (2002) poses the question of whether the use of specific-purpose SDRs for allocating resources to global public goods is consistent with their use for stabilization purposes as originally intended, and if so, what should be the nature of the institutional changes required to bring that about. His response to these questions is that, with minor modifications, it is possible to issue development SDRs for supplementing aid and providing global public goods in a manner that does not compromise international stabilization.

The idea that development SDRs will not harm global stabilization is even more strongly put across by both Clark and Polak (2002) and also by Stiglitz (2003). The latter has written that:

This scheme would not be inflationary: rather it would offset the inherent downward bias of the current regime. Relative to global income—some US$40 trillion—the magnitudes of monetary emissions would be minuscule (Stiglitz 2003: 5).

There appear to be quite strong arguments for the issuance of SDRs, both the regular and the specific. But the arguments against cannot be dismissed.

CHAPTER 4

THE ARGUMENT FOR DEVELOPMENT OF SDR

Stiglitz sums up his discussion of the need for development SDR as follows:

In effect, these reserves are a commitment of the world to help each other in times of difficulty…….This policy would end the logic of instability that is built into the current system, for it would allow some deficits without inevitable crisis' (2003: 5).

As noted earlier, the idea behind the calls for these new issues of SDR is basically to provide developing countries an opportunity to devote resources that would otherwise have been devoted to enlarging reserves to providing services that facilitate development. The new SDRs are expected to create opportunities for development indirectly since they do not directly add to the expendable resources of the recipient country.

But the calls for development SDRs go beyond the need for less expensive reserves, as we saw with Stiglitz (2003). The growing calls for the creation of development SDRs are also closely associated with the need for a faster development of global public goods a la Soros (2002) and Stiglitz (2003). The argument is that effective delivery of global public goods enhances the achievement of the development goals of poor nations. Some of the more comprehensive argumentation for the creation of development SDRs has been put together by Clunies-Ross (2002). In his preamble to the arguments for considering various ways for mobilizing resources for social and economic development, including development SDRs, he indicates that the methods and resources must be (i) technically and administratively accessible; (ii) unlikely to impose any unduly high excess burden of costs through misallocation; (iii) equitably distributed; (iv) not politically out of the question for ever, and (v) so far not fully exploited. Clunies-Ross (2002) sees the attraction of SDR as a source of globally available funds, first, in the fact that it is created by an international institution, hence belonging to the world as a whole, and making it useful for the maintenance of the global public goods for global stability and full employment of resources. Second, he anticipates that the rise in the resulting world income and output may either equal or exceed the value of the funds assigned for the purpose. Third, since SDRs come to national monetary authorities without payment, and their uses are somewhat restricted, those countries with more than adequate reserves could give them up for global causes that impose minimal overt sacrifices on the countries foregoing them (Clunies-Ross 2002: 26).

Wade (2002) has had an interesting look at the Soros proposal for new SDRs, and notes that, the 'proposal focuses public attention on apparently arcane monetary issues, which have a huge impact on the performance of the world economy yet receive rather little public attention'. He suggests that the injection of a modest amount of US$27 billion of SDR equivalent under the proposal for the first issue makes it doable, and this could produce better performance from the world economy as a whole. Wade (2002) sees the link made by Soros between monetary/payments issues and the supply of global public goods as credible 'and the mechanism of choosing which goods will be supplied, by whom, and financed by whom, is an interesting one when put alongside the present arrangements. In Soros' proposal there is a group of eminent persons or independent jury, working with a trust fund, and chosen for the purpose of deciding which global public goods may be funded. This is not left to the World Bank, currently, the most significant supplier of global public goods, to determine.

Wade (2002) notes that even though the proposal was quite modest in scale, it could easily be enlarged to make it a significant contributor 'to solving the chronic tendency in the world economy at large towards excess capacity reflecting insufficient demand'. If the possible uses of SDR were broadened, Wade expects the allocations of these development SDRs, which favor poor nations, to raise their consumption significantly. He expects such a growing consumption to lead largely to an increasing demand for goods from industrial economies. In effect, industrial economies do not necessarily lose by consenting to the creation of the development SDRs,

Having observed that international agreement on assistance to poor nations often takes too long to achieve, Clunies-Ross (2002) notes that the Soros proposal for regular SDRs to be issued to member countries, with the richer ones among them donating theirs to aid and global public goods, has the advantage of ensuring that allocations to such aid and global public goods do not have to wait for universal agreement.

The Argument 'Against' Development SDRS

The arguments against the issuance of development SDRs are basically an extension of the arguments made against regular SDRs. These have been summarized by Lissakers in the Pocantico Report (2003) as (i) legal, referring to the requirement that there must be long-term global need to supplement international liquidity; (ii) moral, that nonconditional financing encourages bad policies; (iii) efficiency, implying that the SDRs are unlikely to go to the developing countries; and (iv) historical, suggesting that the environment of floating exchange rate regimes and the existence of multiple media for reserve holdings made SDRs unnecessary. But these are the points that Clark and Polak (2002) argue against strongly. In effect, the main arguments against the issue of development SDRs on account of international stabilization are derived from the anxiety that not enough measures may be put in place to restrain the IMF from 'flooding' the financial markets with excess new liquidity and then cash-strapped poor nations will go on a spending spree. This is what makes the US Congress not want to ratify the 1997 proposal for a development SDR.

In addition to the above arguments, most of the points of concern that have often been raised about the use of SDRs for development are centered on a couple of issues. These are, first, that it is not obvious what advantages the use of SDRs brings to poor developing nations that are not derived from traditional aid packages; secondly the impact on the stability of the world economy is not clear, and finally, the institutional adjustments that are required for creating the special SDRs that affect country quotas are probably not politically appealing to industrial economies and hence not likely to happen.

Wade (2002) points out the fact that Soros is not clear on what the poorer countries would do with their SDR allocations. He notes that beyond the effect to be generated by the global public goods, it is not obvious what direct benefits countries would receive.

'Presumably, the direct benefits are those they could have had all along from conventional SDRs, and the Soros proposal does not contain anything new in this respect'.

But Clunies-Ross (2002) discusses even more extensively the issue of difficulty in identifying the potential benefits from development SDRs. He sees a possible problem with generating enough desire on the part of potential SDR holders to want them, particularly when the recipient of the SDR is not a central bank but a trust set up to administer global public goods after these allocations have been transferred to it by a recipient central bank. The problem arises from the obligation of interest payments on total cumulative allocation. Evidently the donor nations will have no desire to pay interest on a donation they have made to an international agency that is not necessarily in a position to pay interest when it seeks to exchange these for hard currency. He explores a number of possible uses of the development SDR as follows:

If the global fund were to provide guarantees, for example, of markets for new drugs or vaccines, these assets could be held costless against the call to make good the guarantees without having in that contingency to raise large amounts in the financial markets. Or, if one of the functions of the fund were to reduce the debt burden of highly indebted poor countries, buying out their debt by exchanging it for the proceeds (and the obligations) of SDRs could be valuable to these debtor countries even though it left them with interest obligations at international short-term rates. The servicing obligations would be much more favorable than those attached to many of the loans that might be available to developing and transitional economies (though less so than those on IDA loans).

He suggests that this 'quirk of SDR arrangements does take some of the attractiveness from the Soros and similar schemes' (Clunies-Ross 2002: 28).

It has been suggested that new proposals for the creation of development SDRs ignore the question of how to entice the US government into accepting the proposals (Wade 2002). It is not obvious that if the new SDRs are seen as additional grants to developing nations, the US government will be enthused about it. Aside from its reluctance to see a reduction in the demand for dollar reserves, the US government is also not very interested in seeing the IMF become a central bank to the world.

Indeed Wade (2002) also suggests that the Soros proposal does not say enough on the governance issues related to the creation of SDRs. The lack of clarity leaves the question of how the global public goods would be prioritized unresolved. In the Soros proposal, infectious diseases, judicial reform, education, and bridging the digital divide are prioritized for attention. But this is observed to be different from the priority list of the G-7 countries. For the World Bank, infectious diseases, environmental improvement, trade promotion and greater financial stability should be the top on the list for global public goods. Under the New Partnership for African Development (NEPAD), the priority areas are given as (i) peace, security and governance; (ii) investing in Africa's people; (iii) diversification of Africa's production and exports; (iv) investing in ICT and other basic infrastructure, and (v) developing financing mechanisms. It is obvious that several different lists are possible and accommodating all of them may lead to a longer list that may not easily lend itself to feasible agreed actions. This point is buttressed by the fact that the Stiglitz list is only a subset of all of these.

Proposed mechanisms for creating a development SDR

A number of the proposals for the issue of development SDRs do not provide details of how this can be done. A good example of this is the Stiglitz (2003) paper. Details of what mechanisms may be applied in creating new SDRs for development can at best be pieced together from several sources, and this is done in this section.

The Articles of Agreement of the IMF and the creation of a development SDR

A complication would arise in the creation of development SDRs if it were planned to make an allocation other than in exact proportion to IMF quotas. This would require an amendment of the IMF Articles of Agreement, and it would therefore impede the use of SDRs in ad hoc schemes intended to benefit particular groups of countries. If there were no changes in the allocation quotas, in order for high-income recipients of SDR to give them up simply as grants to others would require no alteration of the IMF Articles of Agreement. It has been pointed out by Boughton (2001) that the Fund's executive board has already altered the working practices to allow recipients of SDRs to use them as grants. The Fund is indeed in a position to name a global fund that receives the grants from SDR recipients as a 'prescribed holder', as has been done for some international institutions. This will allow the global fund to hold SDRs and also to trade them with central banks.

As indicated earlier, complications could also arise with respect to recipient countries making donations of their receipts in terms of how interest payment obligations could be handled, if those making the donations were to be relieved of the obligation of being net payers of interest based on their cumulative allocations. Obviously, if the SDRs were more like regular currency, this problem would not arise, but making it that way would require making the Fund more and more like a central bank, and that is going to be a major problem.

Clunies-Ross (2002) discusses at length various scenarios for dealing with the interest payment issue, assuming industrial countries were to decide to follow the Soros proposal for donating any new issues of SDR immediately to a global fund. The likely outcome would be that the wealthier nations would essentially be providing only a termless loan at a standard short-term interest rate to the global fund or poorer recipient countries, and this may be utilized in any of the manners earlier discussed. It is indeed the lack of clarity about whether donor countries should continue with the interest payment or not that is the main issue. Making the donor countries pay the interest effectively turns the SDR into additional financial assistance to the recipient without affecting the structure of the IMF.

Conditions for creating a development SDR and links to debt relief

It is important to point out that the Soros proposal for donations was intended to overcome the difficulty that alteration of the allocation of SDRs by quota was considered unlikely to happen soon. The voluntary donations, while quotas remained, were, therefore, a way of ensuring less antagonism from some industrial economies. Clunies-Ross (2002) suggests, however, that there might be possibilities for other allocations, where once again, considerable discretion was given to the management of the Fund, as was indeed the case with the 1997 Fourth Amendment of the Articles of Agreement. He suggests that if there was a move to empower the management to create SDRs for low-income and middle-income countries or for countries with high degrees of volatility in their gross foreign exchange receipts, these need not create large conflict with the Soros proposal for a regular allocation by quota and then donation since that could be done at a second stage of the process.

If there is to be a special allocation outside the quota, who should be eligible for it? In the Soros proposal, the SDRs going to the global fund are all from donations, so there is not a major problem. But it should be possible to link the gains from new development SDR to the current initiatives on debt-relief and the attainment of the Millennium Development Goals. If the concern with new SDRs were the likely effect of a rapid expansion in international liquidity, one could limit the Clunies-Ross' proposal for low- income and middle-income countries to cover only the HIPC countries for consideration in the special allocation. It is observed from the enhanced HIPC Initiative that countries will continue to borrow even as they receive relief to settle other obligations in the pursuit of poverty reduction goals. It is important that payments on these do not slow down growth. It is obvious that debt relief must be recognized by creditor countries as additional to new and increased ODA with a focus on enhancing and sustaining both growth and poverty reduction explicitly. New SDR that provides HIPC countries with an opportunity to engage in further debt exchanges certainly enhances the benefits from their involvement from the HIPC Initiative.

There is tension between quick debt relief and comprehensive country-owned poverty reduction strategies. The solution to this problem is to make countries focus on their medium- and long-term development frameworks, showing the anticipated growth paths and how these provide for poverty reduction. In this situation, new SDR that creates new comfort levels in reserve holdings allows countries to pursue development programs of a longer orientation than the shorter-term programs that they have been used to in the last two decades under the directions of the Bretton Woods institutions. Essentially, the development SDRs will provide them with termless credit facilities that have somewhat reduced short-term interest rates. In effect, a specific or development SDR may be essential so long as there are HIPC countries that need greater liquidity than their trade volumes would permit and want greater flexibility in dealing on the international financial markets.

Timing the creation of SDR to support developing countries

Linked to the conditions for creating development SDRs is the issue of their timing. The report of the Zedillo Panel (UN 2001) indicates that there should be an immediate resumption of the issue of regular SDRs. Throughout that report, there is emphasis on the need to augment financial support to developing countries in a manner that deals with their cyclical problems related to the nature of their engagement with world trade. When compounded with the cyclical nature of international capital flows, especially private, the need to develop mechanisms that are countercyclical cannot be over- emphasized.

In line with this thinking, there is very widespread belief that the IMF must have ample authority to introduce new liquidity into the global system at specific times only, particularly if it helps to contain contagion in times of crises. Mohammed (2000) has indicated that the Independent Task Force of the US Council on

Foreign Relations proposed a contagion facility to be funded by pooling a one-off allocation of SDR. The emphasis on development SDRs being issued only when they are globally necessary or on rare occasions is usually within the context of situations where failure to intervene would lead to negative consequences for the world economy generally (Mohammed 2000).

Clunies-Ross (2002: 29) also suggests that in order to stabilize world activity, any intervention would have to be counter-cyclical, 'high when other sources of reserves are falling or demand for reserves is growing or when the rate of growth of world trade and activity is falling or appears to be about to fall; low or negative in the opposite case'. The more fundamental question is whether the Fund can, politically speaking, be allowed to operate in this very responsive manner. It would require a decision-making structure that used considerable discretion in determining when to intervene and when not to.

The possibility of using less discretion and more rules is also discussed by Clunies-Ross (2002). He observes that a possible criterion might be to ensure that the rate of the rise of total non-gold reserves matches the trend rate of growth of world trade. There should at all times be enough SDRs to meet this reserve requirement without increasing the reserves of national currencies; and this is very much compatible with the assessment by Clark and Polak (2002) on the demand for reserves. While this rigid approach is likely to suffer from the peculiarities of particular developing economies, depending on how policy is conducted and the scope of involvement in world trade, it looks like it provides some basis for greater objectivity in determining when to intervene and when not to intervene. It is important to keep in mind, however, that the requirements for international liquidity reform and development finance have their own tensions considering the long-term nature of the latter and the potential fluidity of the former.

Proposed Institutional Re-Organization For Creating A Development SDR

The forms that a development SDR may take are often linked to the question of whether the IMF should increasingly behave like a central bank. Clunies-Ross (2002: 28) has suggested that in order to overcome the interest problem that arises from the Soros proposal, as earlier discussed, 'it would be possible in principle to re-frame the whole system, so that future issues of SDRs or equivalent were more like a regular currency'.

He suggests further that this was the general direction in which SDRs were moving under the Second Amendment to the Articles of Agreement in 1978 and other decisions taken about that time. A major problem he sees with this approach, however, is the likely political opposition that it would generate.

Mohammed has noted that: developing countries would continue to press for an exploration of the merits of establishing an effective international lender of last resort, i.e. one able to create international liquidity freely and to deploy it rapidly to deal with widespread financial crises (2000: 201).

For the developing countries, the IMF needs to have the authority and structure to take decisions and act upon them, like independent central banks do. While the Soros proposal deals with the problems of providing support for development largely through informal agreements to transfer reserves from one party to another, there appears to be a major demand from developing countries for the formalization of such arrangements (Wade 2002). Clunies-Ross (2002) suggests that it is possible to begin with the informal approach to providing additional support for development with SDRs, but providing for a more formalized way of bringing about international stabilization in future allocations. This would be on the basis of greater discretionary authority to the Fund's structures, working through the managing director's recommendations to the board of governors, in concert with the executive board. The managing director may be authorized to recommend that allocation in a particular year be made to a certain group of countries only.

As the process of selective allocations of SDR is formalized, it is inevitable that the IMF would have to act a little more like a central bank. And that requires an amendment of the Articles of Agreement: to provide more powers to its existing governing institutions, and possibly also delegation by them, or further amendment, to give more actual decision-making power to say a technical committee (operating of course under guidelines that the governing institutions had laid down) (Clunies-Ross 2002: 30).

Putting together ideas from Soros' proposal and sentiments from the Zedillo Panel, Clunies-Ross (2002) outlines five stages that may be followed in promoting the use of SDRs for stabilization and for the provision of global public goods. At the first stage, the Fourth Amendment to the Articles of Agreement will have to be ratified by the US Congress in order to allow the 1997 allocation to proceed. This is followed at the second stage by the high-income or industrial economies agreeing to donate their new holdings to an appropriately constituted international body for the delivery of global public goods. That body would have to be accepted by all and made a prescribed holder by the IMF. At the third stage, the IMF board of governors agree informally over a period to accept recommendations from the managing director and the executive board to issue and cancel SDRs according to an agreed formula that reflects a relationship between the growth rate of total international reserves and the trend rate of growth of real international transactions.

At the fourth stage, the Articles of Agreement are altered to allow the distribution to be did possibly according to criteria other than the prescribed quota, while such alterations are approved each time by the board of governors, following proposals from the managing director and the executive board. Finally, the Articles of Agreement may be further altered to create a technical body, which will work on the appropriate quantities of SDR to be allocated and how these may be timed. It is this body, guided by the executive board and the managing director, which will generate the information necessary for decision-making by the board of governors.

An assessment of the proposals for a development SDR

There are three issues that confront us in this concluding assessment, namely whether development SDRs are likely to bring significant additional benefit to developing countries, whether a global fund's access to new resources should be considered priority over the requirements of individual countries and, finally, the manner in which new SDR issues may be managed.

Development SDRs versus other forms of assistance

In the work by Clark and Polak (2002) on regular SDRs, they draw attention to what they refer to as 'the allocation of SDRs versus the provision of conditional Fund credit'. The question suggests that the perceived direct benefits of an expanded SDR allocation to developing countries, even if it is not development SDR, need to be more identified. They are obviously bothered about the question of whether regular conditional credit from the Fund does not deal with the problems that new and regular SDRs are supposed to tackle, namely creating the means for increasing reserve holdings. Clark and Polak (2002) cite the IMF's 1965 annual report, which observed that, 'ideally countries' need for additional liquidity could be met by adequate increases in conditional liquidity. In practice, however, countries do not appear to treat conditional and unconditional liquidity as interchangeable'. Clark and Polak (2002) fear that inducing countries to meet their liquidity constraints with increased conditional lending from the Fund would force them to adopt balance of payments programs that may have largely negative consequences for growth and development. But this does not deal with the substitution of conditional credit for new grants. Should new grants not be ultimately preferred to new SDRs. Maybe that is what is intended by proposing the new development SDRs.4 The problem with showing how increased SDR allocations benefit countries directly has been, and will remain, on the discussion table for a long time.

The situation gets even trickier with proposed development SDRs. As indicated earlier, in Wade's (2002) critique of the Soros proposal, he wonders about how developing countries gain directly from a large increase in SDR before giving his own list of what could be done with SDRs. But these are a basic extension of what countries would generally do with owned reserves as opposed to borrowed reserves.

Indeed, there are number of people who have suggested that if the idea behind campaigning for new development SDRs is a simple matter of getting more development assistance for developing countries, one should tackle the issue directly then. This is often responded to with the point that it is more difficult to argue for increased ODA which involves a significant direct cost to one party, namely the Wade (2002) suggests that, 'it is basically a way to arrange for the rich countries to cough up more grants to poor countries. All the fancy talk is really just an elaboration of this very familiar idea'. development assistance donor, then for the SDRs which involve no direct cost to those developed countries.

In our view, the question of whether new SDRs should be created or not, considering the existence of traditional ODA, should ultimately be tied to the question of whether such SDRs substitute for ODA or complement it. The difference between SDRs and other flows to developing countries is the fact that the use of SDRs is determined largely by the recipient, and not by the giver/donor. Recipient countries are therefore free to use these essentially termless facilities over a period, despite the possible low short-term interest costs if they have to transact business with them. A developing country that receives an SDR allocation targeted at such countries basically has the option of using the opportunities created by the facility to increase spending on those items that are not typically funded by donors with ODA, including massively expanded support to the private sector. This characteristic ensures that additional SDR without a declining ODA will give developing countries greater flexibility in the management of their economies than they possibly will have with only ODA. Using them in a complementary manner is what may be useful. But even when SDR is a substitute for ODA, the benefit to donors is that it is politically easier to transfer SDRs than to increase ODA. Even if donors pay interest on the transfers for development projects, the budgetary impact is not necessarily different from borrowing to finance ODA.

A global fund versus individual countries' access to more liquid assets

There appears to be some agreement that industrial economies giving or donating their SDR allocations to a fund for global purposes is a sensible thing to do. Wade (2002: 3) says, 'I need no convincing that the world could do with a more reliable supply of global public goods. This is also what the Zedillo report seems to suggest. But while there may not be an obvious reason why the world should not spend on global public goods, it may be more obvious to some that the greater the resources devoted to global public goods the less of such international resources will be available for individual countries, hence possible tension. It then becomes essential to the poor nations of the world that resources for global public goods can augment returns from national investments in more obvious ways than may appear to be the case initially. It is also essential that expenditure on global public goods do not cause poor countries to spend more trying to stabilize their own economies.

In this regard, Clunies-Ross suggests that when the SDRs are created and allocated to global public goods, while augmenting aggregate reserves, they will not affect the macroeconomic policies of governments by permitting or encouraging additional spending. If the expenditure were made on vaccines, for example, this will increase global demand in money terms. The vaccines may be able to 'pay for themselves' by generating additional output throughout the world, and this 'will depend on how that additional demand is spread across the world and how far its incidence corresponds with that of unemployed resources' (Clunies- Ross 2002: 31).

There could be inflationary pressures if the world's markets were fully employed. He notes that if there was an abundance of unemployed resources in many of the world's markets, 'the real value of the extra output generated (including multiplier effects) may exceed the value of the vaccines, so that the resources devoted to the vaccines 'more than pay for themselves' through the additional resources brought into use'.

It would be even better if governments employed more expansive policies following the injection of new global capital in a state of global recession. In that scheme of things, if the macroeconomic effect of adding to national reserves after new SDR allocations combined with the extra spending on global issues financed by the new assets to increase demand at the right time, and with the right distribution across countries, it is expected that the extra output that is generated is likely to more than offset the value of the resources sequestered to produce the globally- chosen goods. 'Not only could two birds be killed with one stone, but the stone might also pay for itself (Clunies-Ross 2002: 32).

Structuring The Issuance And Management Of New SDR

One area in which the creation of SDRs for global public goods is seen to be likely to generate good outcomes for developing countries is the area of governance. Wade (2002) thinks that Soros' idea of establishing a trust fund, having an independent jury, the shopping for recipient programs, and the addition of SDRs to the reserves of the poorer member countries is important and should be treated seriously. The element of having an independent third party organize the distribution of global public goods reduces the influence of the World Bank in this area and supposedly brings greater transparency and accountability into what poor nations may or may not have. Shopping for recipient programs ensures that developing countries are not saddled with what some international technocrat believes is good for them.

But even more important is the question of which of three possibilities should be adopted in resuming SDR issues: (i) should the IMF allocate the SDRs differentially? (ii) should the IMF allocation follow quotas and then there is an international agreement of donors to transfer according to some formula? and (iii) should the IMF allocation follow quotas and individual members decide how to transfer their allocation? This takes us back to the issue of whether the transfer arrangements should be more formalized or not. There seems to be the growing view that the third option is the way to start, with a gradual shift to more structured transfers later. This is generally seen by supporters of the resumption of SDRs as the best chance of gaining wider support. We tend to be of that view also as they seem to pass the five tests outlined earlier by Clunies-Ross (2002).

Special drawing rights, the dollar, and the institutionalist approach to reserve currency status

The importance of institutions raises the question of whether SDRs are backed by sufficient institutions to become a dominant global reserve currency. Could the IMF promote SDRs, the way the Federal Reserve bolstered the international status of the dollar after its founding? Could the IMF act as a lender of last resort, providing the kind of liquidity in financial crisis that the Federal Reserve did after 2007? I argue in this paper that the institutionalist approach identifies key limits that may prevent SDRs from replacing the dollar in the near or foreseeable future. Unlike the Federal Reserve, the IMF does not presently have the power as an institution to create liquid markets in a currency or to support a currency's reserve status by intervening quickly in financial crises. However, I will suggest in my conclusion that the institutionalist approach may guide reforms to the IMF that have the potential in the longer run to increase the international status of the SDR.

CHAPTER 5

FOUR APPROACHES TO RESERVE CURRENCY STATUS

(a) The institutionalist approach to reserve currency status

I will first outline Helleiner and Kirshner's three explanations for currencies' reserve status, and compare them to the institutionalist approach. While these explanations are not mutually exclusive, they are distinct in underscoring different determinants of reserve status. The first, market-based approach is taken by economists who emphasize the importance of private actors, as opposed to governments. This approach assumes that private actors — such as investors in the bond market, export-importers, or commodity traders — make decisions to use a currency based on its economic attractiveness compared to other currencies (Helleiner and Kirshner, 2010: 7). The economic attractiveness of a currency depends on (1) its stability as a store of value; (2) its liquidity or how easily it can be bought or sold without changing prices; and (3) its network externalities or the fact that many other market actors are already using the currency, making transactions in it more convenient (Helleiner and Kirshner, 2010: 7—11).

Confidence in the dollar, under a market-based approach, would be undermined by rising current account deficits and government debt.

While the market-based approach emphasizes private actors, the second, instrumental approach instead focuses on the decisions of foreign governments as they pursue economic goals (Helleiner and Kirshner, 2010: 12). According to the instrumental approach, the dollar's reserve status would strengthen if foreign governments decided to peg their own currencies to the dollar, or if they continued to purchase dollar debt. Foreign governments may be motivated to support the dollar, based on the monetary peg theory of Ronald McKinnon, or the Bretton Woods II theory of Michael Dooley, David Folkerts- Landau, and Peter Garber. The Bretton Woods II theory argues that countries like China and Japan buy US treasuries with the economic goal of preventing their national currencies from appreciating. A lower value for the renminbi and yen makes Chinese and Japanese exports cheaper and more competitive in the US market (Helleiner and Kirshner, 2010: 12). An alternative instrumental account of reserve currency status is given by McKinnon's monetary peg theory. It claims that countries peg their currencies to the dollar as a means of stabilizing their price level, preventing significant inflation or deflation (Helleiner and Kirshner, 2010: 13; Ronald McKinnon, 2010: 45—68, esp. 64).

A third approach that seeks to explain why currencies gain or lose international reserve status focuses on geopolitical factors. While the instrumental approach highlights the decisions of foreign governments to support a currency based on economic goals like promoting exports or stabilizing the price level, the geopolitical approach bases the decisions of foreign governments on considerations of security, political power, and military alliances (Helleiner and Kirshner 2010: 15—7). For instance, Kirshner claims that Western Europe and Japan supported the dollar in the Cold War, because of their alliance with the US. But now that the Soviet threat is gone, the alliance has weakened. In Kirshner's view, Western Europe and Japan are less likely to bolster the dollar, and are more interested in expanding the international status of the euro and yen (Helleiner and Kirshner, 2010: 15—6; Kirshner, 2010: 195).

An 'institutionalist' approach argues that a currency's reserve status may be bolstered by the institutions that issue the currency. This institutionalist approach differs from the instrumental and geopolitical perspectives in focusing on the decisions of the institution that supplies the currency, and not the decisions of the foreign governments that potentially demand the currency. It also contrasts with the market-based approach, because it shows how confidence, liquidity, and network externalities are not determined solely by private actors in the market. Rather these market factors can be supported or undermined by institutions. After describing in greater detail, the institutionalist approach, I will then apply the institutionalist approach to debates over the IMF Special Drawing Right.

(b) How the Federal Reserve, as an institution, enhanced the dollar's reserve status

To see how institutions might enhance the international role of a currency, consider the Federal Reserve's actions to increase dollar liquidity after the recent financial crisis. Since the dollar is the international reserve currency, it is crucial for foreign businesses and banks to be able to borrow fUnds in dollars. For example, when a South Korean company imports goods from Thailand or services its bonds, it generally does, not pay in South Korean won, but dollars. Most exports from South Korea and Thailand (80 per cent) are priced in dollars, even though only 20 percent of those goods go to the US (Eichengreen, 2011: 2, 168). For businesses and banks to service their obligations, they need access to dollars. The problem is that in a financial crisis, banks and financial markets are unwilling to loan dollars, causing a severe shortage of dollar liquidity. If it persists, both foreign and domestic businesses may default.

The key institutional role of the Federal Reserve in a financial crisis is to ease the shortage of liquidity by lending dollars on a vast scale. As Ben Bernanke, the Chairman of the

Federal Reserve, declared in a speech, 'serving as a "lender of last resort" has been central banks' key weapon against financial panics for hundreds of years' (Bernanke, 2010a). Although foreign central banks may loan dollars out of their foreign exchange re- serves, there is a danger that their reserves may be exhausted in a financial crisis. If a foreign central bank's dollar reserves drop below a safe mini- mum, there may be a run on the currency and an even deeper financial panic.

The Federal Reserve's solution to this problem was to meet the world's demand for the dollar liquidity by establishing 'central bank liquidity swap lines', beginning in 2007—2010, and extended from 2010—2012 (Bernanke 2010b). The swap lines provided dollar liquidity for 14 central banks, including the European Central Bank, the Bank of England, the Bank of Korea, and the Bank of Japan (Board of Governors of the Federal Reserve System, 2011). Drawing on the swap lines, a foreign central bank could sell its national currency to the Federal Reserve in exchange for dollars. The dollars could then be loaned to a country's banks and businesses, easing the dollar liquidity shortage and stemming the threat of default. After an agreed-upon time period, 1 to 84 days later, the foreign central bank is obligated to buy back its currency at the same exchange rate, returning the dollars and paying a market-based interest rate to the Federal Reserve.

The largest amount of dollars that the Federal Reserve extended at any one time in swaps was $580 billion in December 2008 (Fleming and Klagge, 2010). But what is less widely known is that the cumulative value of the 569 swap lines extended from 2007—2010 was over $10 trillion ($10,057,401,900,000) (Board of Governors of the Federal Reserve System, 2011).[2] Admittedly, this money was lent over three years and not simultaneously, and it was all paid back with interest. But the total size of the swap lines, amounting to $10 trillion worth of transactions, indicates the major institutional role of the Federal

Reserve in promoting the international reserve currency status of the dollar. The Federal Reserve supported the dollar's reserve status by guaranteeing sufficient dollar liquidity during the financial crisis.

This institutional role is not new. One of the notable contributions of Eichengreen's Exorbitant Privilege is to show that the Federal Reserve pioneered the international reserve currency status of the dollar by supporting the currency's liquidity soon after its founding. For a currency to be liquid, there must be a large market in assets denominated in that currency, so that they can be rapidly bought or sold, and converted into cash, without significantly changing their price. A large market requires many buyers and sellers who are willing to trade in those assets. But when a currency is in the early stages of taking an international role, that market might not exist, or the buyers and sellers might be too few to provide sufficient liquidity. Since the assets are less liquid and are relatively novel, investors must be paid a premium to hold them. This interest rate premium makes it more expensive and less appealing to raise funds in bonds or commercial paper denominated in that currency.

The market-based approach acknowledges that liquidity is one of the key qualities required in a reserve currency. But it does not explain how liquid markets in a currency originate. Perhaps one potential explanation is that, once an economy grows sufficiently in size, investors will create a large and liquid market themselves. However, this explanation is belied by how the US had surpassed Britain in GDP by 1870, but lacked an international market in dollar assets until 1913, when the Federal Reserve was created. The insight of the institutionalist approach, I contend, is that it shows how liquid markets in a currency can arise. Institutions can increase the size and liquidity of a market in two ways. First, they can trade large quantities of assets denominated in a currency like the dollar, reassuring investors that they can easily find a buyer, or seller. Since the market is liquid, investors do not need to worry that selling would be difficult, or that it would reduce the price of their remaining assets. Second, institutions can also work to educate investors about a new asset. Investors who are more familiar with an asset will then reduce the risk premium of raising funds in it, and this encourages the market to grow further. As the market grows, its liquidity increases, attracting more investors in a virtuous circle.

The institutionalist account of how institutions can create liquid markets, expanding a currency's international status, is illustrated by the Federal Reserve's efforts to promote the dollar trade acceptance market, as de- scribed by Eichengreen. Acceptances were crucial in funding trade, since exporters needed funds to pay for shipping and other bills before the exported goods arrived overseas (Eichengreen and Flandreau, 2010: 3). To provide credit to exporters, banks created financial instruments called 'trade acceptances'.3 Before the Federal Reserve Act of 1913, American merchants could only acquire trade credit overseas in a foreign currency, most often pounds sterling in London (Eichengreen 2011: 14—5). This greatly limited the international role of the dollar in financing trade. The Federal Reserve Act changed US financial law, permitting American banks to create dollar trade acceptances, but the market was initially small and illiquid.

At this stage, the Federal Reserve stepped in to increase the liquidity of the dollar trade acceptance market as educator and market maker. It aggressively promoted dollar- denominated trade acceptances to expand US trade and to increase the dollar's international influence (Eichengreen, 2011: 29). The Federal Reserve pursued these aims by educating investors about dollar trade acceptances and their attractiveness as investments. It also expanded the market by buying trade acceptances on a large scale. Within a few years, 'the Federal Reserve Banks were the dealers' dominant counterparty' (Eichengreen, 2011: 29). The Federal Reserve's purchases stabilized and lowered the discount rates of dollar trade acceptances, making the market more attractive. As liquidity increased, the market grew quickly. Although no US trade was financed by dollar acceptances before 1913, 'by the second half of the 1920s, more than half of all US imports and exports were financed by bank acceptances denominated in dollars' (Eichengreen, 2011: 30).

Advocates of the market approach might reply that US exporters would have turned to dollar trade acceptances without the Federal Reserve. Re- placing sterling with dollar acceptances had the advantage of removing exchange rate risk, for American traders. However, this criticism of institutionalism overlooks how the market in trade acceptances grew much more rapidly because of the Federal Reserve's intervention. As Eichengreen writes, the dollar rose to rival sterling in the mid-1920s 'as a result of some very concrete actions by the Fed to promote the dollar's international role' (Eichengreen, 2011: 6). In particular, he calculates that Federal Reserve purchases of trade acceptances led banks to increase their holdings of acceptances twice as quickly as they would have without government action (Eichengreen and Flandreau, 2010: 18). Banks were more willing to deal in dollar trade acceptances, knowing that the market was liquid and that they could rely upon on the Fed to purchase acceptances. By increasing the liquidity of the trade acceptance market, the Federal Reserve acted as an institution to enhance the international status of the dollar.

The institutionalist approach raises the question of whether SDRs are backed by sufficient institutions to become a dominant global reserve currency. In the next section, I begin by defining SDRs and outlining proposals to expand their use. I then follow Eichengreen in expressing skepticism about whether SDRs can replace dollars as a global reserve currency in the near or foreseeable future. The main problem, I will argue, is that the IMF as an institution currently lacks certain key powers possessed by the Federal Reserve. However, I will conclude the paper by suggesting the possibility that if the IMF makes major institutional reforms in the much longer term, it could increase the international role of the SDR.

Why SDRs Are Not Currently A Viable Alternative To The Dollar: An Institutionalist Criticism

Since SDRs is an unusual asset, with several properties that distinguish them from a freely usable currency, it is important to start by defining what SDRs are and how they are valued, before explaining why Zhou and Stiglitz have sought to expand their role. I will argue that Eichengreen overlooks two crucial properties in his definition of SDRs — first, they are not claims on the IMF, as he believes, but potential claims on the freely usable currency of IMF member states. Second, he does not discuss how countries must pay interest on the SDRs they have sold. Because Eichengreen overlooks this property of SDRs, he does not mention a key disadvantage associated with their misuse: the rising debt burden from SDR interest payments.5 This disadvantage may grow if the general allocations of SDRs greatly increase. After clarifying the definition of SDRs, I will outline Zhou's and Stiglitz's proposals to expand the role of SDRs as an international reserve asset. I will then suggest the limits of these proposals by using an institutionalist approach.

SDRs are a composite reserve asset that was first created by the IMF in 1969. Its value was initially set at one SDR .888671 grams of gold, then equivalent to one dollar (IMF, 2010a). After the replacement of the Bretton Woods system with floating exchange rates, the IMF redefined the SDR in 1973, basing its value on a basket of sixteen currencies. At first, the basket's inclusion of many minor currencies made it excessively complex (Eichengreen, 2011: 138—9). To simplify the asset and encourage its use, the IMF in 1981 narrowed the SDR's basket to five currencies: the German mark, French franc, British sterling, Japanese yen, and US dollar. Today the SDR basket is composed of four currencies, with the euro taking the place of the mark and the franc. The Executive Board of the IMF reviews the percentage of the currencies in the SDR basket regularly every five years to reflect their importance to the world economy, as measured by the currencies' share of global exports and foreign exchange reserves (IMF, 2010a, 2010b). After the latest revaluation in 2010, the basket of currencies is now 37.4 per cent euro, 9.4 per cent yen, 11.3 per cent sterling, and 41.9 per cent dollars (IMF, 2010b).

To avoid misunderstanding, it should be emphasized that the basket serves only as a basis to calculate the SDR's value. The SDR is not literally a bundle of currencies, such that, when a country holds SDRs, it automatically possesses a certain amount of euro, yen, sterling, and dollars. Nor is the SDR backed by currencies held by the IMF. Rather, SDRs are potential claims on the freely usable currencies of other IMF members. For SDRs to be exercised, a state must first sell SDRs to another state in exchange for dollars, euros, or other currencies (Eichengreen, 2011: 138). SDRs cannot be used directly in transactions involving private parties, such as market intervention and the financing of international trade (Eichengreen, 2011: 7, 57; IMF, 2011a: 7). This is because private parties are not authorized to hold SDRs under Article XVII of the Articles of Agreement (IMF, 2009a: 13). Only states that are members of the IMF and certain international organizations can hold SDRs.

Since SDRs are not privately held or traded, states cannot rely on banks or the open market to convert special drawing rights. Nor can states sell their SDRs to the IMF. The role of the IMF is limited to facilitating the conversion through either one of two means — voluntary trading arrangements or the designation mechanism. Under the voluntary trading arrangements, the IMF can match two states that want to conduct a voluntary exchange of SDRs for a freely usable currency (IMF, 2009a: 14—5). If Australia wants to sell SDRs for dollars, it would contact the IMF, and the voluntary trading arrangements would find a suitable exchange partner (say, China), that would purchase the SDRs. This process typically takes 5 to 10 business days. If there are no countries that want to voluntarily purchase SDRs in the amounts needed, the IMF can activate its designation mechanism. The IMF would designate a country with a strong external position to buy the SDRs in exchange for dollars or other freely usable currencies.

The designation mechanism has not been activated for nearly a quarter century, and the IMF is reluctant to invoke it (IMF, 2009b: 23). However, the designation mechanism may be more problematic in the future if SDR allocations were to increase greatly. States might then seek to exchange their SDRs for freely usable currency on a scale exceeding the capacity of the voluntary arrangements. Under the designation mechanism, other states could be required non-voluntarily to purchase much larger amounts of SDRs. Although Eichengreen does not discuss this issue, the IMF admits the problem when it reports that 'expanding the volume of SDR allocations would increase the contingent claim on all other participants in the SDR department, who could be required under the designation mechanism to provide freely usable currencies. The IMF notes that 'this requirement could quickly become burdensome' (IMF, 2011a: 7). Given the possibility that the designation mechanism could become burdensome, a number of surplus account states may refuse to vote for future SDR expansions. States seeking to sell their SDRs may be unsure whether they will be able convert their holdings reliably into freely usable currency. This difficulty may make states more reluctant to replace the dollar with SDRs in their reserves.

A Criticism Of Eichengreen's Definition Of SDRs

While Eichengreen is clear in explaining how SDRs are valued, and how they cannot be used in transactions with private parties, he introduces some confusion in defining SDRs themselves. He defines SDRs as 'book-keeping claims on the IMF' (Eichengreen, 2011: 137). The problem with defining SDRs as 'claims on the IMF' is that it may mistakenly suggest the IMF is obligated to exchange SDRs on demand for the currencies in the basket or their equivalent value in dollars, the same way that the US Treasury was obligated to exchange dollars for gold on demand during the Bretton Woods era. In fact, the IMF explicitly states that the SDR 'is not a currency, nor a claim on the IMF' (IMF, 2011b). Instead, it is 'potentially a claim on freely usable currencies of IMF members' (ibid.). An exchange of SDRs for freely usable currencies does not draw on the IMF's own resources, but depends on states buying SDRs through either the voluntary trading arrangements or the designation mechanism. Rather than defining SDRs as 'bookkeeping claim on the IMF', it would be more accurate to define SDRs as a composite reserve asset, which is potentially a claim on freely usable currencies of IMF members.

In defining Special Drawing Rights, Eichengreen also overlooks the important fact that a state's SDRs have two components one of which is an asset, and the other a liability. The asset consists of a state's holdings of SDRs. The holdings can change, increasing when the state buys SDRs or decreasing when it sells SDRs. It is an asset because IMF pays every member state interest for its SDR holdings. The second component is a state's allocation of SDRs. A state's allocation is assigned by the IMF, and does not change when a state buys or sells SDRs. It is a liability, since a state is charged interest on its SDR allocation. The SDR interest rate charged on allocations is the same as the rate paid on holdings. The interest rate is calculated 'based on a weighted average of representative interest rates on short-term debt in the money markets' (IMF, 2010a).

Normally, states do not earn or lose any money on SDRs, as long as their SDR holdings and allocations are equal. States are credited for quarterly interest on their SDR holdings, but they are charged the same quarterly interest on their SDR allocations, leaving no net interest payments. When the IMF creates SDRs, making what is called a 'general allocation', it simultaneously raises a state's holdings (assets) and allocation (liabilities) by the same amount. Suppose that the IMF creates 100 billion SDRs in a general allocation. It distributes one billion SDRs to Australia and one billion SDRs to China. Australia now has one billion SDRs in holdings, and one billion SDRs in allocation. The interest that the state pays on its allocation is equivalent to the interest it receives from its holdings, resulting in no net interest payments for Australia.

This situation changes when a state sell part of its SDR holdings. Sup- pose that Australia decides to sell its entire SDR holdings, converting them to dollars. It invokes the IMF voluntary trading arrangements and sells one billion SDRs to China in exchange for dollars (about $1.6 billion at current rates). After the sale, Australia's holdings or assets in SDRs have dropped to zero, and earn no interest. However, its allocation of SDRs remains the same, at one billion SDR, and Australia must pay interest on its liability. The country now has a net interest payment, which it is charged every quarter until it 'reconstitutes' its SDR holdings. Australia would reconstitute its holdings if it bought back enough SDRs to match its allocation.

When Australia incurs an SDR deficit, the interest payment goes to the IMF, but it is ultimately transferred to China. This occurs because China's SDR holdings doubled after it bought SDRs from Australia. China then earns interest on two billion SDR of holdings/assets, but it pays interest on only one billion SDR in allocation/liabilities. The general rule is that states earn quarterly interest when their SDR holdings exceed their allocations. States are charged quarterly interest when their SDR holdings fall below their allocations (IMF, 2011b). In this process, the IMF does not need to make interest payments from its own resources. The interest earned by SDR surplus states is paid exclusively by the interest charged to SDR deficit states, though the IMF does serve as an intermediary (IMF, 2009a: 13).

The dual nature of SDRs as both an interest-earning asset and interest- charging liability is highly relevant, because it raises concerns about the potential misuse of SDRs, which Eichengreen does not discuss. Low in-come countries (LICs) or states that are financially unsound might sell enough of their SDRs to incur interest charges that they may not be able to pay. These states may not be in a financial position to buy back their SDR holdings and end their interest payments. Even if they can pay the quarterly interest, the charges may be high enough to consume a large portion of a government's budget, reducing economic growth. As the IMF warns, the misuse of SDRs may '[contribute] over time to an unsustainable debt burden (e.g., as the SDR rate rises)' (IMF, 2011a: 8). In this case, 'not only may macroeconomic stability be compromised, but also potentially the member's ability to pay charges on their allocations or eventually reconstitute their holdings' (IMF, 2011a: 8).

Some might contend that debt sustainability is not currently a problem with SDRs, due to the low SDR interest rate. The SDR interest rate is only 0.42 per cent (IMF, 2011c), and it might be argued that the low rate makes SDR debts sustainable. The total number of SDRs in circulation is also limited to 204 billion, comprising 'less than 4 per cent of global reserves' in 2011 (IMF, 2011a: 6). Since the number of SDRs is small, the scope for their misuse is thought to be narrow. The difficulty with this argument is that the SDR interest rate is only temporarily low. The SDR interest rate is based on the three-month treasury bills of the US, UK, and Japan, and the three-month Europe, a representative interest rate in the European money market (IMF, 2011c). Interest rates on these bonds are unusually low due to the recession. The SDR interest rate has traditionally averaged 5.5 percent (IMF, 2009a: 7—8). At these higher interest rates, the debt burden on low income countries would be heavier if they sold their SDRs.

While low income countries may not incur large debt burdens as long as their allocations are relatively small, the Zhou and Stiglitz proposals would greatly increase the number of SDRs. The size of the general allocations needed to make a meaningful change in the compositions of reserve assets, as the proposals envision, would be staggering. Even if the IMF were to increase the share of SDRs in global reserves from 4 per cent to only 13 per cent, the expansion would require the IMF to allocate the equivalent of $200 billion (about 133 billion SDR) every year for the next 15 years (IMF, 2011a: 6). In that event, the SDRs in circulation would exceed two trillion. Low income countries would have much larger SDR holdings, and if they sold them, they could incur unsustainable debts burdens. This problem would be exacerbated by the fact that the IMF Articles of Agreement give states the unconditional freedom to use their SDRs (IMF, 2011a: 9).

Why Zhou and Stiglitz want to expand the role of SDRs

Given the issue of debt sustainability, why would Zhou, Stiglitz, and the UN Commission of Financial Experts propose that SDRs replace the dollar as the leading international reserve currency? The primary reason they cite is the instability of the current international financial system. Since the end of Bretton Woods, there have been an increasing number of financial crises, with the 2007— 2009 financial crisis being the most severe.[7] A major cause of financial instability is the growing imbalances that have been created by the use of a national currency, the dollar, as the dominant international reserve currency (Stiglitz, 2010: 157). The dollar's dual functions as both a national and international currency raise a crucial problem, called the 'Triffin Dilemma'. Named after the economist Robert Triffin, the dilemma is that the United States must run a large current ac- count deficit to satisfy the global demand for liquidity in the international reserve currency. On the one hand, if the US supplies sufficient dollars, the rising current account deficit will undermine long-term confidence in the dollar, threatening its value. On the other hand, if the US does not supply the demand for dollars, the world's money supply will shrink, causing deflation, reducing economic growth, and slowing global trade and finance (on the Triffin dilemma, see Blyth, 2003: 240; Eichengreen, 2011: 50—4; Stiglitz, 2010: 157—8; Zhou, 2009: 1).

Both Zhou and Stiglitz believe that the Triffin Dilemma could be avoided if the global economy relied on a supersovereign reserve asset (Stiglitz, 2010: 158). The asset would not be issued by a single state or function as a national currency. Instead, it would be an international asset issued by the IMF. The Fund would regulate the supply of global liquidity according to a clear and orderly set of rules (Zhou, 2009: 1). This would eliminate the problem, found in a dollar dominated system, of the United States producing too little or too much global liquidity. The US produces too little liquidity when the Federal Reserve reduces the money supply to fight domestic inflation, as it did in the early 1980s under Paul Volcker. This lack of liquidity places deflationary pressure on the world economy. The US produces too much liquidity when the Fed expands the money supply to counter domestic recessions, as it arguably did in the 2000s after the dot com crash. This places inflationary pressure on the world economy. In either case, the problem is that the issuer of the reserve currency might pursue national economic goals that are at odds with broader global needs. If a super-sovereign reserve asset replaced the dollar, the global supply of liquidity would match global demand more closely, leading to a more stable international economy. Zhou claims that 'the SDR has the features and potential to act as a super-sovereign reserve currency' (Zhou, 2009: 2; see also Stiglitz, 2010: 158).

Besides providing a more consistent source of liquidity, expanding the use of SDRs, according to Zhou, could address the problem of maintaining the value of international reserves. This is particularly an issue for China, which has built up vast dollar reserves by exporting goods to the United States. It is estimated that '65 percent of China's $2.5 trillion of reserves are in dollar-denominated assets', and China controls 'nearly half of all US treasuries in the hands of official foreign owners' (Eichengreen, 2011: 135). China is worried that its dollar reserves might drop sharply in value as a result of US debts (Stiglitz, 2010: 164). The United States is running enormous fiscal and current account deficits, partly to supply the world with liquidity (as predicted by the Triffin Dilemma), and partly to finance wars, tax cuts, and anti-recessionary spending. The US might be tempted to inflate away the real value of its debt by expanding the money supply.

Investors fearing inflation would respond by selling their dollar assets, and the value of China's dollar reserves would plunge.

While China might preemptively sell its dollar assets before their value eroded, it would be a costly strategy. To alter its reserves, China would have to sell a massive number of treasuries, triggering the very sell-off it wants to avoid (Eichengreen, 2011: 135). The solution that Zhou proposes to this difficulty would be for China to exchange its dollars for another reserve asset slowly, away from the market. An IMF 'substitution account' would allow China to trade its dollar treasuries for SDR-denominated bonds. China could then diversify its reserves outside of the market, and reduce the risk that its portfolio would be harmed by dollar depreciation (Zhou, 2009: 3).

The substitution account, however, would be an imperfect solution to dollar reserve depreciation. I would caution that if China resorted to a substitution account, investors might lose confidence in the dollar, and sell it off. The problem might not be as sudden as in the case of China selling its dollar assets on the open market, but investor confidence is in part based on what others are doing, and if the largest holder of dollar assets were to divest through a substitution account, investors would take it as a sign that the dollar could not be trusted to maintain its long-term value.

In addition to supplying a reliable source of global liquidity and at- tempting to stabilize the value of international reserves, another reason to expand the use of SDRs, cited by Stiglitz but not Zhou, is the issue of equity or fairness. Under a dollar reserve system, states must maintain sizeable dollar reserves to guard against capital outflows during financial crises. States need dollars to pay for imports, commodities, and inter- national loans, which are largely priced and settled in dollars. During a financial crisis, banks and the bond market may be unwilling to loan dollars, except at punitively high rates. States could turn to the IMF, but the loans are subject to pro-cyclical conditions that would impose austerity, force drastic cuts in expenditure, and prolong recessions (for a criticism of austerity policies, see Blyth, in press). Rather than depending on the IMF or the market for dollars during an emergency, states learned the lesson after the 1997 East Asian financial crisis that they should hold large dollar reserves (Stiglitz, 2010: 161—2). As a result, exporting states have accumulated nearly $800 billion of additional reserves a year, close to tripling their dollar reserves from 5.6 per cent of world GDP before the East Asian crisis, to 13 per cent of world GDP at the end of 2009 (Stiglitz, 2010: 162).

Stiglitz argues that the dollar dominated system is unfair because it forces countries to accumulate large dollar reserves instead of investing domestically. The dollar reserves are then lent to the United States, typically at very low interest rates. Adjusted for inflation, the return on US treasuries is negative (Stiglitz, 2010: 163). The poorly paying loans amount to a transfer of resources — $3.7 trillion worth in 2007 — from developing surplus countries to wealthy deficit countries. The money that flows from the developing world allows the United States to spend a trillion dollars more than it produces, and it fuels asset bubbles (such as in real estate and the stock market) that lead to financial crises. The unfairness is that developing country resources could have been invested domestically to finance economic growth and greater consumption for the poor, but instead it must be invested overseas in dollar assets to safeguard against capital flight. In fact, according to the UN Commission, the 'transfer of resources to the reserve currency countries . . . exceeds in value the foreign assistance that developing countries receive from the developed countries' (Stiglitz, 2010: 163). A reformed system might avoid this problem by giving developing countries greater access to a reserve asset — the SDR — that can be used as a source of emergency liquidity during a crisis. In an SDR dominated system, countries would spend less on accumulating large dollar reserves, and more on domestic investment, economic growth, and human development. The result would be a more equitable system.

A fourth reason for SDRs, according to Stiglitz, extends beyond the well-being of developing countries, and includes the interests of wealthier countries. Developing countries must amass enormous dollar reserves to protect themselves against financial crises and unpredictable capital flows. These reserves can only be accumulated by building current account surpluses and saving the proceeds. The level of reserves reached 13 percent of global GDP and 32 per cent of emerging market GDP by the end of 2009 (IMF, 2010c: 6). But if developing countries are saving on a massive scale, they are not spending trillions of dollars a year. This nonconsumption depresses global aggregate demand and slows economic growth for both developing and developed countries (Stiglitz, 2010: 162). The reduction in global aggregate demand from developing country savings is, to an extent, offset by the spending of developed deficit countries, like the United States. However, this arrangement, besides being inequitable, may not be sustainable. Deficit countries are reducing their spending in the aftermath of the financial crisis. If both deficit and surplus countries are trying to save, the result is lower economic growth for all. Stiglitz proposes that SDRs could reduce the need for developing countries to accumulate massive reserves, freeing money to be consumed and increasing global aggregate demand (Stiglitz, 2010: 162—3).

An Institutionalist Criticism Of SDRs

While accepting the criticism that the dollar system may be unfair, unstable, and lower-growth, I would ask whether the SDR proposal is backed by sufficient institutions to succeed. On this ground, there is understandable skepticism about the near-term efficacy of SDRs from an institutionalist perspective, as Eichengreen suggests. However, I will conclude, contrary to Eichengreen, that there is greater room for institutions to change or for new ones to be created. Institutionalism can guide, in the very long-term, reforms in the IMF that would allow it to promote a greater international role for the SDR by supporting the asset's liquidity.

One of the functions of an international reserve currency is to provide emergency liquidity in a financial crisis. The dollar has the twin advantages of (1) being backed by the Federal Reserve, which can act quickly in crises; and (2) being freely usable, as it does not have to be converted into other currencies before being used in transactions with private parties. By contrast it would be much slower to rely on SDRs (Eichengreen, 2011: 145). Since

SDRs are not freely usable in private transactions, foreign central banks would have to activate the voluntary arrangements of the IMF, waiting 5 to 10 business days before their SDR holdings could be converted to freely usable currency, like the dollar (IMF, 2009a: 14). Given that central banks often have to act in hours when intervening in currency markets, a 5 to 10-day delay would be 'an eternity in a crisis' (Eichengreen, 2011: 138). The damage to foreign currencies and businesses could be irreparable by that time. The IMF acknowledges the delay of converting SDRs when it writes: 'with their use limited to the official sector, official SDR holdings provide an imperfect reserve asset, as they cannot be used directly for market intervention or liquidity provision' (IMF, 2011a: 4).

If a country needed more SDRs than it possessed in its holdings, there would have been an even longer wait as the IMF approved a new allocation of SDRs. Before any SDRs can be issued, 85 per cent of IMF members by voting power must agree to the allocation, further slowing action in a financial crisis (Eichengreen, 2011: 57, 141). Because the IMF requires an 85 per cent super-majority before issuing SDRs, as well as 5 to 10 business days before converting SDRs, the Fund as currently structured is institutionally unsuited to support the SDR as a reserve currency.

Another institutional difficulty with SDRs is the proposal for the substitution account. One reason for expanding the role of SDRs, discussed above, is that it could enable China and other countries with large dollar reserves to exchange their dollar treasuries for SDRs-denominated bonds through a substitution account. This would allow China to diversify its reserves outside of the market, and reduce its exposure to dollars. The problem with a substitution account is that the IMF does not have the power to determine who would bear the exchange risk. Who would suffer the loss if the dollar assets in the exchange account were to depreciate in value? As Eichengreen recalls, the idea of the substitution account was proposed in the past, during a previous episode of dollar weakness in 1978 (Eichengreen, 2011: 65). It was not implemented, due to the refusal of both the United States and the other IMF member states to bear the losses from a decline in the value of the account's dollar assets. The IMF admits that this problem remains (IMF, 2011a: 12; see also Eichengreen, 2011: 142). Although a substitution account might work if the IMF as an institution was able to impose a binding risksharing agreement to distribute the losses, the Fund has no such power.

A third institutional problem is that there may be insufficient agreement among the IMF member states to allow the Fund to issue enough SDRs to make a meaningful change in the composition of the world's reserve assets. Even if agreement could be reached on the amount of the SDR allocations, their distribution could be more divisive. The question of who would get the SDRs could be more controversial once the amount of SDRs greatly increases. Currently, they are distributed according to states' IMF quotas, which are set according to the size and openness of economies. The criteria favor the rich countries receiving the most SDRs. For example, in the 2009 general allocation of SDRs made in response to the financial crisis, the IMF distributed 182.6 billion SDR, then equivalent to $250 billion. The general allocation was largest ever made; seven times larger than the number of SDRs that had been created up to that time. Before then, the IMF had only created 21.4 billion SDR, then equivalent to $33 billion, in the entire period from 1969 to 2008 (IMF, 2009c). But the majority of the new general allocation of SDRs went to wealthy countries. Emerging market and developing countries received less than $100 billion worth of SDRs, of which only $18 billion were assigned to low-income countries (IMF, 2011b). Once future allocations become much more sizeable and frequent, countries could be dead-locked over how SDRs should be divided (Eichengreen, 2011: 141).

It might be argued that the some of the shortcomings of SDRs could be overcome if they became freely usable. Suppose that the IMF and member states issued SDR- denominated debt on a large scale, the way the United States government issues treasury bonds. Private investors would then be able to buy, sell, and hold SDR-denominated debt. This SDR bonds would be denominated or valued in SDRs, promoting the use of SDRs as a unit of account and store of value. But they would not payout SDRs to their holders or enhance the use of SDRs as a means of payment (IMF, 2011a: 11). A more radical reform would be to amend the IMF Articles of Agreement, allowing private investors and banks to hold and trade official SDRs (IMF, 2011a: 10). SDRs could then be used in private transactions as a means of payment, and states would no longer have to wait to convert their SDRs to dollars or euros before intervening in the market or financing international trade. Zhou and Stiglitz would approve of these developments since they would remove one of the main disadvantages of SDRs (Zhou, 2009: 3).

I would reply, however, that there is currently an institutional problem with issuing SDR-denominated securities. The Articles of Agreement do not authorize the IMF to issue SDR debt on the scale necessary to create a liquid market and to replace US treasuries as the main store of value in the international financial system. In the IMF's words, 'expanding the issuance of notes in regular intervals . . . would entail a large shift in the role and financial structure of the Fund, requiring an amendment to the Articles of Agreement' (IMF, 2011a: 12). Issuing IMF debt securities would be even more controversial than SDR allocations, since it would be unprecedented. I would add that it is unclear how the IMF would raise funds in order to meet its expanded debt obligations. Unlike the United States, the IMF has no tax income on which to draw. Perhaps the IMF could pay for its obligations by investing its borrowed money, but that would require an enormous institutional transformation to manage trillions of SDRs in investments. Given that the IMF has institutional limitations that prevent it from issuing enough SDR debt to create a liquid market, it is difficult for the SDRs in the near term to become a freely usable currency that can substitute for the dollar.

What Is The Federal Reserve Bank And What Do You Need To Know About It?

For over a century, the privately owned and operated Federal Reserve Banking system has controlled this nation's money supply and credit. This institution and its economic policies are an enigma to most government officials and American citizens. To understand the Federal Reserve Bank, we have to first look at how it operates. We can then understand why our founding fathers were opposed to such a system for the United States of America.

The Federal Reserve is what is known as a central bank. This bank is not regulated by the United States government. It creates the nation's money supply, loans it back to the government at interest, and regulates interest rates on the money it loaned out.

However, the Federal Reserve, also commonly called "the Fed," does not loan out money held in its vaults. Instead, it creates new money for circulation by adding credits to an account. Thus, they are creating new money that never existed before.

How much money can be created out of nothing? The Fed is only required to hold ten percent in reserves, and can loan out ninety percent. One of the Federal Reserve's publications states, "Of course, they (the banks) do not really pay out loans from the money received from deposits. What they do when they make loans is to accept promissory notes (money) for credits to the borrowers account."

Actual currency is relative to the amount of new loans in demand. In short, our system is based on debt. New money cannot be created unless banks issue new loans.

The Federal Reserve is a private bank. It loans America it's currency at interest like any other bank, and process works like this. The federal government needs to make more money. It has the Federal Reserve print reserve notes (money) worth a set value. The federal government then prints treasury bonds, which is basically a promissory note to pay back the loan of the currency at interest. In simple terms our government is in debt to the Federal Reserve as soon as the money is created.

If the government is in debt to the Fed, who makes the money, and the only way to get out debt is make more money, and the people who make the money are charging interest; how would the debt ever be paid off?

It doesn't.

As stated by the great scientist and creator of the light bulb, Thomas Edison wrote, "If our nation can issue a dollar bond, it can issue a dollar bill. The element that makes the bond good, makes the bill good, also. The difference between the bond and the bill is that the bond lets money brokers collect twice the amount of the bond and an additional 20%, whereas the currency pays nobody but those who contribute directly in some useful way. It is absurd to say that our country can issue $30 million in bonds and not $30 million in currency. Both are promises to pay, but one promise fattens the usurers and the other helps the people."

Our founding fathers were very aware of this problem and fought it from the time of the colonies. As Benjamin Franklin states in his autobiography explaining the Currency Act by the Bank of England in 1764, "The colonies would gladly borne little tax on tea and other matters had not been that England took away from the colonies their money, which created unemployment and dissatisfaction... The inability of the colonists to get power to issue their own money out of the hands of King George III and the international bankers was the PRIME reason for Revolutionary War."

Many other founding fathers agreed that our country should issue and regulate its own money. At the Constitutional Convention in 1787, Thomas Jefferson stated, "If the American people were ever allow private banks to control the issue on their currency first by inflation, then by deflation, the banks and their corporations which grow up around them, will deprive the people of all property until their children wake slaves on the continent their fathers conquered... I sincerely believe that banking institutions are more dangerous than standing armies. The issuing power should be taken from the banks and restored to the people to whom it properly belongs."

Also, James Madison said, "History records that the money changers have used every form of abuse, intrigue, deceit and violent means possible to maintain their control over governments by controlling money and it's issuance."

Throughout American history; there has been a battle to keep banking interests from controlling this nation's money supply. A few central banks have come and gone during our Nation's history.

Andrew Jackson recognized the connection between the international banking interests and central banks. In his inaugural address, he states, "It is not our own citizens to receive the bounty of our government, over 8 million in stock of this bank is held by foreigners...controlling our currency, raising our dependency...and holding thousands of our citizens in dependence would be more formidable than a military power of an enemy."

Andrew Jackson fought throughout his presidency to remove the central bank that preceded the Federal Reserve. By the end of his term, he had accomplished the total removal of

SPECIAL DRAWING RIGHTS (SDR) AND THE FEDERAL RESERVE

central banks in America. Of course, the battle waged on through the decades.

Our country remained mostly free of the banking interests until 1913, when the Federal Reserve act was passed in to law. In actuality, the history of the Federal Reserve goes back before 1913, to the economic panic of 1907. The panic of 1907 was the first major economic crisis; stocks dropped and banks collapsed in mass. The knowledge of "special interests" manipulating the market was widespread as stated by Frederick Allen in Life magazine, "The Morgan interests took advantage, to precipitate the panic, guiding it shrewdly."

Even though, a congressional hearing in to the panic of 1907, led by Senator Aldrich was convened. Senator Aldrich conclusion was that another central bank was needed to keep panic of 1907 from happening again, "This trouble could be averted if we appointed a committee of six or seven public spirited men like J.P. Morgan to handle the affairs of this country". After this hearing a secret meeting between banking interest and senator Aldrich took place on a small island of coast of Georgia called Jekyll Island. That meeting was described by Frank Vanderlip in February 9, 1935, in the Saturday Evening Post, "I was secretive, indeed as further as any conspirator. Discovery, we knew, simply must not happen, or else, all our time and effort would be wasted. If it were to be exposed that our particular group had gotten together and written a banking bill. That bill would have no chance of passage by Congress."

The bill that was written was called the Aldrich Plan. Many knew this was just an economic takeover of the country as quoted by Senator Charles Lindbergh, "This act establishes the most gigantic trust on earth. When the president signs this bill the invisible government by the monetary power will be legalized...The worst legislation crime of the ages is perpetuated in this banking bill...The Aldrich Plan is the Wall Street plan. It means another panic, if necessary, to intimidate the people".

Once Woodrow Wilson became president, the Aldrich Plan was rewritten and given another name; The Glass-Owen bill. This new bill remained almost identical to its previous version. Congress appointed an Ohio lawyer to investigate the bill. He testified in front of the committee saying, "The bill grants just what Wall Street and the big banks for twenty-five years been striving for, private instead of public control of currency. The Glass-Owen bill does this as completely as the Aldrich bill. Both measures rob the government and the people".

Even with major congressional opposition, the Federal Reserve Act was passed on Christmas Eve when majority of congress was at home for the holidays. President Woodrow Wilson quickly signed it into law.

With the passing of this law, many people were outraged from politicians to scientists. The Senate Chairman on Banking and Currency stated, "A super-state controlled by international bankers and industrialists is being set up here, acting together to enslave the world for their own interests...The Fed has usurped the government".

After Woodrow Wilson left office, later despaired by his role in passing the Federal Reserve Act, writes, "Our great industrial nation is controlled by its system of credit. Our system is privately concentrated in the hands of a few men...By very reasoned their limitations, chill and cheek and destroy genuine economic freedom. We have come to be one of the worst ruled, one of the most completely controlled and dominated governments in the civilized world. No longer a government by free opinion. No longer a government of conviction and vote of the majority, but a government by the opinions and duress of small group of dominate men."

On March 4, 1933, during Franklin D. Roosevelt's inaugural address he said, "Practices of the scrupulous money changers stand indicted in the court of public opinion, rejected by the hearts and minds of men." Shortly, after his election, President

Roosevelt signed the Gold Seizure Act which by law forced Americans to turn over all but a small amount of gold in their possession to the Federal Reserve. All the American gold, that totaled 700 million ounces of gold (70% of world's gold) was rounded up and placed in Fort Knox.

By the 1950s the gold in Fort Knox was given regulation control to the Federal Reserve Bank. Until this time there had been an audit on the gold every year, but the last audit done was by Eisenhower in 1954. In 1982, President Ronald Reagan appointed the Gold Commission to determine how much gold was owned by the United States. The conclusion from this commission was that United States Treasury owned no gold and that it was owned by the Federal Reserve.

In 1985, President Reagan created the Grace Commission to investigate where the Income Tax money was spent by the government each year. The commission conclusion was that 100% of income taxes were absorbed by the interests on the debt owed to the Federal Reserve.

At the end of 2008, our country fell in to another depression, which is the Federal Reserve's job to prevent. Their solution was to print more money and bailout the banking corporations, thus putting America and its citizens in to greater debt during a time of depression.

Since the creation of the Federal Reserve, it has maintained total control over America's currency and economics. The national debt in time the Federal Reserve was passed in to law was $2,912,499,269. After 100 years of the Federal Reserve control, the national debt is $12,296,232,673,031. This is an astronomical 42,200% increase in the national debt, and most of the debt was incurred with no regulation from the United States government at all.

Understanding the 1913 Federal Reserve Act

The law sets out the purpose, structure, and function of the Federal Reserve System. Congress can amend the Federal

Reserve Act and has done so several times. Before 1913, financial panics were common occurrences because investors were unsure of the safety of their bank deposits. Private financiers such as J.P. Morgan, who bailed out the government in 1895, often provided lines of credit to provide stability in the financial sector. The 1913 Federal Reserve Act, signed into law by President Woodrow Wilson, gave the Fed the ability to print money and policy tools to ensure economic stability.

The Federal Reserve System created the dual mandate to maximize employment and keep prices stable.

The Fed System

The 12 Federal Reserve banks, each in charge of a regional district, are in Boston, New York, Philadelphia, Cleveland, Richmond, St. Louis, Atlanta, Chicago, Minneapolis, Kansas City, Dallas, and San Francisco. The seven members of the Board of Governors are nominated by the president and approved by the U.S. Senate. Each governor serves a maximum of 14 years, and each governor's appointment is staggered by two years to limit the power of the president. In addition, the law dictates that appointments be representative of all broad sectors of the U.S. economy.

Current Federal Reserve Board

Jerome H. Powell (Chair)
Richard H. Clarida (Vice Chair)
Randal K. Quarles (Vice Chair for Supervision)
Michelle W. Bowman
Lael Brainard
Christopher J. Waller
Current Federal Reserve Bank Presidents
Name of President Bank Location-District
Eric S. Rosengren Boston-1
John C. Williams New York-2
Patrick T. Harker Philadelphia-3

Loretta J. Mester Cleveland-4
Thomas I. Barkin Richmond-5
Raphael W. Bostic Atlanta-6
Charles L. Evans Chicago-7
James Bullard St. Louis-8
Neel Kashkari Minneapolis-9
Esther L. George Kansas City-10
Robert S. Kaplan Dallas-11 Mary C. Daly San Francisco-12 Fed Powers

In addition to printing money, the Fed received the power to adjust the discount rate and the Fed funds rate and to buy and sell U.S. Treasuries.[20] The Federal Funds Rate— the interest rate at which depository institutions lend funds maintained at the Federal Reserve to one another overnight—has a major influence on the available credit and the interest rates in the United States and is a measure to ensure that the largest banking institutions do not find themselves short on liquidity.

Through the monetary tools at its disposal, the Federal Reserve attempts to smooth the booms and busts of the economic cycle and maintain adequate bases of money and credit for current production levels.

Central banks across the globe use a tool known as quantitative easing to expand private credit, lower interest rates, and increase investment and commercial activity. Quantitative easing is mainly used to stimulate economies during recessions when credit is scarce, such as during and following the 2008 financial crisis.

CHAPTER 6

HOW THE FEDERAL RESERVE WAS FORMED

The Federal Reserve is widely considered to be one of the most important financial institutions in the world. The Fed can either be a benign help or a cantankerous challenge, and its style is usually a function of the Federal Reserve's board of governors. Its monetary policy decisions can send waves through not only the U.S. markets, but also the world.

America Before the Federal Reserve

The United States was considerably more unstable financially before the creation of the Federal Reserve. Panics, seasonal cash crunches and a high rate of bank failures made the U.S. economy a riskier place for international and domestic investors to place their capital. The lack of dependable credit stunted growth in many sectors, including agriculture, and industry. Americans early on, however, also did not want a central bank, as they saw this as a model based on the Royal Crown and its Bank of England. New America did not want to be made in the image of Britain, and also favored a more decentralized state-by-state approach to its political economy.

Still, there were some early attempts. Alexander Hamilton, the first Secretary of the Treasury, was instrumental in the formation of the first national bank in America, known as The Bank of the United States. Located in Philadelphia, Pennsylvania, within Independence National Historical Park, the structure was completed in 1797 and stands today as a National Historic Landmark. It was one of four major financial innovations at the time, including the U.S. government's assumption of the state war debts, the establishment of a mint, and the imposition of a federal excise tax. Hamilton's aim with these measures was to establish financial order, national credit, and resolve the issue of fiat currency.

However, this first attempt at an American central bank was short-lived, and its charter was not renewed (it was reestablished later for another short period of years, as the second Bank of the United States, which was even shorter- lived). Hamilton proposed the Bank of the United States in 1790, and it opened in Philadelphia the following year. In April 1792, it opened a New York branch, Wall Street's second bank (then becoming the Bank of New York). These central banks lasted a total of eight years before being forced to close by congress.

J.P. Morgan and the Panic of 1907

After many decades of lacking a central bank, it was J.P. Morgan who ultimately forced the government into acting on the central banking plans it had been considering off and on for almost a century. During the Bank Panic of 1907, Wall Street turned to J.P. Morgan to steer the country through the crisis that was threatening to push the economy over the edge into a full crash and depression. Morgan was able to convene all the principal players at his mansion and command all their capital to flood the system, thus floating the banks that, in turn, helped to float the businesses until the panic passed.

The fact that the government owed its economic survival to a private banker forced the necessary legislation to create a central bank and the Federal Reserve.

Learning from Europe

In the years between 1907 and 1913, the top bankers and government officials in the U.S. formed the National Monetary Commission and traveled to Europe to see how the central banking was handled there.2 They came back with favorable impressions of the British and German systems, using them as the base and adding some improvements gleaned from other countries. Congress ultimately passed the The 1913 Federal Reserve Act is U.S. -- legislation that created the current Federal Reserve System.3 Congress developed the Federal Reserve Act to establish economic stability in the United States by introducing a central bank to oversee monetary policy. The law sets out the purpose, structure, and function of the Federal Reserve System. Congress can amend the Federal Reserve Act and has done so several times.

The 1913 Federal Reserve Act, signed into law by President Woodrow Wilson, gave the 12 Federal Reserve banks the ability to print money to ensure economic stability. The Federal Reserve System created the dual mandate to maximize employment and keep inflation low. The Federal Reserve was thus given power over the money supply and, by extension, the economy. Although many forces within the public and government were calling for a central bank that printed money on demand, President Wilson was swayed by Wall Street arguments against a system that would cause rampant inflation. So the government created the Federal Reserve, but it was by no means under government control.

The Great Depression

The government soon came to regret the freedom it had granted the Federal Reserve as it stood by during the crash of 1929 and refused to prevent the Great Depression that followed.

Even now, it is hotly debated whether the Fed could have stopped the depression, but there is little doubt that it could have done more to soften and shorten it by providing lower interest rates to allow farmers to keep planting and businesses to keep producing. The high-interest rates may even have been responsible for the unplanted fields that turned into dust bowls. By restricting the money supply at a bad time, the Fed starved out many individuals and businesses that might otherwise have survived.

The Post-War Recovery

It was World War II, not the Federal Reserve, that lifted the economy out of the depression. The war benefited the Federal Reserve as well by expanding its power and the amount of capital it was called on to control for the Allies. After the war, the Fed was able to erase some of the bad memories from the depression by keeping interest rates low as the U.S. economy went on a bull run that was virtually uninterrupted until the '60s.

Inflation or Unemployment?

Stagflation and inflation hit the U.S. in the '70s, slapping the economy across the face, but hurting the public far more than business. The Nixon administration ended the nation's on and off again affair with the gold standard, making the Fed that much more important in controlling the value of the U.S. dollar. The big question for the Fed was whether the nation was better off with inflation or unemployment.

By controlling interest rates, the Fed can make corporate credit easy to obtain, thus encouraging business to expand and create jobs. Unfortunately, this increases inflation as well. On the flip side, the fed can slow inflation by raising interest rates and slowing down the economy, causing unemployment. The history of the Fed is simply each chairperson's answer to this central question.

The Greenspan Years

Alan Greenspan took over the Federal Reserve a year before the infamous crash of 1987. When we think of crashes, many people consider the crash of 1987 more of a glitch than a true crash - a non-event nearer to a panic. This is true only because of the actions of Alan Greenspan and the Federal Reserve. Much like J.P. Morgan in 1907, Alan Greenspan collected all the necessary leaders and kept the economy afloat.

Through the Fed, however, Greenspan used the additional weapon of low interest rates to carry business through the crisis.

This marked the first time that the Fed had operated as its creators first envisioned 80 years before.

Following Greenspan, the Fed has had to navigate the 2008 financial crisis and the Great Recession under the stewardship of Ben Bernanke and Janet Yellen. Then, during the Trump presidency Jerome Powell led the Fed through a period defined by a lack of central bank independence and political bending to lower rates and expand the Fed's balance sheet.

Criticisms of the Federal Reserve continues. Boiled down, these arguments center on the image people have of the caretaker of the economy. You can either have a Fed that feeds the economy with ideal interest rates leading to low unemployment - possibly leading to future problems - or you can have a Fed that offers little help, ultimately forcing the economy to learn to help itself. The ideal Fed would be willing to do both. Although there have been calls for the elimination of the Federal Reserve as the U.S. economy matures, it is very likely that the Fed will continue to guide the economy for many years to come.

5 Need-To-Know Facts About the Federal Reserve

The Federal Reserve holds tremendous power.

Some of the many important roles of the Federal Reserve include setting interest rates, regulating the value of the dollar, and monitoring inflation rates, all of which impact precious metal markets, including silver and gold bullion. With an institution that has so much influence on our economy, it is important to have at least a basic understanding of what the Federal Reserve is and what its role is in the financial sector of our nation.

Here are 5 important facts about the Federal Reserve.
1. The FR is a private organization. When people think about it, many wrongly assume it to be a public institution- the financial branch of our federal government. However, the FR is owned by 12

corporate banks, each of which are owned by regional, commercial, and foreign banks, as well as miscellaneous individuals who have inherited a stake in the system (Rockefellers, Rothschilds, etc.).
2. The Federal Reserve has a monopoly on the currency flow in America. It does so by controlling the amount of loans made by commercial banks. When the amount of new loans increases, so does the money supply; when loans decrease, the money supply declines as well. The FR has the power to determine the amount of new loans (and ultimately the money supply) by doing one of three things:
   - Changing the required reserve ratio
   - Allowing banks to borrow from the FR at a discounted rate
   - Buying and selling bonds
   - The implication of this essentially means that the Federal Reserve has the ability to borrow an infinite amount of money at 0% interest.
3. Inflation is caused by the Federal Reserve paying interest on debt using future money. If all money printed is being used to pay off the principal of the debt, how does the interest on the debt ever get paid? The answer is money that will be printed in the future is applied to interest. Inflation is a natural byproduct of this system.
4. The potential money supply is infinite. Prior to 2008, commercial banks were required to hold at least 10% of deposits as reserves, which limited the amount of money creation possible to 9 times the deposit amount. However, a minor clause in the Emergency Economic Stabilization Act/TARP Act of September 2008 reduced the requirement to 0%, meaning there are no restrictions on the amount of money that can

be created, and there is no longer any protection against runaway inflation.

5. There is a debate over the constitutionality of the Federal Reserve. Strict adherers to the U.S. Constitution argue that the federal government does not have the authority to establish a central bank, especially one with such magnanimous power as the FR. Defenders respond by saying that currency regulation is indeed authorized by the Founding Fathers, and it is simply a matter of interpretation.

How Central Banks Create Money Out From The Thin Air

The Federal Reserve announced a $700 billion Quantitative Easing program on March 15, 2020, to combat the economic impact of the virus outbreak.

The central banks are creating money out from the thin air again. And if you think this doesn't concern you, then you probably live on Mars. If you live in this world, you need to know what is going on with money.

Quantitative easing is quite simply a process whereby the central bank injects more cash into the economy by buying off debts (bad debts in most cases) with cash that doesn't exist prior.

To understand better, let us use an illustration.

Clara buys a toy from Daisy for $100. Clara paid $50 and took on a debt of $50 (which she would pay in installments). The economy goes down and Clara cannot afford her payments to Daisy anymore. Also, the toy is now worth $20. So, Bruno comes to save Clara.

Clara transfers the ownership of the toy to Bruno. But she still gets to use it and play with it. Bruno then writes a check to Daisy (on Clara's behalf) to pay off the complete $50 debt on the toy. But there is a problem. Bruno doesn't have any money.

However, Bruno has authority. Whatever Bruno calls money is money. All Bruno needs to do is to write $50 with a pen on a toilet paper and give it to Daisy. Daisy can then spend this however she wants.

If Daisy is ever challenged about the toilet paper with $50 written on it, she only has to say, "Bruno gave it to me". And it will be accepted. Nobody dares to go against Bruno's wishes.

So, Bruno is the central bank. Clara is the company (or entity) that needs saving during an economic downturn. Daisy is the commercial bank or investment bank etc.

Now, this is where things go crazy. There are cases where Daisy and Clara are the same entities. In fact, this case is the most common. And the complications can go on and on.

If there is an economic downturn, how does Bruno choose who he helps? Definitely, Bruno doesn't help everybody. Bruno only helps those whose failures will bring a significant dent to the society. Bruno only helps the big ones.

The big ones are expected to help the small ones but they can choose not to and get away with it.

The Central Banks

There are 5 top central banks in the world that control the economy and monetary policy of the 5 countries or constituencies where they are based. They include:

The Federal Reserve Bank of America (USA)

Bank of England (England)

European Central Bank (EU)

Bank of Japan (Japan)

People's Bank of China (China)

These are the big Brunos in the world. Interestingly, they are not controlled by the government. They are accountable (sort of) to the government but they are not subject to the government.

Let's talk about the Fed in the USA since it deals with the largest economy and leads all the other central banks.

The Fed

The Fed in the USA was created in 1913 due to the financial turbulence the country had experienced in the years leading up to that. The Fed was created when the act passed the US Congress (and signed into law by the US President) in December 1913. But the real mastermind creation happened in 1910 when a couple of bankers had a secret meeting in Jekyll Island.

In 1971, President Nixon took the US dollar off the gold standard. Hence undercutting the rest of the world who has their currencies pegged to the US dollar. This event is known as the Nixon Shock.

The US dollar currency was basically a gold certificate before 1971. You could redeem physical gold with the currency. But then in August 1971 when President Nixon announced to take the US dollar off the gold standard, there was already a law prohibiting individuals from owning gold. (That law was later repealed in 1974).

What is the implication of this? Before, if the US wanted to create a $20 note, they had to ensure that they had the gold equivalent in their reserve.

After Nixon's announcement in 1971, the US can print money as they wish to. The currency is no longer pegged to anything but the might and reputation of the USA. Think about it this way:

It cost about 15.4 cents (value) to print a $100 note

Most other countries have their currencies pegged to the US dollar through the Bretton Woods Agreement. And so, the agreement had to fail. This turned central banks into a printing press.

Since 1971, the US dollar has been freefalling in value. The price of gold right now is about $1,648 per ounce. And you can check the real-time price of gold whenever you are reading this. Of course, the price of gold has generally been on the rise since 1971. An ounce of gold used to be $35.

SPECIAL DRAWING RIGHTS (SDR) AND THE FEDERAL RESERVE

The graph below shows how gold has been price in US dollar since 1971:

The US economy tumbled in 2008 after experiencing amazing highs in 2006. There are several explanations for what really happened. But the chief of the matter has to do with subprime mortgages (loans). Apparently, too many loans that should not have been given were given. And it created bad debt.

Bad debt is debt that debtor has defaulted in paying. And the underlying asset for the loan has lost so much value that it doesn't make sense to sell it. Even if there is an attempt to sell it, there is no available buyer.

This happened with the real estate market in 2008. And the Fed rushed in to save the day. Over $1.4 trillion was printed to save the economy from the 2008 crisis.

So, Bruno chooses who he helps and there are more toilet papers with numbers written on it.

So, how does it affect you?

How Quantitative Easing Affects You

Assuming you have $50 (in the down market) and you are the richest guy on the street in Bruno's territory. The moment Daisy (which is also Clara in most cases) takes Bruno's check (the $50 written on a toilet paper) to shop, the shop owner takes the money instantly and promises to deliver the merchandise in the future. Hence, the shop owner becomes as rich as you are overnight.

And gradually everyone will know that there is another rich man on the street. Those that sell to you see that and create a demand competition between you and the shop owner (while the supply hasn't changed).

Before, their only demand was coming from you because you are the only one rich enough to buy from them. Now that the shop owner has $50 too, demand has gone up and hence they will increase their price to level the playing field. And the ripple effect will go through the economy until it reaches the smallest item.

Therefore, your $50 can no longer do what it can. It can no longer buy what it can. It has been devalued.

The interesting part of this is not that the shop owner is now as rich as you. Instead, it is that the money is not a result of work done or value created. It was money that Bruno created. What does this mean?

The New Laws of Money

Before quantitative easing was possible, money was a reward for value creation. However, after quantitative easing became a reality, money is no longer a reward for value created.

If you continue to see money as a reward for value created, you would continue to be that rich man on Bruno's street seeing the value of your money can drop further down.

You can try hard to create more value and get paid for it, but Bruno can write numbers on toilet paper faster. And in most cases, he will.

The new law of money is to use money to create value

Knowing who Bruno is and what he is capable of, it is better to get your hands on as much of his toilet paper money as you can and use it to create value for the society.

Instead of being paid for creating value, you get paid to create value. This is the new law of money. And this is what our society runs on today.

How The Federal Reserve Literally Makes Money

The Federal Reserve has vowed to provide up to US$2.3 trillion in lending to support households, employers, financial markets, and state and local governments struggling as a result of the coronavirus and corresponding stay-at-home orders.

Let that number sink in: $2,300,000,000,000.

I have a Ph.D. in economics, direct the Sound Money Project at the American Institute for Economic Research and write regularly on Federal Reserve policy. And, yet, it is difficult for me to wrap my head around a number that large. If you were to stack 2.3 trillion $1 bills, it would reach over halfway to the Moon.

Put simply, it is a lot of money. Where does it all come from?

Congress gave the Fed the ability to create money from thin air. The Fed should wield this enormous power wisely.

Unlike the trillions of dollars, the Treasury is spending to save the economy by bailing out companies or beefing up unemployment checks, very little of the Fed's money actually comes from taxpayers or sales of government bonds. Most of it, in fact, emerges right out of thin air. And that has costs.

Printing green

It is common to hear people say the Fed prints money.

That's not technically correct. The Bureau of Engraving and Printing, an agency of the U.S. Treasury, does the printing. The Fed, for its part, purchases cash from the bureau at cost and then puts it in circulation.

Although you may have heard some economists talk about the Fed figuratively dropping cash from helicopters, its method of distribution isn't quite as colorful. Instead, it gives banks cash in exchange for old, worn-out notes or digital balances held by the banks at the Fed. In this way, the Fed can help banks accommodate changes in demand for banknotes, like those in advance of major holidays or after natural disasters.

These exchanges are dollar-for-dollar swaps. The Fed does not typically increase the monetary base the total amount of currency in circulation and reserves held by banks at the central bank when it distributes new banknotes.

Magicking green

To put more money into circulation, the Fed typically purchases financial assets in much the same way that it plans to spend that $2.3 trillion.

To understand how, one must first recognize that the Fed is a bankers' bank. That is, banks hold deposits at the Fed much like you or I might hold deposits in a checking account at Chase or Bank of America. That means when the Fed purchases a government bond from a bank or makes a loan to a bank, it does not have to and usually doesn't pay with cash. Instead, the Fed just credits the selling or borrowing bank's account.

The Fed does not print money to buy assets because it does not have to. It can create money with a mere keystroke.

So as the Fed buys Treasuries, mortgage-backed securities, corporate debt and other assets over the coming weeks and months, money will rarely change hands. It will just move from one account to another.

Costs Of Magical Money

While the Fed can create money out of thin air, that does not mean it does so without cost. Indeed, there are two potential costs of creating money that one should keep in mind.

The first results from inflation, which denotes a general increase in prices and, correspondingly, a fall in the purchasing power of money. Money is a highly liquid easily exchangeable asset we use to make purchases. When the Fed creates more money than we want to hold on to, we exchange the excess money for less liquid assets, including goods and services. Prices are driven up in the process. When the Fed does this routinely, expected inflation gets built into long-term contracts, like mortgages and employment agreements. Businesses incurs costs from having to change prices more frequently, while consumers have to make more frequent trips to the bank or ATM.

The other cost is a consequence of reallocating credit.

Suppose the Fed makes a loan to the "Bank of Fast and Loose Lending." If the bank wasn't able to secure alternative funding, this suggests that other private financial institutions deemed its lending practices too risky. In making the loan, the Fed has only created more money. It has not created more real resources that can be bought with money. And so, by giving the Bank of Fast and Loose Lending a lifeline, the Fed enables it to take scarce real resources away from other productive ventures in the economy.

The cost to society is the difference between the value of those real resources as employed by the Bank of Fast and Loose Lending and the value of those real resources as employed in the productive ventures forgone.

Uncharted waters

In recent years, the Fed has shown itself to be quite adept at keeping inflation low, even when making large-scale asset purchases.

The central bank purchased nearly $3.6 trillion worth of assets from September 2008 to January 2015, yet annual inflation averaged roughly 1.5% over the period well below its 2% target.

I'm less sanguine about the Fed's ability to keep the costs of reallocating credit low. Congress has traditionally limited the Fed to making loans to banks and other financial market institutions. But now it is tasking the Fed with providing direct assistance to nonbank businesses and municipalities areas where the Fed lacks experience.

It is difficult to predict how well the Fed will manage its new lending facilities. But its limited experience making loans to small businesses — in the 1930s, for example does little to alleviate the concerns of myself and others.

Congress gave the Fed the ability to create money from thin air. The Fed should wield this enormous power wisely.

US is 'printing' money to help save the economy from the COVID-19 crisis, but some wonder how far it can go.

In its frantic scramble to save the American economy, the central bank of the United States seems to have the ultimate superpower.

It works like magic. With a few strokes on a computer, the Federal Reserve can create dollars out of nothing, virtually "printing" money and injecting it into the commercial banking system, much like an electronic deposit. By the end of the year, the Fed is projected to have purchased $3.5 trillion in government securities with these newly created dollars, one of many tools it is using to help prop up the ailing economy during the COVID-19 pandemic, according to Oxford Economics.

"The way you and I have checking accounts in our banks, that's how all these other banks have accounts at the Fed," said Pavlina Tcherneva, an economist at Bard College in

New York. "All the Fed does is literally credit them. They just type it in."

The Fed's goal: to keep markets functioning after they had seized up in fear. The strategy also makes credit easier to obtain, with a bigger money supply and lower interest rates. Without these and the Fed's other emergency measures, the economy would have crashed already, experts say. Fed Chair Jerome Powell said at a recent news conference that these purchases have helped market conditions improve "substantially" in recent weeks.

But an unstated, practical result of the Fed's bond purchases is that it creates money to finance the gigantic debt run up by Congress. The very idea of it tends to explode the heads of those who say dollars should come from work, savings and investment instead of thin air. In the age of a nearly $25 trillion national debt, such "sound money" concepts seem outdated — relics of a bygone era in which the value of a dollar once was based on a fixed amount of gold.

"What we're working with now is fake money, a fake measuring rod," longtime Federal Reserve critic and former Republican presidential candidate Ron Paul told USA TODAY. "It is unbelievable."

In this case, the federal government's bank isn't just creating massive amounts of dollars from scratch. The government also is, in effect, using those newly created dollars to pay down its own debt, this time at an unprecedented scale because of the economy's massive shutdown triggered by the pandemic.

This might sound like a financial fantasy: You mean we can pay our credit card bills by simply pressing a button?

Yes, the government can, unlike people and businesses, though it's a little more complicated than that. The larger question is whether it's sound and sustainable.

The answer depends on whom you ask and how it's managed.

How The Fed Injects Money Into The Economy

The Federal Reserve doesn't literally print paper dollars. That's the job of the U.S. Treasury, which also collects taxes and issues debt at the direction of Congress. At this time of crisis, the Fed instead makes large asset purchases on the open market by adding newly created electronic dollars to the reserves of banks such as Wells Fargo, Goldman Sachs and Morgan Stanley.

In exchange, the Fed receives large amounts of bonds U.S. Treasury securities and agency securities that are backed by bundles of home mortgages.

As a result, markets that had stopped working smoothly started to flow again. Banks get more dollars in reserve and are more prone to lend money without worrying about exhausting their funds because of a run on the bank in a time of panic. Such big purchases of securities by the Fed also effectively increase the money supply and drive down interest rates. This keeps borrowing costs cheap for those who need it.

If the Fed didn't take these and other emergency measures, "the system already would have blown up," said Tim Duy, an economist at the University of Oregon who previously worked in the U.S. Treasury.

"The markets would have crashed 10 times over."

Separately, Congress recently has passed massive spending bills that have swollen the national debt by about $2.4 trillion to help businesses and taxpayers. Much of that money comes from issuing U.S. Treasury securities government debt that is bought by investors who earn interest on it.

Such foreign and domestic investors owned most U.S. public debt as of last year, with the Fed only owning 14% of it, according to the Government Accountability Office.

Now the Fed has even more. Since mid-March, the Fed has bought $1.4 trillion in Treasuries the bulk of the $1.6 trillion in total Treasuries issued during that period to thaw out markets that had frozen because of the current crisis, according to Oxford Economics. The Fed, however, doesn't buy securities directly from the U.S. Treasury. Instead, it purchases previously issued Treasury securities through commercial banks.

The Federal Reserve and Congress have taken extraordinary measures to prop up an economy devastated by the coronavirus pandemic.

The Federal Reserve and Congress have taken extraordinary measures to prop up an economy devastated by the coronavirus pandemic.

In effect, one agency of the government the Fed is creating dollars to buy government debt in the form of securities previously issued by the U.S. Treasury. The Treasury then pays the Fed what it owes in interest on those securities. In turn, the Fed is required by law to return to the Treasury the profit it makes from the Treasury off of these securities.

"It's just kind of a circle in that respect," Duy said.

The same circle also plays a role in the Fed's unprecedented crisis plan to lend more than $2 trillion to businesses and state and local governments. In this case, the Fed also would be creating the money for loans, said former Federal Reserve vice chairman Alan Blinder, now an economics professor at Princeton.

Fed Chair Powell said he expects the loans to be repaid. But what if some aren't? Does it matters? After all, the Fed can just push a button to create money.

Blinder said it does matter because the Fed is required to remit to the Treasury the profits it makes on its balance sheet, which has ballooned by $2.2 trillion to a record $6.7 trillion since mid-March.

"If the Fed would take losses on some of its loans, it would pay less to the Treasury," Blinder said. "The budget deficit would be higher, so it would be as if the Treasury spent more money or taxed less."

This is why Congress, through the CARES Act relief and stimulus measure, also has provided $454 billion for Fed programs in case some loans fail, giving the central bank some political cover in case they do.

Does 'creating' money create an inflation risk?

Paul, the former Texas congressman and author of "End the Fed," predicts such money creation will lead to disaster. He says it will cause overheated financial bubbles fueled by too much easy money in the system a bubble that could burst with painful fallout. Creating too much money that chases too few goods also leads to price inflation, decreasing the purchasing power of the dollar.

But high inflation didn't materialize the last time the Fed created money on a similar scale as part of its efforts to revive the economy during and after the Great Recession. To the contrary, an arguably bigger concern then and now has been persistently low inflation, which eventually could lead to deflation, or falling prices, that prompt consumers to put off spending and hurt the economy.

"With the economy so down, and inflation so low, the fears that these kinds of operations will lead to high inflation in the United States seem very farfetched," Blinder said.

The cause of the current crisis is a pandemic that forced businesses to shut down for weeks, leading both the Fed and Congress to take extraordinary measures. Congress is approving huge amounts of spending on stimulus and relief while the Fed is creating huge amounts of dollars that end up paying for that debt.

This isn't new, Tcherneva said.

"It's just that now the expenditure is so extraordinary, and because we need to pass a huge budget overnight that we are suddenly realizing we didn't tax anyone to get this money, and we didn't borrow it from anyone," said Tcherneva, author of the upcoming book, "The Case for a Job Guarantee." "The government self-finances."

Tcherneva is on the opposite side of the spectrum from Paul. She is a proponent of "Modern Monetary Theory," which argues that the government can always pay its bills by creating more money, minimizing the importance of deficits and debt.

Not every country can do this only those that issue their own currency. And no other country can borrow quite like the United States, whose Treasury securities are in demand worldwide, largely because they are backed by the "full faith and credit" of the U.S. government, a global superpower with a powerful military. But there are limits.

'Is there a limit?'

The Fed's mandate from Congress is to maximize employment and stabilize prices. In doing so, it effectively steps on the gas during times like this and hits the brakes when the economy appears to overheat and prices rise too fast.

Just as it can increase the money supply by creating money, the Fed can also reduce it by making moves that increase interest rates, such as selling some of the securities on its balance sheet, effectively taking money out of the system.

Going too far in either direction at the wrong time can hurt the economy. In this economic emergency, the Fed has signaled it will do what it takes.

The Fed's "lending facilities are constrained by approval of Treasury, and ultimately Congress holds authority over the Fed," said Duy, who publishes a blog on the Fed called "Fed Watch."

"But in theory, the Fed can just keep buying assets," such as Treasury and mortgage-backed securities.

Treasury Secretary Steve Mnuchin tells climate change activist Greta Thunberg to get an economics degree

At the same time, Congress's spending still creates debt from the Treasury that has to be paid back. The Congressional Budget Office recently projected the budget deficit will more than triple to $3.7 trillion in the current fiscal year, with federal debt held by the public at 101% of gross domestic product. How much debt is too much?

Powell told reporters that the U.S. has not been on a "sustainable" fiscal path for some time, noting the nation's debt is growing faster than the economy. He added that those concerns now must take a backseat to getting out of this crisis.

Tcherneva downplayed debt concerns in the long term, noting that Japan is still able to service its debt despite having a debt-to-GDP ratio more than double that of the U.S. in recent years. Japan also issues its own currency.

"We actually don't know how much (debt) is too much," Tcherneva said. "Is there a limit? If the interest on the debt exceeds the growth of the economy, that could be a problem."

She said the Fed has tools that can help keep long-term interest rates below the economy's growth rate, though others would say those rates are mostly controlled by the market.

And, of course, there's the Fed's magic printing machine.

"The United States can pay any debt it has because we can always print money to do that," former Federal Reserve chairman Alan Greenspan said on NBC in 2011. "So, there is zero probability of default."

How an Allocation of International Monetary Fund Special Drawing Rights Will Support Low-Income Countries, the Global Economy, and the United States

The COVID-19 pandemic has taken an extraordinary toll on the global economy and has strained financial liquidity. Global growth contracted 3.5% in 2020—the worst peacetime recession since the Great Depression and will likely inflict long-term scars on the global economy.

The International Monetary Fund (IMF) has warned of a stark divergence in economic growth prospects for advanced economies versus low-income and developing countries. Overall, the IMF projects that 150 economies will have per-capita incomes below their 2019 levels in 2021.

An allocation of IMF Special Drawing Rights (SDRs) would help build reserve buffers, smooth adjustments, and mitigate the risks of economic stagnation in global growth.

Importantly, it could also enhance liquidity for low-income and developing countries to facilitate their much-needed health recovery efforts. Containing the pandemic across the globe is paramount to a robust economic recovery. To this end, Treasury is working with IMF management and other members toward a

$650 billion general allocation of SDRs to IMF member countries. Addressing the long-term global need for reserve assets would help support the global recovery from the COVID-19 crisis. A strong global recovery would also increase demand for U.S. exports of goods and services creating U.S. jobs and supporting U.S. firms.

An SDR allocation is not a catch-all solution. It is part of a package of broader international efforts to support the global recovery. This package also includes robust support from the IMF, multilateral development banks, and debt relief in some cases all alongside countries taking necessary reform steps. Bilateral assistance and debt relief under the G20 Debt Service Suspension Initiative and Common Framework, as well as financial support to the COVID-19 Vaccines Global Access (COVAX) Facility, all remain integral to help prevent long-term scarring from the pandemic and worsening global wealth divergence.

As part of our support for an SDR allocation, Treasury is working with the IMF and other member countries to maximize the benefits and limit the possible downsides of an allocation by enhancing transparency, accountability, and equitable burden sharing.

Below are some common questions about the nature and uses of SDRs and the mechanics of an SDR allocation.

For more information on SDRs please see the IMF's Factsheet.

QUESTION: IS THE ADMINISTRATION TRYING TO BYPASS CONGRESS IN APPROVING AN SDR ALLOCATION?

Answer: As required by U.S. law, the Administration is consulting Congress on our proposed support for an SDR allocation. Under the Special Drawing Rights Act, Congress has authorized the Secretary of the Treasury to support an SDR allocation without additional legislation where the amount allocated to the United States does not exceed the current U.S. quota in the IMF in the applicable five-year basic period. The proposed SDR allocation is below this level. Based on current global liquidity conditions, Treasury does not support an additional SDR allocation beyond the proposed $650 billion at this time.

Treasury would only consider an additional SDR allocation beyond the proposed $650 billion at some point in the future if circumstances justify it at that time.

QUESTION: DOES AN SDR ALLOCATION IMPOSE A LARGE FINANCIAL BURDEN ON THE UNITED STATES?

Answer: An allocation itself imposes no direct cost on the United States. Based on a $650 billion allocation, the United States will receive about $113 billion in SDRs. The idea that an SDR allocation imposes a financial burden arises from potential exchanges of SDRs for U.S. dollars. If countries wish to sell their SDRs to the United States in exchange for dollars, Treasury would exchange SDRs for dollars held in the Exchange Stabilization Fund (ESF).

The U.S. cash position would decline, and federal borrowing requirements would increase. However, the United States would also earn interest on the SDRs we purchased, largely (and perhaps entirely) offsetting any increase in Treasury's borrowing costs. This is the case with our existing SDR resources, and the same process would occur with a new allocation. The differential between the SDR interest rate and the interest rate on Treasuries varies over time, so at times there is a small cost and at other times a small benefit to Treasury. This potential implicit cost is much lower than the benefits of a strong global recovery.

QUESTION: WILL THE UNITED STATES BE REQUIRED TO EXCHANGE DOLLARS FOR SDRS WITH ANY IMF MEMBER ON DEMAND?

Answer: Treasury has agreed to voluntarily purchase SDRs up to a certain level from other IMF members to promote an orderly system of exchange rates and to help provide liquidity support to our global partners. The United States retains the right to refuse to purchase SDRs from any country whose policies run counter to U.S. interests. Many large countries, such as most advanced economies and China, already hold excess SDRs and are very unlikely to request to exchange their new SDRs for hard currency.

Even if there is strong demand for dollars after the potential allocation, the United States is not alone in voluntarily agreeing to purchase SDRs. The IMF spreads the transactions across 32 members who have similar voluntary arrangements. We are working with the IMF to further ensure our potential transactions are proportional to others' commitments.

QUESTION: IS THERE A NEED FOR AN SDR ALLOCATION TO SUPPORT GLOBAL RESERVES?

Answer: In 2016, the IMF estimated the global reserves gap to be $430 billion to $1.4 trillion. This shortfall of international reserves is likely larger now.

In addition, many low-income and developing countries remain constrained in their ability to issue debt in international markets, either to replenish reserves or to finance fiscal spending.

Providing reserves will help prevent countries from engaging in FX purchases that could weaken their currencies and lead to a further buildup of the U.S. trade and current account deficits.

QUESTION: IS THERE A NEED FOR AN SDR ALLOCATION GIVEN THE GLOBAL ECONOMY IS RECOVERING?

Answer: After contracting 3.5% in 2020, the IMF projects a partial recovery in economic growth in 2021 of 5.5%. Yet, this recovery faces significant downside risks, is uneven, and will leave global output below the pre-crisis level over the medium term. Moreover, the global recession has strained central bank foreign exchange reserves in many countries. The proposed SDR allocation will help buffer reserves, supporting governments' efforts to address the health and economic crises. Importantly, an SDR allocation will increase confidence and liquidity needed to promote a global recovery that benefits the American worker and U.S. economic growth.

Low-income and developing countries have been particularly hard hit in this crisis, and we face a critical window to prevent a permanent global divergence between rich and poor countries. The pandemic is expected to reverse the progress made in poverty reduction across the past two decades with close to 90 million people expected to fall below the extreme poverty threshold during 2020-21. Low-income countries have seen their real annual GDP growth decline by about 5% in 2020. The IMF estimates that low-income countries will need to deploy around $200 billion over the next five years just to fight the pandemic and an additional $250 billion to return to the path of catching up with advanced economies. The IMF forecasts the medium-term output losses for low-income countries will be about 6%, compared to 1% for advance economies.

The proposed SDR allocation, by providing liquidity and potential fiscal space, could help low-income and developing countries finance vaccines and other COVID- 19 related spending.

For more information see the IMF's blog post on the pandemic's legacy.

QUESTION: IS AN SDR ALLOCATION A CASH GIVEAWAY?

Answer: SDRs are neither money nor currency, but an international reserve asset. SDRs are allocated by the IMF to IMF members, and can only be used by IMF members and a limited number of international institutions. SDRs cannot be exchanged by private entities, and all transactions involving SDRs must go through the IMF's SDR Department. To use SDRs, a country must find an IMF member willing to provide a usable currency (generally, dollars, euros, or yen) in exchange for SDRs. The transaction is thus an exchange of assets. The country pays an interest rate to the IMF if their SDR holdings are below its allocation.

QUESTION: DOES AN SDR ALLOCATION ONLY BENEFIT RICH COUNTRIES, AS OPPOSED TO THE COUNTRIES THAT NEED IT?

Answer: A $650 billion SDR allocation would provide about $21 billion worth of SDRs in liquidity support to low- income countries and about $212 billion to other emerging market and developing countries (excluding China), complementing existing multilateral efforts to assist countries in need. By comparison, the G20/Paris Club Debt Service Suspension Initiative has delivered about $5 billion in liquidity relief to more than 40 eligible countries as of March 2021. The IMF's concessional lending provided about $13 billion in emergency financing in 2020.

We are working with our international partners to pursue ways for advanced economies to lend a portion of their SDR allocation to support low-income countries. For instance, during the current crisis, several countries have used part of their existing SDR holdings to expand the IMF's concessional financing through loans to the IMF's Poverty Reduction and Growth Trust's (PRGT). Total new PRGT loan resources mobilized since the start of the crisis amount to about $24 billion, of which about $15 billion is from existing SDRs.

QUESTION: IS THERE TRANSPARENCY AND ACCOUNTABILITY IN HOW SDRS ARE USED?

Answer: The IMF already reports the SDR holdings of each of its members on a monthly basis. As part of our support for a new SDR allocation, Treasury is working with our international partners and the IMF on a number of initiatives to improve the transparency of SDR transactions and the effectiveness of how countries use SDRs.

For example, the IMF could expand quarterly country-level data on SDR transactions, breaking out the transactions that occurred each quarter by major categories (e.g., IMF operations and exchanges with other SDR holders). Moreover, we are encouraging the IMF to publish an exante guidance note on how countries could use and account for SDRs, consistent with macroeconomic and debt sustainability and good governance. We are also urging the IMF to conduct an expost review of the results two years after the allocation to describe the various uses. We are working closely with the IMF and other members to advance these initiatives.

QUESTION: IS AN SDR ALLOCATION A LIFELINE FOR DICTATORS?

Answer: The United States retains the right to refuse to purchase SDRs from any countries that we choose, including those under U.S. sanction regimes, and we are working to coordinate with other countries to do the same. Because all IMF members receive an SDR allocation proportionate to their quota share, some countries whose policies the United States opposes will receive an SDR allocation. However, these countries will not necessarily be able to exchange their SDRs for hard currencies. First, the country's authorities must be recognized by the IMF membership. Then, the country would need to find a willing country to provide them with hard currency in exchange for their SDRs. We are working to increase transparency around SDR exchanges.

QUESTION: WILL AN SDR ALLOCATION PUT AT RISK THE DOLLAR'S RESERVE CURRENCY STATUS?

Answer: The dollar currently makes up 57% of global reserves, while SDRs only make up 2%.

After the proposed allocation, SDRs as a share of global reserves would only grow to around 7%, while dollars would comprise about 54%, more than three times the next most significant currency.

Additionally, restrictions on who can hold and transact SDRs and the IMF's role in clearing all SDR transactions significantly limits the ability of the SDR to function as a replacement for the dollars' reserve currency status.

CONCLUSION

It argues that institutions can enhance a currency's reserve status by creating liquid markets and by intervening quickly in financial crises. The institutionalist approach adds to the market, instrumental, and geopolitical perspectives on reserve currency status. The instrumental and geopolitical perspectives examine the decisions of foreign governments that demand a currency. Governments demand a currency as a means of pursuing economic goals (the instrumental view) or to promote their security, power, or military alliances (the geopolitical view). The market-based approach focuses, not on governments, but on whether private actors support a currency, based on its liquidity and stability. By contrast, the institutionalist approach differs from the instrumental and geopolitical views, since it looks at the institutions, like the Federal Reserve or IMF, that supply a currency. The institutionalist approach also differs from the market perspective, because institutionalism explains how liquid markets in a currency originates in the first place. They are created, not solely by private actors like bond investors, commodity traders, and import-exporters, but with the initiative of the public institutions that issue a currency. The process of converting SDRs to freely usable currencies could also be streamlined to make the Special Drawing Right a more perfect substitute for dollar reserves. The IMF would then be better placed as an institution to support the international reserve currency status of the SDR. The second reason why the United States could support these institutional reforms to the IMF draws on a historical precedent. The US allowed the SDR program to be founded in 1969, during a previous period that threatened a shortage of dollar liquidity. The US also approved a sizable SDR allocation in 2009, equivalent to $250 billion, in response to the liquidity shortage created by the financial crisis. Similarly, the US may increase its support for SDRs if it finds that global demands for dollar reserves and liquidity are becoming financially unsustainable.

www.ingramcontent.com/pod-product-compliance
Lightning Source LLC
Chambersburg PA
CBHW072048110526
44590CB00018B/3080